SIX POETS FROM
THE MOUNTAIN SOUTH

SOUTHERN LITERARY STUDIES
Fred Hobson, Series Editor

SIX
POETS FROM
THE MOUNTAIN
SOUTH

JOHN LANG

)((LOUISIANA STATE UNIVERSITY PRESS   BATON ROUGE

Published by Louisiana State University Press
Copyright © 2010 by Louisiana State University Press
All rights reserved
Manufactured in the United States of America
LSU Press Paperback Original
First printing

Designer: Michelle A. Neustrom
Typefaces: Whitman, text; Centuryremix, display

LIBRARY OF CONGRESS CATALOGING-IN-PUBLICATION DATA
Lang, John, 1947–
    Six poets from the mountain south / John Lang.
        p. cm. — (Southern literary studies)
    Includes bibliographical references and index.
    ISBN 978-0-8071-3560-0 (pbk. : alk. paper) 1. American poetry—Southern States—
History and criticism. 2. American poetry—Appalachian Region—History and criticism.
3. Appalachian Region, Southern—In literature. I. Title.

    PS261.L36 2010
    811'.5409975—dc22

                                                                2009027449

The paper in this book meets the guidelines for permanence and durability of the Committee
on Production Guidelines for Book Longevity of the Council on Library Resources. ♾

For Esther

CONTENTS

Acknowledgments ix

Introduction 1

1. Jim Wayne Miller and the Brier's Cosmopolitan
   Regionalism: "You Must Be Born Again" 9

2. Fred Chappell: "Flesh-tree and Tree of Spirit" 38

3. Robert Morgan: "Mountains Speak in Tongues" 73

4. Jeff Daniel Marion: "Measures of Grace" 99

5. Kathryn Stripling Byer: "Laying up Treasures on Earth" 125

6. Charles Wright: "The Energy of Absence" 157

Works Cited 195

Index 205

ACKNOWLEDGMENTS

MUCH OF THIS BOOK WAS COMPLETED during a yearlong sabbatical funded jointly by Emory & Henry College and the Appalachian College Association, which is supported by the Andrew W. Mellon Foundation Trust. Some of the initial research was also funded by summer grants from Emory & Henry College and by a Mednick Fellowship from the Virginia Foundation of Independent Colleges that enabled me to travel to the North Carolina Collection housed in the Wilson Library at the University of North Carolina and to the Appalachian collections of both Berea College and the University of Kentucky. I wish to thank all four of these organizations for their generosity and their confidence in my work. I am grateful as well for the assistance offered by the many librarians at the institutions where I conducted research and for the superb copyediting of Jo Ann Kiser.

I am especially indebted to Fred Hobson of the University of North Carolina, who first encouraged me to consider such a project, who helped me obtain a contract from Louisiana State University Press, and who then read each of the chapters of the book as I completed them, offering many helpful suggestions. My interest in the poets whose work is analyzed in this volume arose, in part, as a result of personal contacts with each of them through Emory & Henry's annual literary festival, an event which, for over a quarter of a century, has brought many of the best writers from southern Appalachia to our campus for readings, the presentation of critical papers, and a public interview, the proceedings subsequently published in a special issue of the *Iron Mountain Review*. My friend and former colleague Robert Denham, who helped to establish the tradition of these festivals and launched the review, continues to inspire with his own recent scholarship on Charles Wright, including two books, *Charles Wright in Conversation* and *The Early Poetry of Charles Wright*, that appeared after my manuscript had been submitted to Louisiana State University Press.

I'm also grateful to the journals, presses, and individuals that granted permission to reprint works on or by Fred Chappell, Jeff Daniel Marion, Robert Morgan, and Jim Wayne Miller. They include the University of South Carolina Press for excerpts from chapters 3 and 4 of my *Understanding Fred Chappell*; *Shenandoah: The Washington & Lee University Review* and *Pembroke Magazine* for essays on Morgan; *Appalachian Heritage* for an essay on Marion; Jeff Daniel Marion and Celtic Cat Publishing for use of poems from *Ebbing & Flowing Springs: New and Selected Prose and Poems, 1976–2001*; and Mary Ellen Miller, literary executor of the estate of Jim Wayne Miller, for use of poems by Jim Wayne Miller.

SIX POETS FROM THE MOUNTAIN SOUTH

INTRODUCTION

IN AN ESSAY ENTITLED "Appalachian Literature at Home in This World," Jim Wayne Miller distinguishes dramatically between what he considers the characteristic orientation of religion in Appalachia and the main thrust of the region's literature. According to Miller, "While the varieties of Protestantism found in the Appalachian region often differ sharply with regard to certain theological points, denominations share a decidedly otherworldly outlook. . . . Yet Appalachian literature is—and always has been—as decidedly worldly, secular, and profane in its outlook as the traditional religion appears to be spiritual and otherworldly" (13). Although Miller's assessment of "the worldly, secular tradition of Appalachian literature" (17) may accurately describe his own poetry and fiction—and that of James Still, the subject of Miller's essay—that assessment does not do justice to the pervasive role that religious and spiritual concerns play in the work of many of the region's finest writers. Yet Miller's essay does identify a crucial tension between traditional religion in the mountain South and the stance adopted by the majority of its best-known literary authors. That stance is one of rebellion, of resistance to the excessive otherworldliness and the harsh judgmentalism of much mountain religion.

While this book focuses on six poets from the Appalachian South— Kathryn Stripling Byer, Fred Chappell, Jeff Daniel Marion, Jim Wayne Miller, Robert Morgan, and Charles Wright—that spirit of rebellion is equally evident in a novel like Harriette Arnow's *The Dollmaker*, especially in the conflict between Gertie Nevels and her dour mother. Gertie challenges her mother's view of Jesus as wrathful judge and envisions instead "a Christ who had loved people, had liked to mingle with them and laugh and sing" (64). Whereas for Gertie "Jesus walks th earth in peace and love" (77), for her mother "Christ is a scourgen th world like he scourged th temple" (64). Arnow makes the pernicious effect of Gertie's mother's view evident when Gertie's five-year-old daughter Cassie is heard speaking of "this sinful Satan-ridden earth" and "this Satan-ridden world" (133), echoing the language of the preacher to whom Cassie has been exposed. Indeed, Gertie refers to the minister, Battle John Brand, as "stampeding the souls of his flock to Christ with his twin whips of Hell and God" (68). The violence of the preacher's methods is made explicit in his nickname, Battle John, and in the image of his twin whips.

In *Appalachian Mountain Religion: A History,* the most comprehensive study to date of the region's religious life, Deborah Vansau McCauley argues convincingly for a distinctive religious tradition in Appalachia's mountain communities (as opposed to its cities, towns, and valleys), a tradition sharply differentiated from that of the mainline Protestant denominations. McCauley refers to "the autonomous, nonhierarchical, nondenominational character of mountain church life" (38) and to these churches' "expressive and ecstatic worship traditions" (15) grounded in "grace and the Holy Spirit" rather than "free will and rational decision" (14). "Mountain religion," she notes, "pursues a distinctly nonrational mode of religious experience" (11), a trait that might help explain some of the skepticism with which mountain religion is met by many of the region's poets and fiction writers.

With the exception of Robert Morgan, however, whose mother was a Southern Baptist and whose father was a member of the Pentecostal Holiness church, the latter one of the two nondenominational groups that McCauley most closely identifies with mountain religion (38), the poets whose work will be analyzed here grew up in mainstream denominations: Presbyterian for Byer, Methodist for Chappell and Miller, Southern Baptist for Marion, Episcopalian for Wright. Yet what mountain religion shares with these denominations, despite the range of worship practices and doctrinal differences both within mountain religion and across these denominations, is an otherworldly stance. Of mountain people McCauley writes, "Their religious identity is atemporal, aligned with the spiritual realm" (440). Although at one point she mentions in passing "the world God created for them [believers] to cherish" (275), McCauley offers no evidence to support her claim that the representatives of mountain religion do, in fact, cherish creation. Instead she comments on "mountain religion's overwhelming emphasis on the spiritual realm—'those things which [are] not seen'" (11; McCauley's brackets), a viewpoint that tends to denigrate the physical world.

A similar stance is evident in Loyal Jones's *Faith and Meaning in the Upland South*, a book that draws heavily on oral history, the self-reported beliefs of mountain folk. Acknowledging that Satan receives more attention in Upland religion than in mainline churches, Jones states, "Satan's domain may be hell, but the main concern is that he has permeated all that is worldly. Upland Christians constantly worry about what is of the world and what is of God. Their struggle is between the worldly and the spiritual—the natural and the supernatural" (76). This conflict is manifest in the remarks of several of Jones's informants, one of whom stresses that "separation from the world" is essential to authentic religious life (85). Another of his informants, a pastor, says, "Through the Fall, we have become the servants of sin and our bodies have become the workshops of Satan" (88), while a third refers to "this sin-cursed world" (92), a phrase strikingly similar to the words of Arnow's Cassie.

The otherworldiness that Miller and Arnow view as deeply problematic goes largely unchallenged by McCauley and Jones, perhaps because it is all too characteristic not only of mountain religion but also of Christianity generally, a religion that has been insufficiently incarnational throughout most of the past two thousand years. Contemporary critiques of historical Christianity by environmentalists—both religious and nonreligious—and by eco-theologians have highlighted Christianity's frequent failure to embrace adequately its doctrines of creation and Incarnation. As early as 1967, Lynn White, Jr., had written in the journal *Science* of Christianity's heavy responsibility for what White called, in the title of his article, "The Historical Roots of Our Ecologic Crisis." Wendell Berry likewise speaks of "the culpability of Christianity in the destruction of the natural world" (93) in his essay "Christianity and the Survival of Creation." In that essay Berry deplores the philosophical dualism, a legacy of Platonism, that has shaped both Western thought and historical Christianity: "a cleavage, a radical discontinuity between . . . spirit and matter, religion and nature" (105). "This dualism," he adds, "is the most destructive disease that afflicts us. In its best-known, its most dangerous, and perhaps its fundamental version, it is the dualism of body and soul" (105), a dualism illustrated all too well by the quotation from Jones's second informant about our bodies as Satan's workshops.

As already noted, Miller's dichotomy between an "otherworldly" religion and a "worldly, secular" Appalachian literature in many ways threatens to reinforce a dualistic perspective. But most of the poets examined in this book view nature not as discontinuous from religion but rather as a source of religious revelation and spiritual insight. Like Ralph Waldo Emerson in his essay "Nature," they see nature as "the symbol of spirit" (1114) and find in natural phenomena ways to speak about the divine. For Emerson, nature is a language that helps convey spiritual truths. The same can be said, as we will see, of Robert Morgan, whose poetry is deeply influenced by Emerson's conception of nature as language and symbol. At the same time, however, most of these poets tend to reject the deep-seated dualism of Emerson's thought, its emphasis on "Idealism," the primacy of spirit or soul, and its relegation of the body to what Emerson calls the "NOT ME" (1107). In *Midquest,* for example, Fred Chappell creates a character whom Ole Fred, the speaker of the poem, addresses as "Uncle Body," a character clearly intended to combat the kind of dualism that Emerson takes for granted and against which Berry warns.

In recent years Berry's call for a renewal of Christian thinking about the creation has been echoed by countless theologians, particularly those conscious of the growing ecological crisis. In *Earth Community, Earth Ethics,* for instance, Larry L. Rasmussen, a Lutheran theologian, invokes an "earth faith" (11) that will reject "the earth avoidance carried in the teaching of *contemptus mundi* (contempt of the world)" (10). Miller's conception of Appalachian literature as "at home in this world" is obviously in sympathy with Rasmussen's rejection of what he terms "the most popular religious metaphor of all, the metaphor of ascetic ascent, throwing off the corruptible things of earth for the precious booty of heaven" (10), a metaphor implicitly rejected as well in the titles of three of Robert Morgan's books of poems: *Land Diving, Groundwork,* and *Topsoil Road.* In order to heighten human care for the earth, Rasmussen proposes that writers create symbols drawn from nature—trees, rivers, mountains, stars— that speak across cultures and religious traditions. And just as Emerson numbered beauty among the four benefits or uses of nature, so Rasmussen contends that "images of beauty bear a moral vision and carry moral weight. They encourage some behaviors and restrain others. . . . Their orienting presence shapes moral imagination and human character itself" (195). By embracing and respecting the natural world, human beings can reverence the divine. At the same time they also acknowledge their dependence on a natural order beyond their capacity to make, an awareness of which generally gives rise to expressions of gratitude, humility, and praise, traditional expressions of religious emotion or religious consciousness of the sort that is apparent in a poem like Chappell's "A Prayer for the Mountains."

Such recognition of humanity's ultimate dependence on nature, both uncultivated and cultivated, is all too rare in an age when many people appear to believe that food originates in supermarkets. But the poets on whom this book focuses suffer no such delusions. With the exception of Charles Wright, all grew up on farms or had a grandparent living on a farm. These writers' roots, then, are deep in the soil, a point worth underscoring about Appalachian literature more generally. In a recent essay on Appalachian poetry, Jim Clark has traced the influence of Donald Davidson and the Vanderbilt Agrarians on Jesse Stuart, James Still, Don West, and Jim Wayne Miller, all of whom studied at Vanderbilt. In a broader study of twentieth-century southern literature, *Reclaiming the American Farmer,* a book that includes chapters on such first-generation native Appalachian authors as Stuart, Arnow, Elizabeth Madox Roberts, and Olive Tilford Dargan (Fielding Burke), Mary Weaks-Baxter argues that the Southern Literary Renaissance itself, during the decades from 1900 through 1960, built upon a redefinition of the South in terms not of the aristocratic planter class but rather of the "southern democratic ideals that were largely valued in Thomas Jefferson's notion of the American farmer" (2). The same might be said of the more recent flowering of Appalachian literature, from the 1960s through the present, a renaissance that Miller himself helped to initiate and sustain until his untimely death in 1996. The connection between farming and poetry is celebrated in Fred Chappell's essay "The Poet and the Plowman," which focuses on Vergil's *Georgics* and which highlights "awe of nature, reverence for the earth" as shared emphases of these two vocations (74). Quoting Vergil's admonitions *Nudus ara, sere nudus* (plow naked, sow naked), Chappell remarks, "The words are there to remind us of the ceremonial, and ultimately religious, nature of farming" (76).

Insofar as Appalachian poetry has taken the natural world and agrarian life as major subjects, it has sometimes been criticized as backward-looking, hopelessly nostalgic, and perilously out of touch with current economic and political realities, as Frank Einstein observes in his essay "The Politics of Nostalgia: Uses of the Past in Recent Appalachian Poetry." But in light of the increased attention among eco-critics and eco-theologians to the degradation of our natural environment, Appalachian poetry rooted in both American Romanticism and agrarianism achieves a new level of interest and "relevance." As Lawrence Buell declares (quoting sociologist Ulrich Beck) in *Writing for an Endangered World*, "Only if nature is brought into people's everyday images, into the stories they tell, can its beauty and its suffering be seen and focused on" (1). One of the major effects of the poetry of these six Appalachian writers is to revivify the natural world, to encourage readers "to see the miraculous in the common," in Emerson's phrase in "Nature" (1134).

Yet the authors who are the subject of this study are not self-conscious eco-poets. Their profound interest in nature arises not from environmental consciousness but from a reaction against the drastic dualism of the religious tradition in which they were raised (although, as will become evident, Charles Wright is something of an exception here, for the diction of his poems is steeped in dualistic terminology). Much of their work reflects, though to different degrees, what Robert Morgan calls in *Good Measure* the importance of "coming out from under Calvinism" (142), what he labels its "terror and exclusions" (25), as well as its dissociation of God from the natural world, which Rasmussen describes as "the Calvinist insistence that the finite cannot hold the infinite" (272). While these six poets come out of a range of denominational backgrounds, none of them, as adults, have aligned themselves with any organized church. All, however, address religious concerns and/or make use of religious diction and metaphors. Whether they define themselves merely as a "God-fearing agnostic" (Wright) or see themselves as only an "ethnic Protestant" (Miller), religious motifs shape their work. The Dantean quest in Chappell's *Midquest* also appears in Wright's poetry, although with much different results. Ultimately, what links these poets, amid their varied responses of faith and doubt, is their allegiance to this world, their celebration of nature, their resistance—again with the complex exception of Wright—to the otherworldliness that has plagued Christianity in general and the churches of the Appalachian region in particular.

The much-noted "love of place" in these writers, their deep affection for the mountains and for other natural phenomena, becomes a means of "placing the soul," in Norman Wirzba's phrase, of discovering the spiritual in the things of this world. However skeptical these poets may be about traditional religious belief, they seem to concur with Rasmussen that human beings encounter the divine, if at all, not by fleeing this world but by embracing it. In Rasmussen's words, "Experiencing the gracious God means, then, falling in love with earth and sticking around, staying home" (280).

In an age of increasing mobility and heightened rootlessness, the term "home" continues to have singular resonance, both individual and collective. The term has often been appropriated in Christian hymnody to designate heaven, an eternal, otherworldly refuge (however much its features may resemble this world's). Consider such hymns as "This World Is Not My Home," "A Poor Way-faring Stranger" (someone who is "just a-going over home"), and "Will the Circle Be Unbroken?" (yes, "in a better home a-waiting in the sky"). Over against such otherworldliness, the poets analyzed in this book tend to set the native ground of the physical world. "Singing the way home," in Jeff Daniel Marion's phrase, they immerse themselves in natural landscapes infused with a spiritual dimension, at least for Byer and Chappell and Marion and Morgan. For Wright, too, the physical world is often a realm of grace, of religious revelation, however fleeting—although Wright seems unable to sustain his momentary glimpses of divine presence even as his poetry enacts an ongoing quest for spiritual insight. Miller alone among these poets appears to lack a strong religious consciousness in his poetry, though he certainly makes significant use of religious subject matter and adapts religious metaphors for his own purposes.

Perhaps my choice of poets deserves some comment. I have been guided, first of all, by their poems' attention to the kinds of issues already discussed in this Introduction. Charles Wright, for instance, has repeatedly spoken of "language, landscape, and the idea of God" as his three principal subjects. Fred Chappell foregrounds religious matters not only by adopting the motif of Dantean pilgrimage in *Midquest* but also by opening and closing *First and Last Words*, his book of prologues and epilogues, with poems based upon the Old and New Testaments. I have been guided, second, by my sense of the high artistic quality of many of these writers' poems and other works. Miller and Marion may not be widely known outside Appalachian literary studies, but both poets merit a larger readership. The current efflorescence of writing by authors from the Appalachian region, which Robert Bain and Joseph M. Flora have called "a

Renaissance within a Renaissance" (14), is almost unimaginable without the example Miller set and the encouragement he provided, while Marion's skillful editing of the literary journal *The Small Farm* from 1975 to 1980 provided an outlet for many of the region's writers, including Morgan and Chappell, both of whom have achieved national reputations. Chappell shared the Bollingen Prize with John Ashbery in 1985, and Morgan's novel *Gap Creek* was an Oprah Book Club selection in 1999. Kathryn Stripling Byer, who succeeded Chappell as North Carolina's poet laureate, has won the Lamont Poetry Prize for *Wildwood Flower,* and Charles Wright, the most widely celebrated of these authors, has received the National Book Award for *Country Music* (1982) and both the Pulitzer Prize and the National Book Critics Circle Award for *Black Zodiac* (1997). Were this study more comprehensive, it could easily include such additional poets from the region as Lynn Powell, Ron Rash, Michael Chitwood, and Diane Gilliam Fisher, all of whom respond in powerful ways to the religious heritage that has been so important a force in Appalachian culture.

As Hyatt Waggoner demonstrates, however, in *American Poets: From the Puritans to the Present,* such religious concerns have been a constant in the poetry of our nation as well (and often its fiction, one might add). Given the country's Puritan heritage, how could it be otherwise? Morgan's phrase "coming out from under Calvinism" might be—and has been—usefully applied not only to Dickinson and Whitman but to Hawthorne, Melville, and Faulkner. The poets examined in this book thus participate in an ongoing debate about the locus of our allegiance as human beings, a debate given greater urgency by the ecological costs of Christianity's tendency, until recently, to denigrate the earth and the natural world for the sake of a heavenly home. As writers from the mountain South who have helped to shape a renewed sense of regional identity in Appalachia, these poets also stand in sharp contrast to the "placelessness" that Leonard Lutwack considers a fundamental motif of much twentieth-century literature. Rootedness, not deracination, is their theme as they seek to sing the way home.

1

JIM WAYNE MILLER AND
THE BRIER'S COSMOPOLITAN
REGIONALISM

"You Must Be Born Again"

THE QUEST FOR HOME is clearly among the central motifs in Jim Wayne Miller's poetry, as it is in his novel *His First, Best Country* (1993), the last book-length publication he completed before his early death of lung cancer three years later at age fifty-nine. Miller is widely considered the progenitor of the ongoing renaissance in Appalachian literature, an awakening he dated from the 1960s. Loyal Jones, the longtime director of the Appalachian Center at Berea College, says of Miller, "He was the natural heir to Cratis D. Williams, the father of Appalachian studies" ("Brightest" 45), and Fred Chappell states, "If it were not for Miller, the Appal lit movement might have foundered before it got started" (qtd. in Leidig 2). Through his numerous essays and reviews, his work as an editor, his role as a poet-in-the-schools, his frequent readings and workshops, and his published poems, Miller inspired and encouraged other writers in the mountain South, helping to create a sense of literary community and justifying Robert Morgan's claim that "[Miller] has done more for Appalachian writing in our time than anyone else" (*Good Measure* 27).

Born in 1936 in Buncombe County, North Carolina, about fifteen miles west of Asheville, Miller was raised there on a small farm near Leicester. Both sets of his grandparents farmed, his maternal grandparents running the farm on which Miller's parents lived. As a high school student Miller read Horace Kephart's *Our Southern Highlanders* and heard Dr. Willis Weatherford, a trustee of Berea College, speak on behalf of that institution. Miller enrolled there in 1954, majoring in English, and later attended Vanderbilt University, where he earned a doctorate in German, with a dissertation on nineteenth-century German poet Annette von Droste-Hülshoff. Miller once told an interviewer that the German authors who most influenced him, also including Eduard Mörike and Theodor

9

Storm, "tended to be regional writers of their place." "There's a phenomenon in German literature," he added, "that's known as *Heimatsliteratur,
heimat* meaning homeland. So *Heimatsliteratur* is writing that is sort of
consciously regional" (Beattie 257). Among Miller's teachers in his mi-
nor field (American literature) at Vanderbilt were Donald Davidson and
Randall Stewart, and Miller has noted in his essay for the *Contemporary
Authors Autobiography Series* that it was his mistaken expectation of studying with the Fugitives/Agrarians that prompted his initial interest in Vanderbilt ("Jim Wayne Miller" 282).

After completing his doctorate, Miller accepted a position as professor
of German language and literature at Western Kentucky University, remaining there in the Department of Languages and Intercultural Studies
throughout his academic career. Miller's training at Vanderbilt thus provided him with an international, not just a regional, perspective on which
he was able to draw when he turned his attention to his native Appalachia. Miller's recognition of the important ways in which literature can
assist in defining group identity heightened his consciousness of the role
his work could play in the Appalachian identity movement of the 1960s
and 1970s.

That movement gained impetus from the renewed attention to the region during the War on Poverty in the early 1960s. It also grew out of a
desire to subvert the stereotypes that had originated in the fiction of such
non-native Local Color writers as Mary Noailles Murfree and John Fox, Jr.
Although native Appalachian writers of the generation before Miller—
authors such as Thomas Wolfe, Elizabeth Madox Roberts, Jesse Stuart,
Louise McNeill, James Still, and Harriette Arnow—had already addressed
these distortions of mountain people and their lives, the stereotypes persisted. The heightened political consciousness of the 1960s and the new
national focus on Appalachia's economic woes led to renewed interest in
the region's history and culture among Appalachians, for many of whom
the very term "Appalachian" was still relatively new.

Miller chose to stand at the center of this effort to define (or redefine)
the region's identity, to recover its past, and to shape its future. Many of
Miller's essays, still uncollected, address the nature and purpose of public education in the region, with Miller insisting that Appalachia's children must have at least a portion of their own experience mirrored in
curricular materials. This assumption is one Miller derived from Donald

Davidson, as Miller makes clear in his essay "A Post-Agrarian Regional-ism for Appalachia," an essay published in 1980 to commemorate the fif-tieth anniversary of the publication of *I'll Take My Stand* (67–68). A year later Miller published *I Have a Place*, an anthology of Appalachian writ-ing, both literary and historical, for use in public schools. Miller hoped that such materials might help prevent the frequent out-migration of the region's better educated young people. As he wrote in his essay "Appala-chian Education: A Critique and Suggestions for Reform," "The success-ful school will teach students how to live better at home" (17). Yet Miller also emphasized, in the "Note to the Teacher" in *I Have a Place*, that the book was intended to be used only as a supplementary text; it was not meant to promote provincialism (192).

Miller's insistence on the local and regional as a corrective to an ex-clusively national and international focus arises not only from his identi-fication with Appalachia but also from his commitment to an aesthetics that he traces to Emerson. In the essay "Regions, Folk Life, and Literary Criticism" Miller quotes approvingly Emerson's advice in "The American Scholar" to "sit at the feet of the familiar" and to remember that "things near are not less beautiful and wondrous than things remote" (qtd. on 181). "Accepting Things Near," the title of another of Miller's essays, is a central principle of his poetry, as it is of William Stafford's, whose phras-ing Miller cites. In "Regions, Folk Life, and Literary Criticism" Miller also quotes Emerson's pronouncement, "a fact is true poetry, the most beauti-ful of fables" (184). The Emerson who finds the miraculous in the com-monplace resonates with Miller, who says in "Accepting Things Near," "I am in love with the ordinary, the common place. I like to make the or-dinary shine—by holding it in just the right light" (17). For Miller, espe-cially in his poems of the 1980s and 1990s, that light often depends on surprising yet apt figurative language, on startling juxtapositions, and on humor, both lighthearted and sharply satirical.

Given the all-too-common tendency among some literary scholars to use "regional" as a derogatory term, what Miller calls "a term of relega-tion" ("Anytime" 2), Miller's emphatic rejection of provincialism needs to be underscored. Although he concedes that identification with a region and its traditional culture can be—and has at times been—an obstacle to desirable change ("Anytime" 10), he looks forward to a redefinition of the terms "regional" and "regionalism" that will free them of their weight of disparagement ("People Waking Up" 72). Moreover, he intends for his own work to represent a more inclusive perspective. As he explains in his essay for the *Contemporary Authors Autobiography Series*, "While my work is associated with the southern Appalachian region (and, I hope, is a genuine expression of the region), I have never wanted to be associated with anything less than a cosmopolitan regionalism, an awareness of our little histories and local traditions compatible with national and international perspectives" ("Jim Wayne Miller" 290). Miller's aim, then, is to blend the universal and the particular rather than to treat the regional as somehow antithetical to the universal.

Just as Miller wants to dissociate himself from provincialism, so he seeks to avoid accusations of nostalgia and sentimentality. In the preface to his second book, *The More Things Change the More They Stay the Same* (1971), a collection of what Miller calls "song-poems" grounded in political protest, Miller observes, "Trying to live on nostalgia is like trying to live on a diet of sugar water" (unpaged). But Miller also contends that nostalgia can be useful when "what is often taken for nostalgia for the past contains those very ideas and images that have a future" ("Appalachian Studies" 109). In fact, one of Miller's essays bears the paradoxical title "Nostalgia for the Future," an essay in which Miller unites past and future when he remarks, "The future derives its strength, its potency, from the past" (19).

What are the "ideas and images" from Appalachia's past "that have a future," according to Miller? Among what he calls the "distinguishing features of the shared history and collective experience revealed in the work of Appalachian writers," Miller lists "a sense of the past working still in the present," "a sense of close attachment to the earth," and "a determination to endure" ("Appalachian Writing" 420), and he associates that attachment to the earth not only with the region's agrarian past and such images as the farm and farmhouse but also with more generalized images drawn from nature—birds, deer, fish, rivers, trees—that reveal a sense of connection to place and provide a source of deep emotional satisfaction.

Miller's poetic career began with the publication of *Copperhead Cane* in 1964, a book that focuses upon the familial past through a sequence of twenty poems (plus the dedicatory title poem) about the poet's maternal grandfather, Fred Smith, who died in 1962. Although the collection contains eleven additional poems, Miller's best work here appears in the

sequence, which consists primarily of sonnets, many of them about activities associated with farming and the natural world such as hanging
tobacco, burning tobacco beds, mending fence posts, hunting, and fishing. Elegiac in tone, this sequence demonstrates Miller's mastery of traditional forms "wrought out of my gnarled grief," as he says in the opening
poem. Like the copperhead cane of the book's title, the poems become a
means of support amid such grief.

Miller returned to the subject of his grandfather's death in his third
book, *Dialogue with a Dead Man* (1974), which reprints in the first of its
three parts fifteen of the poems from the sequence that dominates *Copperhead Cane*, along with one new poem, "Old Man All My Life." In part 2,
"Dialogue with a Dead Man," Miller writes both in traditional forms like
the sonnet and in free verse, but the major departure from the earlier
collection occurs in the poem "Listening," in which the grandfather begins to speak for himself. Identifying himself with an agrarian lifestyle in
"Trellis," a sonnet variant, the grandfather remarks:

> For my life was heat of the sun, strain and sweat
> of man and mule mingled in newground.
> The grating plowpoint darted from root
> to stump to rock, snapping singletrees
> and tracechains . . . (30)

Miller's diction evokes farm life while his sound effects—the plosive *t*'s
and *p*'s of "grating," "plowpoint," "darted," "root," and "stump," along with
the hard *c* of "rock"—reflect the harsh conditions of that mode of life.
That the grandfather's death has resulted in the farm's decay becomes evident in the poem's sestet, in which the grandson speaks:

> Now sloe-eyed cattle are swishing flies
> in black shade where you left saplings standing.
> Bees pasturing honeysuckle are rising
> and drifting down at the springdrain trickle.
> Your life is a trellis I train verses up,
> just as these roses climb the weathered porch.

In these lines cultivated fields have returned to woods and bees have assumed the farmer's task of "pasturing." Yet here the poet relates his poetic
vocation to his grandfather's farming and to nature's flowering, just as he

does in the following poem, whose printed appearance on the page takes the shape of a mountain, when he states, "I break / these poems / like mountain / newgrounds" and claims to be "Drawing a verse as straight as / any furrow you [his grandfather] ever turned" (31). The image of the trellis affirms the poet's dependence upon his grandfather, but as an image drawn from the world of gardening, it also suggests the vital interconnectedness of humanity and nature and the importance of cultivating nature.

Part 3 of *Dialogue* is entitled "Family Reunion." Added to Miller's manuscript at the suggestion of the book's editor at the University of Georgia Press, the poems in part 3 are less unified than those in the preceding sections and are generally of lesser artistry. But the section's title poem once again reinforces Miller's theme of the interrelationship of past and present by asserting that the dead are also present at this family reunion: "They are looking out of the eyes of children" (78). Despite this closing poem's positing of continuity, however, Miller has acknowledged that it was his sense of loss, both personal and cultural, that impelled him to write about his grandfather. Responding to an interviewer's question about the "evolution" in his books as he moved toward *The Mountains Have Come Closer* (1980), Miller notes, "Your question suggests to me that maybe one of [the] reasons why I wrote poems about my grandfather . . . was because I was mourning not just a man but a particular way of life" (Woodhull 16).

Although this statement should probably be attributed more to hindsight than to the poet's original intent, by the late 1970s Miller's poems were moving toward a more explicit focus on regional issues, not just personal experience. During this time Miller had begun using a persona he called the Brier, an epithet applied to Appalachians who had moved north of the Ohio River to cities like Cincinnati, Dayton, Columbus, Detroit, and Indianapolis. This out-migration itself reflected the region's troubled economy: the loss of farming as a livelihood and the boom-or-bust fluctuations in the coal industry. According to Miller, "The Brier is a kind of quintessential or typical or representative mountain man" (qtd. in Arnold 209). "My appropriation of the figure," he says in his previously cited autobiographical essay, "represented a movement beyond personal experience to a point where I could write of the collective experience of several million southern Appalachians known to other Americans chiefly through the stereotypes found in popular fiction, in movies, and on television. . . . [T]he Brier . . . accommodated my own experiences, my grandfather's, and the experience of other southern Appalachians who bore ascribed identities into a period of wrenching change" (286–87). This statement makes it clear that the figure of the grandfather persists within the persona of the Brier, and in such later poems as "Brier Coming of Age" and "In This Dream" from *Brier, His Book* (1988), the grandfather continues to serve an iconic role.

The first book of poems in which the Brier appears, however, is *The Mountains Have Come Closer*, Miller's most carefully structured and tightly unified collection, for which he won the Thomas Wolfe Award. The volume's title seems to derive from the closing lines of the penultimate poem in *Dialogue*, "Visitors," in which Miller writes, "After last night's storm the air / is so clear, even the mountains / have moved closer" (77). But the title also illustrates Miller's heightened sense of identification with the mountains, an intensified emotional (not just geographical) proximity. And better than any other collection of Miller's poems, this book demonstrates the crucial role that the quest for home plays in his work, as several critics have noted. Don Johnson, for instance, argues that "*The Mountains Have Come Closer* explores the implications of the loss of home for the rural Appalachian" ("Appalachian Homeplace" 133), while Wade Hall views the Brier as Miller's "Appalachian version of the archetypal wayfaring stranger" (29) who draws on "a storehouse of home memories" to sustain him (31). For yet a third critic, Marianne Worthington, a principal theme of the book is "recovering and repossessing an Appalachian heritage and culture that has dissolved into a nightmarish postmodern landscape" ("Lost" 144).

The Mountains Have Come Closer contains forty poems divided among three sections of unequal lengths. Part 1, "In the American Funhouse," as its title indicates, includes several poems that employ surrealistic, disorienting images, a trait it shares with poems from parts 2 and 3 as well. All but one of the poems in part 1 use first-person singular pronouns (the exception being the mock horoscope of "If Your Birthday Is Today"). The opening poem, "Saturday Morning," depicts the speaker's house as a ship "plowing / gently . . . through / a moderate green sea of grass and wild onions" (3). Miller's nautical imagery in this poem confirms his use of the journey motif while simultaneously negating the customary association of

plowing with the land. The last of the eleven poems in part 1, a poem entitled "Going South," reminds readers of the journey anticipated in "Saturday Morning" while also pinpointing the direction to be taken, a movement back to the speaker's origins, origins linked to the natural world in
the poem's final stanza, in which "the only story worth the telling" is that
"a black river / of birds turned slowly and flowed south" (16)—a *turning*
that foreshadows the call to "conversion" announced in parts 2 and 3.
"Going South" also anticipates part 2 because in that poem the speaker
envisions his own death and thus prepares the reader for the motif of rebirth proclaimed in the title of part 2: "You Must Be Born Again."

Even before that explicit call for rebirth, Miller invokes the agrarian
past in one of the book's finest poems, "A House of Readers":

> At 9:42 on this May morning
> the children's rooms are concentrating too.
> Like a tendril growing toward the sun, Ruth
> moves her book into a wedge of light
> that settles on the floor like a butterfly.
> She turns a page.
> Fred is immersed in magic, cool
> as a Black Angus belly-deep in a farm pond.
>
> The only sounds: pages turning softly.
> This is the quietness
> of bottomland where you can hear only the young corn
> growing, where a little breeze stirs the blades
> and then breathes in again.
>
> I mark my place.
> I listen like a farmer in the rows. (14)

Miller's figurative language and imagery ("like a tendril," "cool / as a Black
Angus," "the quietness / of bottomland") establish continuity between the
human and natural worlds, linking culture and agriculture as the poet
"listen[s] like a farmer in the rows." In the presence of this impulse to
grow through reading, the inanimate ("a wedge of light") becomes animate, settling on the floor "like a butterfly." The relative brevity of the poem's syntactical structures underscores the quiet confidence of the speaker's pronouncements, especially in the two one-line sentences of the final

stanza, a confidence the reader is invited to share through Miller's use of the conversational "you" in line 11. The serenity that marks this moment owes a great deal to the agrarian landscape the poem evokes.

The first-person pronouns used in part 1 disappear in the second and third sections of the book once the representative figure of the Brier gains prominence. As Miller explains in an interview with Loyal Jones, "The Brier is the persona I adopted after I stopped being able to say 'I'" (62), a statement that expresses the plight of the person described in "No Name," the second poem in part 2. Finding himself "settled in a suburb, north of himself" (28), the Brier comes to realize what the title of part 2 announces, although the rebirth Miller portrays occurs in secular terms and is largely a product of renewed identification with ancestral figures, particularly the Brier's grandparents and mother. In "Turn Your Radio On," for example, the person spoken of as "he," while living in a northern city, is described as "try[ing] to keep a sense of direction south" (21), an effort he compares to tuning in to a far-off radio station. He also uses a shoebox of family photographs to awaken memories of home, focusing on his grandparents:

> Weathered and home-made like the chairs they sat in, and like the house
> and barn, so comfortably in place, they looked like one another.
> Something about the way they sat spoke to him through his own thoughts
>
> all the way from the mountains, like a powerful transmitter: this place
> belongs to us, their faces said, and we belong to it. (21–22)

The sense of being rooted in place that these lines convey recurs in "Bird in the House," in which the unnamed "he" portrays his ancestors' and his childhood neighbors' "rooted lives" as "great trees, his summer shade" (32). Yet the title of this poem refers to this figure's plight as he confronts the abandoned farms and homes once inhabited by these people, with Miller comparing that persona to "a sparrow beating its wings at a window inside / the emptied house" (32). Fleshless bones are also a prominent image in part 2 because the Brier recognizes the difficulty of recovering a sense of belonging to this altered landscape, as is also evident in a poem like "Down Home," which, despite its title, focuses on the returning Brier's estrangement from his native place.

At almost the exact center of this book, however, Miller places "Restoring an Old Farmhouse," the twenty-first of the volume's forty poems and the tenth of the twenty poems that comprise part 2. This poem is paired with the preceding poem, "Down Home," by their shared emphasis on feelings that the poet no longer embraces. In the latter poem, in fact, Miller writes of "Dismantling country feelings," an idea made more emphatic by its placement in a separate stanza. But the subsequent two-line stanza immediately adds, "Tearing down, building up again / from what was salvaged" (29). The work of reconstruction outlined in this poem reflects Miller's commitment to grounding the future on what is valuable from the past, for the restoration proceeds by utilizing materials from the old farmhouse. In the words of the poem's final stanzas,

> A coming shape, a new room and view,
> rose from old flooring.
>
> Two times mingled. Fresh sawdust
> spumed yellow as sunlight from old timber. (29)

Not only does this passage vividly illustrate Miller's theme; it also exemplifies his skillful use of diction, sound effects, and figurative language. In both stanzas the "coming," the "new" and "fresh," arises from the "old," with the long vowel sounds of "shape" and "view" and "rose" and "old" expressing the expansiveness of the new possibilities the poem envisions. The internal rhyme of "new" and "view" in the first line quoted is echoed by "Two" and "spumed" in the first syllable of the third and fourth lines, thus interweaving the stanzas. The verb "spumed" is both apt and vigorous, while the simile "as sunlight" firmly embeds the restorative process in the natural world, the sawdust's color aligning this human construct (the house) with nature.

Such alignment of the human and the natural worlds is a principal strategy throughout *The Mountains Have Come Closer*. In "Light Leaving," for instance, Miller compares nightfall to "his mother's black hair falling over her neck / and down her back when she loosened her combs in the evening" (30), a comparison that domesticates the onset of darkness. In "His Hands" the hands "snuffling about / in his pockets for cigarettes" resemble "a dog / tracking a mole" (24), and in "Bird in the House" people's "stories on the porch at night" are equated with "rain on the roof" (32), a metaphor that reflects Miller's belief in the nurturing, life-enhancing power of storytelling. Sometimes Miller relates the human to cultivated

nature, as when he refers to "any small farm of flesh" (23), a phrase reminiscent of Thoreau's remark in *Walden* about those who "find it labor
enough to subdue and cultivate a few cubic feet of flesh" (1809).

Part 3 of *Mountains* obtains its title from the longest poem in the
collection—in fact, the longest poem Miller ever published—"Brier Sermon." That sermon takes as its text the imperative that gives part 2 its
title. Eight shorter poems precede this section's title poem, with the first
of them, "Harvest," evincing the poet's contentment as he considers his
career. Although the poem opens with self-deprecating references to the
poet's life as "weathered and old-fashioned," "his shriveled wisdom [hang-
ing] like peppers / and shuckybeans from a cabin rafter," the poet is heart-
ened when he recalls the songs—that is, the ballads—brought to North
America by his ancestors, "songs that still remembered the salt salt sea /
and held all past time green in the month of May / and made all love and
death and sorrow sweet" (43). Comparing his poems to these songs, Miller
thinks of them "gathered / up in books, kept on a shelf like dry seeds / in
an envelope" (43), seeds that will germinate upon planting. Just as his
ancestors transported themselves to a new land, so their descendants in
contemporary Appalachia are often in transit to new places: "Now they
moved mountains to the cities," the poet notes, immediately adding, "and
made all love and death and sorrow sweet there" (43). Miller's repetition
of this phrasing at the end of successive stanzas emphasizes that mountain people need not abandon their cultural heritage in moving outside
Appalachia, a theme on which he dwells at length in "Brier Sermon."

"Harvest" concludes with two brief, contrasting stanzas that articulate
Miller's poetic credo:

> Heaviness was always left behind
> to perish, to topple like a stone chimney.
>
> But what was lightest lasted, lived in song.

In these stanzas form mirrors content, for Miller devotes two lines, appropriately, to heaviness and just one line to lightness. At the same time,
he makes the first stanza more prosaic, even awkward, especially in the
phrasing of its simile. Had Miller written "like a chimney stone" instead
of "like a stone chimney," the line would have had an iambic pentameter
rhythm. Instead, Miller saves that rhythm for the poem's final line, where

the meter is reinforced by the alliteration of the *l*'s on stressed syllables in three consecutive feet.

Most of the other short poems in part 3—for example, "The Brier Losing Touch with His Traditions," "He Sings Ballads," and "The Brier Reviewing Novels"—deal with the stereotypes that plague Appalachia and its people. Or, as in "Abandoned" and "How America Came to the Mountains," the poems portray the destructive impact of mainstream America on mountain culture. Contemplating out-migration in "Abandoned," the "hundreds of coves and hollers / fallen silent," the Brier compares his life first to an abandoned house, then to an even bleaker household scene that composes the poem's final stanza:

> Or else his life became the house
> seen once in a coalcamp in Tennessee:
> the second story blown off in a storm
> so stairs led up into the air
> and stopped. (46)

Such images of desolation are countered by the image of the restored farmhouse at the center of the book, by experiences of ongoing delight in "Shapes" (45), and by the Brier's reference to his current residence in "As If, Kentucky," a place name that evokes the power of the imagination (fueled in part, presumably, by memory) to create alternatives to the status quo embodied in "Is, Illinois" (48).

"Brier Sermon—'You Must Be Born Again,'" the collection's final poem, extends this vision of alternatives, the didacticism implicit in its title leavened by Miller's humor and irony. The Brier delivers this sermon not on Sunday, significantly, but on Saturday, and he preaches *sans* Bible, details meant to indicate the secular nature of this rebirth. Yet the Brier quotes scripture with authority, not only the imperative "You Must Be Born Again" but also—and just as important—the first four words of Jesus's statement, "In my father's house are many rooms" (53; John 14:2). For the Brier his auditors' rebirth depends on their reclaiming the home left to them by their foreparents, on their affirmation of the things of value in that inheritance. "The house our foreparents left had a song, had a story," the Brier proclaims (54). "If you're lost," he adds, "I say it's because / you're not living in your father's house" (55). Miller makes it clear, however, that inhabiting, or re-inhabiting, that house is not a matter of physical but of psychic relocation. Nor is it a matter of returning to the past, as the Brier points out:

> . . . you don't have to live in the past.
> You can't, even if you try.
>
> . . . .
>
> You don't have to think ridge-to-ridge
> the way they [your foreparents] did.
> You can think ocean-to-ocean. (55)

Here the Brier becomes a spokesperson for Miller's cosmopolitan regionalism and for the power of loving memory. The primary sin which the Brier denounces is forgetfulness (56), but he also deplores his listeners' willingness to accept the outside world's stereotypes of mountaineers (61).

Asked what being born again is like, the Brier responds with paradoxical statements that echo biblical texts: "It's like becoming a little child again / but being grown up too"; "It's being old wine in a new bottle"; "It's going back to what you were before / without losing what you've since become" (63). Perhaps most important, "It's being at home everywhere" (63), a declaration that underscores the possibility of leaving the mountains physically without losing what the Brier calls "the spiritual ground" beneath one's feet (60, 62). This idea of "being at home everywhere" is one Miller anticipates in *Dialogue with a Dead Man* both in "On Native Ground" and in "The Bee Woman" (57, 76).

In "Brier Sermon," however, no one is converted by the Brier's words, and at poem's end he finds himself standing almost alone on the sidewalk across from the Green Stamp Redemption Store, an emblem of the commercial values of contemporary America. When traffic stops at the street corner, the Brier disappears "behind a motor home" and has vanished when that vehicle pulls away. Although some critics have seen the motor home as an image of American rootlessness, that vehicle can also be seen as an apt symbol of the Brier's capacity to move about the country while remaining psychologically and emotionally at home because the Brier carries home with him through memory and imagination. For Miller, it seems, the mountains can come closer wherever one's geographical home happens to be, including Bowling Green, Kentucky, well outside Appalachia, where Miller spent his adult life.

In his essay "Reading, Writing, Region," Miller speaks of the themes

the Brier embodies: "continuity and change, identity, and the compli-
cated relationship of southern Appalachia to what we are pleased to call
'mainstream America'" (126). These themes are also evident in Miller's
second gathering of Brier poems, *Brier, His Book* (1988). As if to confirm
the Brier's capacity to maintain his identity amid change, the book opens
with "The Brier Moves to a New Place," a rural place of "A hundred and
twenty acres, three barns, a house" in the words of the opening line (3).
Yet this place is available to the Brier largely because, as other poems report, rural America is vanishing. The following poem, "Country People,"
for example, contradicts its title by focusing not on people but on the
physical artifacts—corn wagon, garden plot, gate, cistern, smokehouse,
barn—that remain on the abandoned farm, the first four speaking in first
person in the absence of people. Similarly, in "Small Farms Disappearing
in Tennessee," a title taken from a newspaper headline, Miller details the
loss of farmland to real estate development, suggesting that there is "a
syndicate dismantling farms / on dark nights" (31). While comic hyper-
bole lightens the tone of this poem, the problem that Miller addresses is
all too real, as Sharyn McCrumb recognized in using this poem as an epigraph to her novel *The Rosewood Casket* (1996).

   Brier, His Book is not as tightly organized as *The Mountains Have Come
Closer;* yet the collection is essential to an understanding of Miller's emphasis on people's connection to the land, to a specific locale in contact
with nature. In "A Turning," a title that invokes not only change, not only
the movement of the plow or the poet's pen at the end of a row or line,
but also religious conversion, the mood of the poem alters when "One
blade of birdsong / has turned the hollow of his [the Brier's] mind a deep
green / lapping bay where thoughts swarm like shoaling redhorse" (16).
Earlier in the poem the bird's song "springs up like a single blade of grass"
(16), an image that, in conjunction with Miller's highlighting of the color
green, recalls Thoreau's view of "the grass-blade" as "the symbol of perpetual youth" in *Walden,* in the chapter entitled "Spring" (1970). Equally important in the lines quoted from Miller's poem is the simile involving the
shoaling redhorse, for in Miller's novel *His First, Best Country* the arrival of
the redhorse in the creek testifies to springtime's return. "Then miracles
could happen again," Miller writes there, before repeating in prose the
experience recounted in "A Turning" (106–7). The Brier's "conversion"
in "A Turning" is followed by the prose poem "The Faith of Fishermen,"

in which divers discover gigantic catfish below a dam. In the fishermen's words, "We need to know wonders are still alive at the base of the steel and concrete world we've made" (17), a need that Miller associates with all human beings.

The crucial importance of nature is further underscored in the title of part 2 of *Brier, His Book*, "Land & Language." "Written on the Land," this section's opening poem, compares farmers to writers in its opening stanza, the farmers "pushing plows for pens," creating a "story" and a "language" now "unintelligible" in contemporary America—though that writing is clearly more substantial than the writing on water described in the poem's concluding stanza, an activity that results from the flooding of this farming community by the Army Corps of Engineers to create a reservoir (29–30). Such erasure of Appalachian countryside is also the subject of Don Johnson's *Watauga Drawdown* (1990) and Ron Rash's *Raising the Dead* (2002). And with the disappearance of the agrarian lifestyle that this farmland supported, language itself alters, says the poet: "words melt—firedog, milkgap, singletree, sundad" (38). Other words persist, however, particularly names that witness to humanity's former—and still recoverable—intimacy with and pleasure in nature. In a poem simply titled "Names" Miller comments at length on the classical and biblical origins of many of the names common in Appalachia. He also acknowledges names taken from the Cherokee and names grounded in local experience and "wry reflection on it," names such as Sandy Mush, Rabbitham, and Bearwallow (45). But Miller concludes this poem by emphasizing the beauty of the natural world as a source of names and by giving precedence, once again, to the commonplace:

> . . . if the lofty and the grand [classical and biblical names] were humbled
> in the homemade frames and faces of sang diggers,
>
> farmers and squirrel hunters, the homely and low
> discovered their own dignity and beauty
>
> on Sugar Creek, at Snow Hill Gap, in Piney Grove. (46)

Miller's preference for the homemade and the homely is evident in these egalitarian lines, with their echoes of Emerson and Whitman.

As the final poem in part 2 shows, however, Appalachia's—and America's —primordial "green wilderness" has been cruelly ravaged (47). In "The

Brier's Pictorial History of the Mountains," Miller writes, "Cut up and bleeding, the land lies breathing hard, / in places torn and gouged beyond all healing, / in others beautiful and blessed as ever" (49). And so in part 3 of *Brier, His Book,* which includes just four poems under the title "The Country of Conscience," Miller presents the Brier as social critic and spokesperson for national and international, not just regional, concerns. "Why Rosalie Did It" targets the provincialism of small-town life, which is also one of the objects of Miller's social critique in "The Brier Plans a Mountain Vision Center." The focus on vision in the latter poem and on the link between seeing and saying again recalls Emerson, who defined the poet as seer and sayer. Many of the poem's lines echo ideas present in "Brier Sermon," as when the Brier laments that "still few saw farther than ridge-to-ridge" (56) or promises that with the improved vision provided by his center, "They'd see that the longest memory also saw the farthest up ahead" (58).

What distinguishes the portrait of the Brier in *Brier, His Book* from that in *The Mountains Have Come Closer* is that in the closing pair of poems in the later book the Brier embodies the cosmopolitan regionalism about which he had only preached in *Mountains.* "Brier Ambassador," for instance, depicts the Brier on an airline flight to and from Washington, DC, on some unspecified "Brier business" (59). But what the poem highlights is the Brier's profound commitment not to that intentionally vague business agenda but rather to "rivers, lakes, and ponds" (60), that is, to the ongoing health and vitality of nature, on which all human life depends. In an apparent allusion to and inversion of Thoreau's desire to "fish in the sky, whose bottom is pebbly with stars" (1859), Miller has the Brier "fish / for rivers, troll for lakes and ponds" (60). Looking down from the airplane, the Brier sees a lake that resembles "a long-haired man, islands / for eyes, arms outstretched, a crucified Christ" (61). References to Christ are extremely rare in Miller's poetry, so this one seems somewhat contrived or forced until the reader reflects on the despoiled landscape of Appalachia resulting from clear-cut timbering, strip mining, and mountaintop removal.

The book's final poem, "The Country of Conscience," at first seems totally unconnected to the Brier. Dedicated to Czeslaw Milosz, the Nobel Prize-winning expatriate poet from Lithuania, this poem announces its premise, "There are two of every country," in its opening line (62). According to Miller, one of those dimensions of a person's identity depends on landscape, language, and culture, including distinctive foods, and is thus decidedly local or regional. The other derives from abstract political forces aligned with the state and operates on the national level in ways that are often highly artificial, undercutting more local identities. Although the Brier is never mentioned by name in this poem, he is clearly a dissident figure in Miller's poetry, a "refusenik" in relation to the American mainstream. Thus Miller's own regionalist impulse finds a parallel in the resistance of the Baltic countries to the Soviet Union's hegemony, and that parallel leads Miller to enact one kind of cosmopolitan regionalism, namely his recognition that his own (and the Brier's) position vis-à-vis mainstream America is not unique to Appalachia. What Miller says about the Soviet Union applies directly to the quest for authentic regionalism in the United States:

> What's really there, rooted deep,
> keeps coming back: a state of diverse nations,
> countries within a country, nations rooted
> deep in time, rooted deep in place,
> and hardier than rootless uniformity.
>
> . . . .
>
> Deep-rooted speech climbs columned memory,
> leafing out into songs and stories,
> as ivy scales a wall.
> A land and people finds it has a voice,
> discovers a tongue to say itself. (65)

The last five lines in this passage may be read as the manifesto of the Appalachian literary renaissance that Miller helped launch, though they obviously have broader implications as well. Equally striking in those lines is Miller's use of the singular verb "finds" and the singular pronoun "it," unexpected grammatical choices that assume the oneness of the land and its people.

The country of conscience of this poem's title is ultimately a realm of the imagination that houses what Miller calls the individual's "image of himself and what man is / that lives, sprite in a spring, / beyond the state's dominion" (68). It is that image, which can be collective as well as individual, that enables people to "travel everywhere on native ground," as

Miller writes in *Dialogue* (57), because that vision of wholeness, of the past alive in the present, of kinship with nature, of home, cannot be destroyed. The waters that the Brier ambassador sought to protect reappear in the concluding lines of "The Country of Conscience," lines in which Miller addresses the reader directly. In the country of conscience the imagination's vision of identity is restorative, as it is in Frost's "Directive." In Miller's words,

> you lie on your stomach at a bold spring,
> a blue hole nobody knows is there but you
> (you've always known)
> and drink your face. (68)

This striking closing image is meant to imply not self-absorption but self-definition, one of the greatest needs of Appalachian people given the prevalence of negative stereotypes of the region.

Poems like "The Country of Conscience" and "Brier Sermon," it must be conceded, do not contain Miller's best writing, for the poems are too didactic and too discursive, despite the poet's efforts to ground them in descriptive detail and fresh figurative language. Some of Miller's best poems of the 1980s go largely unread, unfortunately—such poems as "Poetry Workshop," "Thinking about My Poems," "Teaching," and "A January Poem"—because they appeared in *Vein of Words* (1984) and *Nostalgia for 70* (1986), both published by Seven Buffaloes Press, which had few resources to promote the books. After Miller's death Gnomon Press reprinted *Mountains* and *Brier, His Book,* along with six uncollected Brier poems, under the title *The Brier Poems* (1997), but that volume omits at least a dozen other uncollected Brier poems and reprints nothing from Miller's five other volumes of poetry. Of the poets analyzed in this book, Miller is one of the two who are least well known outside Appalachia. To some extent that dearth of critical attention is understandable, for as Miller's poem "Report to the Public Service Committee" reveals, Miller spread himself very thin playing so many different roles in the region's literary renaissance. His poetry perforce often took a back seat to his essays and lectures and workshops.

Miller also tends to be pigeonholed as an exclusively Appalachian author, a view that misrepresents both the variety of his poems and the breadth of vision that his concept of cosmopolitan regionalism encourages. Such pigeonholing has arisen inside as well as outside Appalachia, as Miller noted in his essay for the *Contemporary Authors Autobiography Series:* "With regard to critical reception," he states, "I have sometimes felt myself in much the same situation as my 'Brier Losing Touch with His Traditions': reviewers and readers insist on seeing me as an 'Appalachian' writer and are disappointed when I am not 'Appalachian' enough for them" ("Jim Wayne Miller" 290). In other essays Miller rejects the romanticizing of mountain landscapes, even going so far as to assert, "I have no literary enthusiasm for mountains. I am not interested in mountains as mere landscape—or in any place as mere topography or terrain. What interests me, as a poet, is people in their place: how they have coped, what they have come to be as a result of living in that place" ("I Have a Place" 85). Nonetheless, for Miller the sense of place is strongly tied to the natural world, one part of which is the mountains themselves. Contact with nature is a recurring source of satisfaction in Miller's poems, and his figurative language repeatedly interweaves the human and natural phenomena, as in "His Hands": "Fish hung in his veins, shadows fanning. / Birds circled his farthest green thoughts" (*Mountains* 24).

Yet unlike the other poets treated in this book, Miller does not appear to find within nature the presence of spiritual realities that transcend the physical world while also being immanent in it. For all his familiarity with Emerson and his endorsement of many of Emerson's ideas about the poet's function, Miller does not seem interested in Emerson's view of nature's capacity to symbolize or mediate spirit or spiritual truths. When Miller deals with religious figures such as preachers, his stance is typically critical or satirical, and when he uses religious terminology, as he does in "Brier Sermon," it is usually to encourage secular conversions that lack any specific religious dimension.

In a 1988 interview with Loyal Jones, Miller refers to himself as an "ethnic Protestant," a phrase that entails no particular creedal commitment but that does indicate a major source of what the poet calls his "sentiments and basic attitudes" (72). As has already been suggested, nowhere is that predilection for religious diction and attitudes more apparent than in *The Mountains Have Come Closer*, with its last two sections entitled "You Must Be Born Again" and "Brier Sermon." Poems in other collections, too, reveal Miller's attraction to religious terms, images, and metaphors. Yet a careful examination of those poems—and of Miller's work as a whole—demonstrates that his primary allegiance is to the things of this world apart from their spiritual implications or any traditional religious resonance they might have. In this respect, Miller offers a significant contrast to his fellow western North Carolina poets Fred Chappell and Robert Morgan, in whose work the religious is a far more vital presence and the quest for spiritual revelation a major impulse. Nor does one find in Miller's poetry the intense struggle between faith and doubt that marks Charles Wright's work. Miller seems almost unique among the mountain poets of his generation in having escaped the burden of what Morgan calls "coming out from under Calvinism" (*Good Measure* 142), though Miller's poetry certainly does, at times, evince his dissatisfaction with traditional religion and its representatives.

In addition to his interview with Loyal Jones, Miller addresses religion directly in only one other published interview, an interview conducted by Edwin T. Arnold some ten years earlier. Contrasting two poems—"The Reverend Mr. Thick" and "Brier Sermon"—Arnold asks Miller, "What role does religion play in your poetry? . . . What is your attitude toward religion in your poetry?" (220). Miller's response to these questions both affirms religious impulses and distances him from any particular religious viewpoint:

> It would seem from those two examples that I would have an ambivalent attitude, and that may be the case. I can find certain religious practices, certain narrow theological views just as amusing, just as ridiculous as the next person. On the other hand, I think that a religious impulse is a genuine and authentic thing. There's nothing sham about it, although there's lots of sham religion in the news nowadays. I think it's superficial to take the old view that everyone who is caught up in religion or is concerned with religion is either stupid or uneducated or that all ministers are Elmer Gantrys or Jimmy Joneses. In some ways I find it difficult to differentiate [between] a religious approach to one's experience and a broadly philosophical or even an aesthetic approach. . . . I do not have any denominational affiliation. . . . I would rather be eclectic and find a genuine religious impulse anywhere in the world or from any period in the history of the world and not put on the blinkers of any particular denomination. (220–21)

I have quoted this comment at such length because it invites readers to consider whether Miller's poetry does, in fact, reflect such a "genuine religious impulse," however eclectic, and to what extent that poetry represents more of a philosophical or aesthetic attitude rather than a religious one. As "The Reverend Mr. Thick" reveals, many of the preachers in Miller's poetry are negative figures of whom the poet strongly disapproves. If they don't illustrate "sham religion," they clearly embody the worst features of a narrowly judgmental Protestant fundamentalism. The Rev. Mr. Thick appears in the fourth poem in Miller's first book, *Copperhead Cane*, a poem that Miller chose to reprint in *Dialogue with a Dead Man*. In the former volume Miller omits the honorific term "Mr." from the title, referring to the minister simply as "The Reverend Thick," a surname that seems appropriate to both the pastor's body and his mind. The poem is an Italian sonnet about Miller's grandfather's funeral, with the poet using the octave-sestet structure of that traditional form to underscore the preacher's focus on the meal that precedes the funeral rather than on the service itself:

> Commissioned to preach your funeral, the Reverend Thick,
> The one you thought a fool, not looking thinner,
> Rejoiced in God's great bounty, your daughter's dinner.
> He ate, unless I mistake my arithmetic,
> Of God's golden drumsticks four, no less
> Than three wings, two necks, a gizzard, rolls untold,
> Then started a story (already we felt consoled),
> But had to break it off to do his office.
>
> Leaning on the lectern, mating trite trope to trope,
> Backed by the dollars and cents on Sunday's roll,
> He plunged us into doubt about your soul;
> Then when the women wept he gave us hope.
> Just as in life, the calmest man about,
> You were the least concerned, the least in doubt. (unpaged)

The tone of this poem, clearly, is one of pervasive irony.

Despite the elegiac impulse that underlies *Copperhead Cane,* its poems offer little or no traditional religious consolation in the face of death. The book's repeated images of hunting might be said to imply spiritual questing, but the overriding impression is one of death's finality, with no explicit allusions to the possibility of resurrection. In "Hound and Hook," for instance, the poet writes, "With hound and hook I hunt and fish that night / Your shadow stepped into beyond the light." In another poem, "October Burley Barn," the speaker remarks, "You went the moldy route through mystery," with the term "mystery" coming as close as Miller does in this volume to representing a religious sensibility. The book's second-to-last poem, however, "After Love," returns to a vision of death's apparent finality:

> Spent waves of locked love's undulation,
> Now rippled coolness comes,
> We two apart in rapt death's imitation.
> How quaint abstracter sums
> Would seem if death should prove
> A coolness after love.

In its diction and rhythm this poem seems to owe a debt to Dickinson, who in one of her poems refers to the moment of death as an entry into "Conjecture's presence" (46).

"After Love" is one of some fourteen poems from *Copperhead Cane* that Miller chose not to reprint in *Dialogue with a Dead Man*. Some of the omitted poems (e.g., "The Fencepost II" and "Horse Knob II" and III) would have partially lightened the darker tone of the first poem in each sequence. Some of the other omitted poems, had they been included, would have made the tone of *Dialogue* grimmer, as with the three poems under the heading "In Tippletown" and the ominous "Among the Hives." The first and third poems of the "Tippletown" sequence, near the end of *Copperhead Cane,* return to the negative images of preachers apparent in "The Reverend Thick." One preacher is presented as evidence that "Tippletown's all oddities," while the first-person plural "we" of the third poem spend Sunday walking through town, detached from the "static gospel whining" of neighbors' radios in the early morning and equally remote from a noontime setting in which "preachers raged from radios / Of love, their words dishwater slopped on grass."

While Miller moderated the tone of *Dialogue* by omitting some of these harsher poems, the later book contains little to suggest that religious consolation plays a significant part in his ongoing attempt to come to terms with his grandfather's death. In "Listening," for instance, the grandfather declares, "For I'm not in the ground, nor the sky either. / I am a live man walking with you, / wanting to throw a shadow into life" (28). And in

"Last Words" he advises his grandson, "You'd do well to remember, / I lost my hold on life but still crave earth" (40). The hope of continuity, of survival, that this book tenders resides in nature's cycles and in memory's power to sustain and resurrect, not in religious visions of an afterlife. In Miller's work death's triumph is limited not by God but by nature: "forever tree-shading / summer was and is and summer will be," as the poet affirms in "On Native Ground," the final poem in the "Dialogue with a Dead Man" sequence (57). Death's power is also limited by reproductive cycles within the human community. The book's concluding poem, "Family Reunion," grants a qualified resurrection to the dead and diminishes the impact of death by linking death to shadows alternating with sunlight. The poem's last three stanzas read:

Here the living and dead mingle
like sun and shadow under old trees.

For the dead have come too,
those dark, stern departed who pose
all year in oval picture frames.

They are looking out of the eyes of children,
young sprouts
whose laughter blooms
fresh as the new flowers in the graveyard. (78)

These lines demonstrate that *Dialogue* does provide consolation in the face of death, but that consolation is not distinctively religious.

The crucial volume for any assessment of religious elements in Miller's poetry, as already indicated, is *The Mountains Have Come Closer*. Here readers will find none of the satirical portraits of preachers that appear in *Copperhead Cane* and in a poem like "Cripple Creek Revisited" from Miller's second book, *The More Things Change the More They Stay the Same*. In "Cripple Creek" the otherworldliness of the preacher is emphasized by his apolitical stance and by the response he makes to the "Feller come in from the poverty war": "Said the preacher to the man from OEO [Office of Economic Opportunity], / 'To hell with their bodies, I'm savin souls!'" (unpaged). In *Mountains* such figures are replaced by the resourceful, multifaceted Brier, one of whose roles is that of street preacher in "Brier Sermon."

As has been shown earlier in this chapter, the Brier is generally a figure of resistance who refuses to surrender to mainstream America's devaluation of Appalachia and its people. Yet except for the maxim "You must
be born again," which gives the second section of *Mountains* its title and
serves as the subtitle for the Brier's sermon, there is little of a substan-
tively religious nature in this collection. True, Miller incorporates biblical
allusions in such poems as "A Plague of Telephones" and "Brier Sermon,"
but when religious terms appear in these poems, they are usually emptied of their traditional religious significance or they are applied to secular phenomena. Thus, in "Chopping Wood" Miller refers to "the resurrection and miracle of rest / after labor" (23), and in "Born Again" he depicts
memory, not divine agency, as the instrument of rebirth (37). In "On the
Wings of a Dove," bluegrass music, white lightning, and meditation along
the French Broad River transform the speaker's depression. The white
doves that rise out of the speaker's ribcage (35) are only distantly related
to the dove of the Holy Spirit, though Miller appears to invite the reader
to recall such religious associations with his poem's title. Similarly, in
"Shapes" the poet begins in a mood of depression as he observes "people
flowing out of the mountains, / leaving like a line of clanking coalcars"
whose departure leaves him as "damp and heavy" "as charred wood in a
rained-out fire" (45). Although fire is one of the traditional symbols of
God's presence (the burning bush, the tongues of fire emblematic of the
Holy Spirit), the fire imagery that Miller employs in the remainder of
the poem is oriented toward the human, not the divine. The shapes to
which the poem testifies are very much of *this* world, as the closing stanza
attests:

> When he found deer tracks on the logging roads
> his life grew light and dry.
> Near the weathered silver of old barns
> his life caught fire
> and he studied shapes in the flame of his own spirit. (45)

The final phrases here, "in the flame of his own spirit," disclose the decidedly anthropocentric nature of Miller's poetic vision.

Only in "He Remembers His Mother" are Miller's religious terms and
images filled with their traditional religious significance rather than being reduced to either emblems of nature or facets of individual psychol-

ogy. Yet here these memories cause the speaker a sense of discomfort, a grave unease: "Under the leafy tangle of his senses / death and religion always gliding, gliding, / snakes in a dark green swale of creeping kudzu" (31). The image of snakes darkens the mood of this poem, and the closing stanza again links religion with the fact and fear of death as the speaker recalls attending church with his mother:

> High overhead the churchhouse creaked,
> an old ship's rigging. They sailed in a storm
> of hymns, slammed to the trough, rolled to the crest
> of sermons, the cemetery trailing always
> in their wake, acres of heaving ringing buoys. (31)

These buoys signal danger, sounding the alarm of mortality, cementing in the speaker's mind the association of death and religion, perhaps also alluding to the terror tactics of fire-and-brimstone sermons. It may be these very tactics that led Miller to his pronounced rejection of any "denominational affiliation," to his identification of himself as merely an "ethnic Protestant."

The poet's narrowly circumscribed religious perspective is equally apparent in "Brier Sermon—'You Must Be Born Again.'" The poem opens with the Brier addressing his auditors, distancing himself from their general conception of a preacher: "You may say, Preacher, where is your black Bible? / Why ain't you preachin down sin? / You may say, Preacher, why ain't you talkin about hell?" (52). The implicit judgmentalism of these references to sin and hell plays no part in the Brier's vision of rebirth. Yet he later acknowledges that he is preaching about sin, what he calls "the sin of forgetfulness" (56), a forgetfulness "that's a sin against ourselves" (61), not against God. The Brier urges his auditors, "Don't run off and leave the best part of yourself. // And what is that best part? It's spirit" (59). The term "spirit" remains undefined in this poem, but it clearly refers to emotional and psychological qualities in contrast to things physical or material. After insisting that he's not talking about physical death, the Brier proclaims:

> I'm talking about spiritual death.
> I'm not talking about life after death.
> I'm talking about life before death.
> I'm saying that if you're dead in life,

> spiritually dead in life,
> you must be born again,
> you must be born again and again and again. (63)

When the Brier inquires rhetorically, "What's it like—being born again?"
(63), he responds, "They're born again to sights and sounds and tastes"
(64). In other words, the rebirth he promises focuses on a recovery of
spirit achieved through the senses, through immersion in the things of
this world. While the Brier firmly rejects believing in nothing (52–53),
his faith centers on human capacities and human achievements.

Almost every commentator on this poem has agreed with Miller's own
assessment in *Kentucky Poetry Review* that the change to which the Brier
invites his auditors "is compared to religious conversion, though it occurs
in a secular context" ("Letter" 61). As Miller comments in his interview
with Loyal Jones, "The 'Brier Sermon' is not a religious poem. It employs
a concept—the concept of being born again—as a metaphor for talking
about a new understanding and a new view of one's history and heritage"
(71). For Stephen Mooney, then, the Brier "urges [people] to seek rebirth
into a more personal, more regionally centered consciousness that is akin
to spirituality in its power" (63)—akin, but not identical with. For Don
Johnson, "The genius here lies in the poet's humanization of the ritual,
his divesting both the father's house and the notion of rebirth of exclusively religious connotations and re-mythologizing them in terms of personal and cultural resurrection" ("Appalachian Homeplace" 132). For
J. W. Williamson, in his essay entitled "Appalachian Poetry: The Politics
of Coming Home," this poem is "the single most ambitious distillation of
Appalachian politics yet to appear in this Appalachian renaissance" (73).
Miller would, indeed, have found the label "political writer" far more
congenial than "religious writer."

Yet I don't want to oversimplify Miller's often complex use of traditional religious language and beliefs. Although only a handful of the poems in *Vein of Words* and *Nostalgia for 70* involve such religious concerns
or religious diction, one of the best of those poems, "Original Red: A
Short Story," a tribute to Robert Penn Warren, critiques the loss of "the
Protestant nerve" so evident in Warren's fiction. The reductivism of the
modern outlook is reflected in such ironic lines as "Spirit is something
felt at ball games . . . // Quests are *idees fixe*, and only weirdos map / caves

of guilt" (*Vein* 44). According to this poem, "We've put our faith in an-
tibiotics and mental hygiene" (44). From the contemporary perspective,
Miller adds, "most / of the facts of life are economic" (45). The speaker
of this poem finds the erosion of the Protestant moral and religious vision
anything but comforting and praises Warren for confronting his readers
with that vision.

It is primarily in Miller's later Brier poems, both those collected in
Brier, His Book and *The Brier Poems* and those still uncollected, that the
poet continues to explore his relationship with traditional religious belief—or, at times, unconsciously reveals his attitudes toward it. In "The
Brier Moves to a New Place," for example, the first poem in *Brier, His
Book*, the Brier longs for the stability that he associates with a church
building: "He wants to be like that church by the trout stream— / patient,
trailing gravestones behind it / like fish on a stringer" (4). Just a few pages
later, however, in "On Trammel Creek," it is the Brier who "came trailing / two trout on a stringer" (12), and the image of the church has been
reduced to little more than a place for him to rest and smoke and share
some moonshine with a stranger he meets. Although Miller comments
ironically on the Brier's sense of decorum ("He never drank whiskey / on
the church house steps / when a service was in progress" [14]), it's also
evident that the Brier never frequents the church house. Sunday is his
day for fishing—and not as a fisher of men. Significantly, "The Brier's Pictorial History of the Mountains" contains no images of or references to
churches, despite their ubiquity in the Appalachian countryside. And the
Whitmanesque concluding line of "The Brier Plans a Mountain Vision
Center," though it refers directly to religion, reduces that concept to a
vague mysticism: "Maybe they'd see that sitting down in the evening and
looking into the distance was religion, too" (58). In the one poem in *Brier,
His Book* that mentions God directly, moreover, "The Country of Conscience," the reference occurs parenthetically and the context is anything
but positive:

> (Pray you are not targeted for some leap forward,
> pray engineers of affluence aren't sent your way.
> You may be swept, while God is looking the other way,
> like a sparrow into the checkered grille
> of a cruising Cadillac.) (63)

The fundamental commitment of both the Brier and Miller himself is made explicit in "Bhagavad-Brier," one of the previously uncollected poems reprinted in the posthumous *Brier Poems*, where it concludes the book. Unconvinced by the transcendental asceticism of the *Bhagavad-Gita*, the Brier confesses his adamant attachment to the natural world: "Always he returned / to the laurel hells and dirt roads of his senses, / craving smoked ham and redeye gravy" (158). The playful particularity of such images may partly undercut the Brier's allegiance to the physical world, but the poem's closing lines confirm his preference for the things of *this* world: "In the darkness of his senses, a spiritual frog, / he didn't desire the kiss of an eastern princess / to translate him into a noble soul" (159). These lines fail to indicate, of course, how the Brier might respond to a Western princess, but Miller's poems afford little evidence that either he or the Brier would choose to embrace any specific Western religious traditions. While the title of Miller's 1993 chapbook, *Brier, Traveling*, might be said to invoke the figure of the pilgrim, the Brier has tended to move away from traditional religious consciousness toward a deeper and deeper engagement with the secular.

In tracing that movement, I don't mean to imply that Miller's work is in any way weakened by the direction it has taken. Miller's poetry is notable for its vivid imagery, its inventive figurative language, its humor and playfulness, and its powerful commitment to things Appalachian. As the poet writes of his labors in the uncollected Brier poem "Unsalaried, He Deals in a Service":

> He had . . . to keep
> his mind clear for the job—which was to invent them,
> to show them, in their place, to themselves and one
> another, to set them in the center of a world
> that knew them, since it flowed out of their lives,
> encircled them, and ran back again, deep and never
> ending. (5)

The Appalachian region owes Miller a profound debt of gratitude for this service, for he has helped to provide the people of this region with a renewed sense of home and of place linked inextricably with nature while at the same time he has insisted on a more expansive, elastic sense of regional identity within a national and global community. As subsequent

chapters will show, however, Miller's conception of Appalachian literature as "decidedly worldly, secular, and profane in its outlook" does not
do justice to the profound spiritual questing of many of southern Appalachia's other major poets.

2

FRED CHAPPELL

"Flesh-tree and Tree of Spirit"

ALTHOUGH FRED CHAPPELL and Jim Wayne Miller, both born in 1936, grew up in adjoining counties in western North Carolina, the two authors did not meet until their literary careers were well advanced, as Chappell himself notes in an essay on Miller (8). Like Miller, Chappell was raised on his grandparents' farm, about three miles outside Canton, a paper-mill town some twenty miles west of Asheville. His parents helped work that farm but found that they needed to supplement their meager agricultural income by teaching school and later by operating a furniture store. As Chappell's essay "The Poet and the Plowman" makes clear, his experiences on that farm helped shape not only his childhood and adolescence but also his very conception of life and of his poetic vocation. For Chappell, the poet and the farmer are linked by their "awe of nature" and their "reverence for the earth" (74). A tribute to Vergil's *Georgics,* "The Poet and the Plowman" also reveals the premises of Chappell's religious views, which ground faith in nature's wonders, in the intricate design evident in the universe itself. Chappell writes of Vergil's sense of "the ceremonial, and ultimately religious, nature of farming" (76), states that "the largest purpose of the *Georgics* is not to dignify, but to sanctify, honest farm labor" (77), and notes that "the poem is full of stars," images that reflect Vergil's belief that "the Roman state is not founded upon the soil, it is founded in the universe" (77). Chappell goes on to state: "And so were all the other civilizations which managed to endure for any length of time. If poets do not wish to study these matters and treat of them, they shirk their responsibilities and fail their society" (77).

Commenting on these quotations from Chappell's essay, critic George Hovis remarks, "In this passage Chappell makes explicit his belief in the spiritual harmony that exists between yeomen and the cosmos. The language here is as confrontational as anything found in the Agrarians' manifesto *I'll Take My Stand*" ("When" 413). In the mid-1960s Chappell became friends with Allen Tate, one of the original Agrarians, while both were teaching at the University of North Carolina at Greensboro, where Chappell began working in 1964. "The Poet and the Plowman" opens with a reported conversation between Chappell and Tate, with Tate conceding, "But we would make dreadful farmers, Fred, you and I" (73). Yet while Chappell did indeed leave his family's farm for a Duke University education and a career in academe, most of his fiction and poetry, as he told interviewer Tersh Palmer, "is set in the mountains on the farm outside Canton" (406). When another pair of interviewers assumed that Chappell would not want to return to living on a farm, he replied, "If I could make a living, I would do it" (Patterson and Lindsey 70). As Don Johnson rightly observes, in an essay tracing the influence of the *Georgics* in Chappell's work, "Chappell's poetry, its urbanity and erudition notwithstanding, nevertheless remains firmly rooted in the homeplace soil of the southern Appalachian mountains" (171).

While neither Vergil nor Chappell idealizes agrarian life, instead acknowledging its "difficulties and dangers" (74), they both consider farming a means of keeping oneself attuned to a natural order originating in the divine. Chappell's poetry often performs a similar function. In "Towards a Beginning," an essay published in Jeff Daniel Marion's journal *The Small Farm,* Chappell refers to the poet's "traditional role as celebrator of divinity and of the created objects of the universe" (97–98), and in "The Function of the Poet" he embraces the reader's expectation that poets will "find a new way to praise something of our lives, and a new object to praise" (37). The impulse to praise is central to Chappell's Bollingen Prize-winning *Midquest* (1981), as it is also to Marion's poetry. But Chappell's religious views, like Miller's and Marion's, often involve biting critiques of the clergy, especially of ministers of a fire-and-brimstone cast, like Canary of the "Ugly Holies" in *I Am One of You Forever* (63) or the preacher in the early short story "The Two Ministries" who denounces the created order in ways totally antithetical to Chappell's incarnational aesthetic. According to that preacher, "This world is foul with sin, . . . this world is a vale of filth and misery" (152), and he goes on to voice a Gnostic dualism all too prevalent in the Protestantism of the southern mountains—and in Pauline Christianity itself—when he adds: "It's your soul you got to worry about, not your body. The flesh is evil" (153). Much of Chappell's poetry, especially in *Midquest,* aims to combat the otherworldly emphasis of such a viewpoint. At the same time, however, Chappell's work, far more than Miller's, reflects a profound religious impulse that attempts to bring into fruitful balance the traditional binary oppositions—body and mind, flesh and spirit, time and eternity, humanity and nature—that have shaped Western thought, without slighting the claims of either term in these pairs. Raised a Methodist, Chappell now rejects institutional religion. As he told interviewers Fred Brown and Jeanne McDonald, "I think of myself as a religious person, but no church. I have no interest in organized religion. None whatsoever. I am interested in theology. I read the Bible . . ." (128). In the same interview he notes that one of the reasons he abandoned organized religion is that it seemed to promote racial prejudice (130). Equally important in this connection, though, is Chappell's distaste for the attitudes expressed by the preacher in "The Two Ministries."

By the time Chappell published his first book of poems, *The World between the Eyes,* in 1971, he had already published three novels and completed the draft of a fourth. In an interview with Hovis, Chappell explained that these early experimental novels—*It Is Time Lord* (1963), *The Inkling* (1965), and *Dagon* (1968)—were marked by "a kind of claustrophobic feeling . . . that derived from a kind of determinism that I could not get out of my fiction. . . . The philosophical ideas stated in the first four novels [including *The Gaudy Place* (1973)] are surely not mine" (71). In contrast to these novels, *The World between the Eyes* situates the poet in a more effectively realized rural setting and dramatizes the ambivalence he feels toward it and toward his family, especially in the eight longer narrative poems that fill nearly half of the book's pages. In fact, as Kathryn Stripling Byer has suggested, those eight poems—"February," "The World between the Eyes," "The Farm," "The Father," "The Mother," "Tin Roof Blues," "Sunday," and "The Dying"—though often separated from one another by shorter lyric poems, can usefully be read as a sequence ("Turning" 89). All these poems run to at least three pages in length, and all but "Tin Roof Blues" speak of "the boy" or "the child" in the third person, a point of view that distances the adult poet from the child's perspective portrayed in the poems.

The World between the Eyes opens with "February," which vividly describes, in a syntax often disjointed and a free verse that frequently employs an iambic base, a hog killing. The child's ambivalence toward this event is captured in such phrases as "dismayed / With delight" and "elated-drunk / With the horror" (3, 4). The communal dimension of this activity is one of its most important features, for Chappell seeks to locate the reader not only in proximity to the natural world but also in relationships with others. Through this "most unlikely prodigious pig" (5), nature affords the family both food and an occasion for affirming friendship and interdependence.

One of the major struggles of the child in these longer poems revolves around his love/hate relationship with his home. In the book's title poem, for example, "rooms of his fathers / Hold him without mercy; he feels / This house about him, a fantastic skin," and likewise senses "that outermost skin, the sky" (12). His mind replete with figures drawn from his imagination (one meaning of the poem's title), he also must confront the objective world, yet a world of symbolic objects perceived as "signs, the total / Sky hieroglyph; his duty to read aright, / To know" (14). Surrounded by such signs and filled with a sense of time "charged past endurance with the future" (14), the child comes to realize that "he's blest in his skins, an old stone / House, and a sky eaten up with stars" (15). Here time and eternity are yoked in the images of house and star, and brooding on both is the figure of the developing poet.

In "The Farm" (which Chappell later revised and reprinted as "The Fields" in *Spring Garden: New and Selected Poems*), the poet takes pains to avoid romanticizing the rural by beginning the poem with the harvesting of hay but advancing temporally to winter, with its "Stupor of cold wide stars" (20) and its "Sky cloudless, / Birdless, merciless" (21). "The world, locked bone," the poem concludes (21). Neither nature nor farming is idealized here, and Chappell depicts similar struggles in the boy's relationships with his father and mother, conflicts presented in two consecutive poems, the latter at the virtual midpoint of the book. The father's judgmental stance in the former mirrors that of James Christopher's father in Chappell's first novel; yet the boy's success in fulfilling the task his father assigns—to discover a new spring to replenish the family's water supply—leads the child to a renewed sense of life's possibilities. Although that hopefulness is promptly shattered in "The Mother," the child is ultimately able to overcome his hostility and rage through humor and a hard-won capacity for detachment. Storming out of the house after a confrontation with his mother, the boy longs to "Squash it from sight with his palm"

(29). Rejecting that option, he retreats into the woods to consider others. Yet the very shapes of his fantasies subvert their appeal: "Could live in the woods and eat bugs! / Or, handily build Snug Cabin, chink it with mud / . . . // Could murder his mother, conquer the world!" (30). By acknowledging the absurdity of his fantasies, the child manages to return home, "his pace . . . deliberately fashioned." Unlike the figure in this volume's "Face to Face," who, standing at his door, decides that "he'll sleep the ditch tonight" (22), the child-poet "stops to take the measure of the family door. / And then he enters" (31). This return home becomes the pivotal event in the poet's psychological and artistic development, an event paralleled in *Midquest* and affirmed in the title of the first volume in the Kirkman tetralogy: *I Am One of You Forever.*

Despite the child's acceptance of home in "The Mother," however, "Tin Roof Blues" and "Sunday" portray additional features of home that the boy finds repugnant. In the former, Canton is imaged as a "port / Of stinks" and an "Obscurely comforting hell" (37). The speaker walks "Past Central Methodist steeple / That cleaves the sky like an axe" (37), a simile that suggests latent violence, especially given the earlier image of the sky as one of the boy's "blest" skins. "Sunday" recounts the fourteen-year-old's disdain for that church and its preacher, the latter compared to a "fishbone in the quick of the gum" (46). Here, in contrast to *Midquest*, the church bells are primarily irritants, and "The big Good Book's the enemy" (46), at least in the hands of this preacher for whom everything is "all white and black" (44), "stark white and black" (45), "white and stark black" (46), the poet's repetition underscoring the minister's simplistic viewpoint. Yet the poet, who distances himself from the "preacher's God" (45), nevertheless describes "Starfall" as a "baptismal current streaming pure / In fire-red sunset" (46) and writes of morning's "unfathomed light" (45). Nature thus promises spiritual resources that this church and its preacher only obscure. In fact, Chappell refers to this church as "Most creatureless house / In the world" (44), a phrase that may be meant to imply the extent to which the otherworldly emphasis of the church's doctrines has severed it from the creation.

The final longer narrative poem in *The World between the Eyes* is "The Dying," which depicts the death of the boy's sister. While this event is invented, not autobiographical, Chappell movingly conveys the boy's anguish, his realization that "he hates his skin" (56), here a symbol of the materiality that betrays his sister to death, although earlier that skin had been one of his blessings. Death has always been one of Chappell's major subjects. Indeed, one of the principal aims of his poetry, it could be argued, has been his desire to reconcile readers to the fact of death. Even though the boy in "The Dying" is not reconciled, instead "Learning at last no justice, learning to be brave / Is bitter" (55), he does have a vision of *"The spirit aching toward the light / . . . / This spirit also held familiar / in arms of light"* (56). It is to the quest for light and for rebirth that Chappell turned in the four books of poems that succeeded *The World between the Eyes,* the four books that together comprise *Midquest.*

Now widely recognized as what Patrick Bizzaro calls "the structural and thematic centerpiece of Chappell's poetic achievement thus far" (4), *Midquest* is an extraordinarily ambitious, complexly structured, deeply humane book. Some five thousand lines in length, it gathers together the previously published volumes *River* (1975), *Bloodfire* (1978), *Wind Mountain* (1979), and *Earthsleep* (1980). Each of these volumes consists of eleven poems, with each volume organized around one of the four elements —water, fire, air, and earth—that Pythagoras and other ancient philosophers viewed as fundamental to all life. Chappell allows each of these elements to assume a variety of meanings and also has them interact with and upon one another, as when he describes "the burning river of this morning / That earth and wind overtake" (*Midquest* 187) or speaks of "the morning flush of loosed wind-spirit, exhalation / Of fire-seed and gusty waters and of every dirt" (98). In *Bloodfire* alone, the image of fire is linked to dawn, to a Rimbaudian derangement of the senses, to the Ku Klux Klan's cross burnings, to sexual desire, to spiritual longing, to Pentecost and the Christian symbolism associated with the Holy Spirit, to hellfire, to the violence of war, to martyrdom (political as well as religious), to hearth and home, to the fevers of physical illness, to natural disasters, to Lucretius's *ignis semina* as building blocks of the physical world, to illumination or revelation, to alcohol ("firewater"), to "fire / As symbolic of tortured, transcendent-striving will" (85), and to many other objects and significations. A similar multiplicity of meanings attaches to the other elements, allowing the poet enormous latitude for the exercise of his ingenuity while at the same time insuring a comprehensive and comprehensible focus for each book. As *Midquest* amply demonstrates, Chappell himself is the kind of "metaphysical professor" to whom Melville refers in the passage from *Moby-Dick* that the poet uses as an epigraph to *River,* an epigraph that also insists, "Meditation and water are wedded forever" (xiii).

In addition to using the four elements as a unifying device within and between volumes, Chappell conjoins the four books that comprise *Midquest* in several other ways. Each volume opens, for instance, with the poet-narrator (variously called Fred or Ole Fred) in bed with his wife Susan on the morning of his thirty-fifth birthday, and each volume closes with the couple back in bed. Susan likewise appears in at least one other poem in each volume. Ole Fred's grandparents and parents speak at length in various narrative poems throughout the four volumes, while yet another unifying character is Virgil Campbell, the country storekeeper first introduced in *It Is Time, Lord.* One poem in each of the four volumes is devoted to Virgil, "who is supposed to give to the whole," Chappell states in the book's preface, "its specifically regional, its Appalachian, context" (x). Each volume also contains a lengthy stream-of-consciousness poem that meditates on such philosophical issues as the relationship between body and mind, flesh and spirit, time and eternity; and each volume contains a poem that portrays a natural disaster appropriate to the element around which that book is organized: a flood, a fire, a hurricane, and in *Earthsleep* death itself. Similarly helping to unify all four volumes are Chappell's varied allusions to and echoes of Dante's *Divine Comedy,* with its quest for moral and spiritual rebirth at the midpoint of one's life. The motif of pilgrimage is implicit throughout *Midquest,* as is Thoreau's equation of morning with moral reform (Thoreau 1855). To interviewer Richard Jackson, Chappell declared, "The whole poem, *Midquest,* is about rebirth" (156), a rebirth grounded in the created world, in a vision of nature's goodness, while at the same time, as the poem's references to various natural disasters demonstrates, the poet recognizes nature's recalcitrance, its capacity for destruction as well as creation.

Chappell subtitles *Midquest* "A Poem," thus indicating the unity of impression to which the work aspires, and which, I believe, it achieves—a unity amid astonishing and engaging variety. The careful design of the book infuses in the reader a sense both of order and of the richness of life's possibilities; yet *Midquest* never slights the struggles that are necessary to attain and sustain such a vision. Ole Fred lacks the certitude of his Dantean counterpart, and Chappell thus makes his pilgrim's affirmations more credible by detailing the "wilderness of doubt" (56) from which Fred's faith ultimately arises. The poet's skillful use of humor and irony, his perfectly timed moments of self-deprecation and self-mockery, strengthen the book.

"Birthday 35: Diary Entry," the second poem in *Midquest*, marks the point of departure for Ole Fred's spiritual quest and provides an effective example of the poet's self-directed humor and irony:

> Multiplying my age by 2 in my head,
> I'm a grandfather. Or dead.
>
> "Midway in this life I came to a darksome wood."
> But Dante, however befuddled, was Good.
>
> . . . .
>
> I'm still in flight, still unsteadily in pursuit,
> Always becoming more sordid, pale, and acute . . . (3)

In the book's opening poem Ole Fred is portrayed as "wishing never to wake" (2). His diary entry helps explain his reluctance by limning the spiritual wasteland he wanders. Yet his response to this emptiness is not to despair but to pray; "Birthday 35" concludes with a prayer that runs for twenty-two lines. A striking admixture of the humorous, the grotesque, the self-ironic, and the sincere, that prayer distances readers from Ole Fred's longing for rebirth without undercutting the sincerity and significance of his spiritual yearning.

That yearning is powerfully portrayed in *Midquest*'s fourth poem too, "Cleaning the Well," with its archetypal descent into the underworld and its confrontation with death. Hauled up into the light, the "most willing fish that was ever caught" (16), young Fred wonders, "Jonah, Joseph, Lazarus, / Were you delivered so?" (16) and remarks, "*I had not found death good*" (17). The prospect of death and the possibility of resurrection preoccupy Fred in many of the book's poems, especially those in *Earthsleep*, for as his grandmother tells him as early as *Midquest*'s third poem, echoing the "dust to dust" motif of Genesis, "It's dirt you rose from, dirt you'll bury in" (12). For her, this thought is more fact than threat, a fact of nature that does not negate her hope of resurrection. Indeed the natural and the supernatural cohabit throughout *Midquest*, as they often do in the Judeo-Christian tradition. Each of the four elements around which Chappell organizes his book assumes religious significance. Water, for instance, often a symbol of materiality, becomes an emblem of the intersection of time and eternity in "The River Awakening in the Sea." Water is also, in baptism, a sacrament, a means of grace, of spiritual regeneration. Fire is both instrument of divine wrath and means of purification. It witnesses to God's presence in the burning bush from which God spoke to Moses and in the tongues of flame associated with the Holy Spirit. Wind—bodiless, invisible, yet observable in its effects—is similarly linked to the Holy Spirit on Pentecost and to the breath of God by which Adam was created out of the dust. In "Second Wind," moreover, it touches Fred's grandmother, after her husband's death, with "the weight of grace" (106). Chappell regularly associates wind with music as well and has said in an interview that "music probably stands in my poems most of the time for exaltation, exalted spirits, ecstatic visionary knowledge" (Broughton 109). As for earth, with its gaping graves, it is the foundation of the Earthly Paradise and the soil from which the "Tree of Spirit lift[s] from the mountain of earth" (*Midquest* 149) to "the Mountains Outside Time" (169).

Midquest is a poem that, at key points, invokes the mythos of Eden and "a final shore" beyond the fevered river of time (141). *River* concludes with a single-line stanza that mentions "the dew-fired earliest morning of the world" (51), while the closing lines of *Bloodfire* anticipate the wind's arrival in the subsequent volume, "wind bearing from the south, / out of the green isles / of Eden" (94). Moreover, implicit in the sleep of the book's final volume is the prospect of awakening. The epigraph from Hawthorne that Chappell affixes to *Earthsleep* speaks of the peaceful transition from waking to the "temporary death" of sleep, comparing that transition to the experience of dying itself: "So calm, perhaps, will be the final change; so undisturbed, as if among familiar things the entrance of the soul to its Eternal home" (*Midquest* 143). Hawthorne's "perhaps" in this passage registers the ineluctable mystery of the human encounter with death, and the sketch from which Chappell excerpts this epigraph is entitled "The Haunted Mind." Yet while the questions death poses are irresolvable for the mind situated on this side of the grave—as the varied definitions of the term "earthsleep" in *Midquest*'s closing poem indicate—Chappell concludes that poem by invoking Dante's vision of God: "The love that moves the sun and other stars / The love that moves itself in light to loving" (187). The first of these lines translates the final line of the *Paradiso,* while the second is Chappell's attempt to capture the tone and spirit of Dante's poem. In the final line of "Earthsleep," Fred and Susan lie side by side "Here in the earliest morning of the world" (187), an image suggestive not of death but of new life. Dabney Stuart, in his essay "Spiritual Matter in Fred Chappell's Poetry," is thus correct in contending that Chappell is "preoccupied with and hopeful of images of release and transformation, which are Christian in their orientation" (48). The Fred who resists waking in the book's opening poem learns to "invite the mornings" (*Midquest* 185).

In addition to tracing this explicitly religious quest, Chappell fills *Midquest* with metaphysical speculation of various sorts. Chappell's repeated probing of philosophical issues, what one critic has called his "abiding concern with Ultimates" (Makuck 180), contributes significantly to both the breadth of *Midquest*'s subject matter and the substantiality of its themes. Yet the book does not simply juxtapose humorous narrative poems with more somber meditative poems. Instead, Chappell's narrative poems address philosophical and religious themes, while his meditative poems are leavened by a buoyant humor that prevents reader and poet alike from taking themselves too seriously. The book's more lyric poems—those, for instance, that open and close each of the four volumes—are similarly infused with philosophical inquiry. In fact, cosmogony is a recurring motif in the initial poems of *River, Bloodfire,* and *Wind Mountain,* introduced in each case by references to "how the world was formed" (2, 56, 98). Myths of origin are also evident in Ole Fred's "slightly different Big Bang theory" in "The Autumn Bleat of the Weathervane Trombone" and in the excerpt from his novel-in-progress in "Science Fiction Water Letter" (41–43). Obviously, a concern for cosmogony also underpins Chappell's use of the four elements to structure *Midquest.* Renouncing the abstraction of Plato's realm of Ideal Forms (as he had done in his early poem "A Transcendental Idealist Dreams in Springtime" [*World* 6]), Chappell draws upon the pre-Socratic naturalistic era in Greek philosophy. What he offers, finally, is a profoundly incarnational view of the relationship between matter and spirit, time and eternity, a view shaped by Christian theology.

This incarnational perspective is most fully developed in *Midquest*'s four long meditative poems: "Susan Bathing," "Firewood," "The Autumn Bleat of the Weathervane Trombone," and "The Peaceable Kingdom of Emerald Windows." The first two are single-sentence stream-of-consciousness poems, each seven pages long, and they thus contrast in structure with the greater formal and syntactical clarity of the latter two poems, differences intended to mirror, Chappell says in the preface, his pilgrim's progress "as the speaker begins to order his life" (x).

"Susan Bathing" incorporates both philosophical and explicitly religious themes while also confirming Chappell's claim that *Midquest* is "in its largest design a love poem" (xi). The epigraph to the poem, taken from Pope's "Windsor Forest," asserts that harmonious confusion, not chaos, governs the world and thus underscores the fundamental outlook of *Midquest*. The poem begins and ends with the word "you," thereby affirming Fred's marriage to Susan. But marriage in *Midquest* assumes a metaphoric significance that extends well beyond that institution's societal role. For Chappell marriage illustrates the union of apparent opposites, not only women and men but also flesh and spirit, humankind and nature, and, in Christian theology, humanity and the divine. Susan herself functions allegorically both in this poem and at other points in *Midquest*. From his sensual response to Susan's presence in the shower, Fred proceeds to establish her identity as an emissary of the divine. Not only does he conjoin his praise of Susan with Gabriel's annunciation to Mary, "Ave, plena gratia" (20), but he also depicts Susan both as divine intermediary (the pilgrim's Beatrice) and as *deus absconditus*. When Susan's body vanishes into the steam from the shower, the poet declares, in lines reminiscent of John Donne's anguished prose,

> Why do you go away? where do you go? will you
> again return from behind the spiritual mists & acquaint again
> my senses? or are you for good ascended into ideal spaces & rely upon
> my hurt memory to limn your shape my heart starves to join, do not
> so scar my will I plead you, for my will is stricken and contort,
> its own most effort has fouled & burst it & only intercession from
> without can restore it . . . (21)

This passage clearly reflects St. Paul's notion of the bondage of the will.

Although Susan's allegorical function remains subordinate to Fred's personal relationship with her, Susan reminds Fred of the powerful claims of both body and soul, the physical and the spiritual. This Beatrice-Susan's "flesh the synonym of love" also causes the poet to profess, "I do believe your spirit has power in air" (22), words that link Susan to Ariel and thus adumbrate a realm beyond the physical. In response to her, the

poet gives voice to "speechpraise," for "unattending beauty is danger &
mortal sin" (19). Praise becomes Chappell's "instrument of unclosing and
rising toward light" (19), a light that brings spiritual illumination, "for
once the mind prepares to praise & garbs / in worshipful robe it enlarges
to plenitude" (19). "Susan Bathing," like *Midquest* as a whole, moves toward an affirmation of love: marital love, love of family and friends, love
of nature, love of language and literature, love of God. As Chappell writes
near the end of this poem:

> it is praise, love is praise, Susan, of what is, and if it be prisoned
> in low earth it shall bound high in air saying like howitzers its
> name and if it be scurried to & fro over cold waste of skies yet
> shall it touch with all its names blade root stone roof . . .
> . . . nowhere would you escape it. (23–24)

Chappell's credo here echoes that of St. Paul in Romans 8:38–39.

In contrast to "Susan Bathing," "Firewood" is less explicitly religious
and more overtly philosophical in its exploration of the relationship between flesh and spirit, matter and mind. It too employs the metaphor of
marriage, however, and discusses the role of art in bonding humanity and
nature. Much more than "Susan Bathing," "Firewood" confronts the fact
of death and attempts to reconcile that fact with the longing for immortality. The wood Ole Fred splits in this poem is destined for his fireplace,
where the sun—imaged as stored in the wood—will be released as heat
and light, "the sun risen at midnight" to ascend "the rose trellis of stars"
(69). Burning, this wood will become "tree of spirit," with Fred's chimney
linking the corporeal and the immaterial and suggesting humanity's dual
identity as flesh and spirit—the world of spirit symbolized, here as elsewhere in Chappell's work, by the stars. The chimney "pins our dwelling /
to the earth and to the stars equally" (69), the poet observes. Yet despite
the beauty and the rhetorical effect of an image like "the rose trellis of
stars," Ole Fred remains skeptical, fearful that "the cold dark will tear our
tree of fire / away complete" (69) and conscious that Lucretius's "seed of
fire ignis semina is seed semina mortuis," that is, seed of death (70). Unable to endorse, as he once did, Rimbaud's conception of "the vatic will"
(71) capable of utterly transforming reality through the powers of the poetic imagination, Fred yields to thoughts of death. For a moment he even
longs to jettison human consciousness in exchange for the apparent con-

tentment of the animal world. Finally, however, he can neither surrender the uniqueness of human selfhood nor evade its often anguished doubts. According to Chappell, "man in / his fallen state is condemned to split the tree / with his intellect all alert and doubtful" (72).

As Ole Fred continues to wonder, "but where / shall I sit when once this flesh is spirit?" (73), the reader should notice that Chappell has undercut the Lucretian view of a purely physical universe in the very formulation of that question. "Firewood" concludes by comparing the ultimately successful splitting of the wood to the annunciation to Mary and by depicting that experience as a kind of baptism: "I'm washed in the blood / of the sun, the ghostly holy of the deep deep log" (73). The punning religious diction here is meant to resolve, to some extent at least, the tensions between secular and sacred, flesh and spirit, time and eternity that this poem examines. Yet, as Ole Fred states in the poem's final lines, "it doesn't come easy, I'm / here to tell you that." Elsewhere in *Bloodfire* he likewise testifies to the difficulties faced by those longing "to be born again into light" (85) when he writes, "our faith must be earned from terror, consummate / Love must be thirsted for, light must be wholly desired" (87).

What the other two long meditative poems in *Midquest* make clear is that, for Chappell, this "ghostly holy" is not to be sought at the expense of the physical world. In both "The Autumn Bleat of the Weathervane Trombone" and "The Peaceable Kingdom of Emerald Windows," the poet refers to a new character, someone whom Ole Fred calls Uncle Body. This figure is intended to subvert the philosophical idealism espoused by Plato, Plotinus, Descartes, and Emerson as well as the otherworldliness of a Christianity too often misled by Gnostic and Neoplatonic thought. For the Emerson of "Nature," personal identity was purely a mental or spiritual phenomenon; even one's body belonged to the category of the "NOT ME" (1107). The playfulness and linguistic exuberance of both these poems reflect the expansiveness of the poet's sense of selfhood. In "The Autumn Bleat" fall is less a time of decay than of rebirth. As the title's term "bleat" implies, the trombone's music is scarcely elegant, but the poem provides a cornucopia of sound effects, of levels of diction and allusion too. "There's something in air in love with rounded notes, / The goldenrod's a-groan at the globèd beauty," Chappell writes, in lines of consciously exaggerated alliteration (110). "Bring me my trombone of burning gold, bring me / My harrowing desire," he adds, paraphrasing Blake's *Milton*. Obviously, Chappell takes risks in such passages as he attempts to communicate Fred's vision of life's fullness; occasionally, those fanciful flights collapse under the weight of their distended diction. In general, however, readers are likely to be borne along by the sweeping sense of elation Ole Fred expresses, by the sheer energy and inventiveness of the poet's words.

Like "Firewood," both "Autumn Bleat" and "The Peaceable Kingdom of Emerald Windows" address the fact of death, but in contrast to "Firewood" the latter two poems actually contain portraits of the afterlife (as does *Earthsleep's* "At the Grave of Virgil Campbell"). At times, these visions of the afterlife are wildly comic, verging on the blasphemous, as when Fred avers that there is "Whiskey-after-Death" (169) and identifies God as "the Holy Bartender" (173). But the different versions of the afterlife that Ole Fred offers all have in common their being grounded upon human relationships and the physical world. In "Autumn Bleat," for instance, he anticipates—with some apprehension—the prospect of spending eternity in the company of his fellow poets. In "Peaceable Kingdom" it is naturalists like Gilbert White and William Bartram, a novelist like Colette, and "rare Ben Franklin" whom he envisions joining, all of them people firmly attached in their earthly lives to the physical world. Moreover, since the phrase "Emerald Windows" refers to raindrops, nature becomes precious in itself, associated through the color green with seasonal rebirth and providing a means of spiritual vision, a window on eternity. At odds with the philosophical idealism of Emerson, Chappell nevertheless seems to concur with the Transcendentalist precept, "Nature is the symbol of Spirit" (Emerson 1114). Chappell's window imagery here is also reminiscent of Emerson's claim that "the poet turns the world to glass" (1183), creating a new means of vision that enables readers to glimpse the spiritual amid or beneath the physical. As Old Fred later remarks in "At the Grave of Virgil Campbell," "Our golden boughs ope the Otherworld" (171).

Yet while Old Fred celebrates nature and renounces Nirvana as "a sterile and joyless blasphemy" (113), he is decidedly unwilling to resign himself to physicality alone, refusing to surrender to matter his powers of mind and spirit. Thus in "Autumn Bleat" he issues Uncle Body a tongue-in-cheek invitation "to swim from Singapore / To Hermeneutics and through the Dardanelles / To Transcendentalism, back through the Straits / Of Hegel right on to Greasy Branch" (113), to hike "the slopes / of stony

Heidegger" and voyage "Around the World in Eighty Tractates aboard / The good ship Wittgenstein" (114). Despite the humor of such a passage, Chappell's book moves comfortably from the homespun philosophy of Virgil Campbell to the *ignis semina* of Lucretius, from Hogback Ridge to the Mountains Outside Time, from flesh-tree to tree of spirit. Just as the Vergil of the *Georgics* identifies the natural philosopher (along with the farmer and the poet) as one of the three kinds of people most attuned to the harmonies of the universe, so Chappell makes philosophical thought one of his book's central activities, along with farming and artistic creation and the religious quest itself.

Perhaps the most persistent philosophical and religious problem that *Midquest* addresses, especially in *Earthsleep*, is human mortality, the inexorable reality that Heidegger terms *Sein zum Tod* (being toward death). "The Peaceable Kingdom" includes the statement "Goodbye I perceive to be a human creature" (156). Yet the tone of that poem is not one of fear or anxiety but serenity. Chappell achieves this effect in part by invoking the utopian vision of the Edward Hicks painting mentioned in the poem's title, in part by making green one of the poem's dominant colors (as that color predominates in several other poems in *Earthsleep*) and in part by organizing the latter portions of the poem around the activity of harvesting hay. That activity, successfully completed despite the threat of rain, lends to the poem an aura of fruition. The poem's quiet confidence is also evinced by the image of the house into which the farming family enters, a meal already prepared, a Bible resting on the table open to "a chapter of Psalms" (157). Again rejecting Platonic idealism's "sleepy flea market of Forms" (158), Ole Fred emphasizes the goodness of creation, informing Uncle Body, "All the world is lit for your delight" (159), an iambic pentameter line whose abridged initial foot intensifies the inclusiveness of the poet's claim. Integral to this vision of oneness with nature are those passages in which Chappell personifies Maude and Jackson, the horses pulling the hay wagon, endowing them with speech. Through this device Chappell bridges the accustomed gap between humanity and nature and suspends the reader's predilection for the purely factual. Chappell's appeal to a wider conception of truth encourages the reader to assent as well to his image of the sun nestling "in the form / In the hay in the world in the green green hand" (157), an image that evokes divine nurture of the creation.

For Chappell both spiritual rebirth and authentic poetic insight depend upon recognition of the wonder and mystery of nature and of human existence itself. And for Chappell that consciousness of nature is intimately connected to the mountain landscape of his native Appalachia. In "Rimbaud Fire Letter to Jim Applewhite," one of the poems in *Firewood,* the young Fred who was expelled from Duke returns to Canton, where he reports he "watched the mountains until the mountains touched / My mind and partly tore away my fire-red / Vision of a universe besmirched" (60–61). The boy harvesting hay in "The Peaceable Kingdom" envisions the barn toward which that crop moves as "heaven" and says: "Barn is home. Home is heaven" (161). At various points throughout the last two books of *Midquest* church bells can be heard "Calling home, home, home, home" (100, 133; cf. 140 and 161), although Ole Fred also cites two opposing views about the locus of home on a single page: "*Earth is home*" and "This world is wind, and homeless" (140). The tension evident in these opposing images conveys the poet's desire to balance the claims of flesh and spirit, time and eternity. "I do not wish to be / Consumed by spirit merely," Ole Fred remarks, on one hand (146); on the other, he insists, "*Time I shall not serve thee*" (184). Elsewhere the book's dual impulse is apparent in Fred's sense that he is both "Restored to earth, returned / from earth" (183). Chappell ultimately refuses to resolve this tension, appending to *Midquest,* as a kind of epilogue, a passage from Shakespeare's *Twelfth Night* in which Sir Andrew and Sir Toby discuss the four elements (188), lines that juxtapose Shakespearean comedy of the body with the book's Dantean "divine" comedy.

But Chappell's affirmation of the spiritual dimension of human identity is evident when Virgil Campbell, who at one point is addressed as "You who were overmuch of earth" (169), is displaced by Susan as Ole Fred's guide, just as Dante the pilgrim's Virgil was replaced by Beatrice. After Fred visits Campbell's grave in the sixth poem of *Earthsleep,* the seventh poem opens appropriately with lines from Canto XXX of the *Purgatorio,* the canto in Dante's epic in which Beatrice appears and the Roman poet vanishes, and one of several cantos Dante devotes to his visit to the Earthly Paradise. Yet *Earthsleep's* seventh poem, "How to Build the Earthly Paradise: Letter to George Garrett," focuses primarily on the physical world whose spokesperson Campbell has been. Its thirteen nine-line stanzas are all end-stopped, a pattern that reinforces the poem's building-block structure as Chappell lists the materials needed for this project: stone, sand, earth, the dead, water, air, plants, animals, people, "the troubadour atoms / dancing / full" (176). Each stanza opens and closes, moreover, with a single-syllable line, as if to suggest the solidity of the workmanship, and the second and eighth lines contain just two syllables per line. The ponderous rhythms these four lines establish and the precision of these stanzas' appearance on the page give the reader confidence in Chappell as builder and successfully prepare for the imagery of rebirth in the poem's closing lines: "New / now you / see me a new man" (177). Moreover, Chappell has Ole Fred ask near the end of the poem about this paradisal vision, "what if it's true already? And / we have but to touch out to see it / among our amidst" (177). For those whose vision is cleansed by love, the poet implies, paradise is here and now as well as in eternity, "the other shore us gathering" (156).

What Chappell manages to accomplish in *Midquest*—and it is no small achievement in what is often considered a postmodern secular age—is to awaken readers to the presence of Spirit, both in nature and in themselves. "The *Book of Earth*," as Ole Fred discovers, is "brimming over with matter, / Matter aye and spirit, too, each / And every page is chock to stupefying" (160). In an era of intensely subjective lyric poetry, Chappell directs the reader's gaze to the objective world, the realm of nature and the human community, praising seventeenth-century British poets like Marvell and Donne and Vaughan because "they had senses / alive apart from their egos, and took delight in / every new page of Natural Theology" (40). *Midquest* is Chappell's contribution to such theology, a book that merits wider recognition as one of the finest long poems in twentieth-century American literature.

Even while working on *Midquest*, Chappell had begun to plan a series of four novels, the Kirkman tetralogy, intended to parallel the four books of verse that compose *Midquest*. Analysis of those novels—*I Am One of You Forever* (1985), *Brighten the Corner Where You Are* (1989), *Farewell, I'm Bound to Leave You* (1996), and *Look Back All the Green Valley* (1999)—is beyond the scope of this study, but interested readers may consult either my *Understanding Fred Chappell* (2000) or *More Lights Than One* (2004), a collection of essays on Chappell's fiction edited by Patrick Bizzaro. Chappell now refers to this entire set of books as "an octave" (*More Lights* 256).

The eight collections of poems that Chappell has published since *Midquest* continue to attest to his identification with the agrarian world of his childhood, to his love of nature, and to his quest for spiritual illumination amid suffering and death. Each of those subsequent volumes has been strikingly different from the others in overall design, poetic structures, and dominant tone; yet all confirm the inventiveness of Chappell's imagination and his mastery of both traditional forms and free verse. The remainder of this chapter will highlight those poems and books that address most directly Chappell's agrarian vision, his celebration of the natural world, and his religious concerns.

The title of his 1985 collection *Source* indicates Chappell's ongoing engagement with ultimates, recalling the cosmogonies and fables of origin scattered throughout *Midquest*. The singular noun of the title points to a single source, reflecting what Chappell calls his "passion for unity" ("Too Many Freds" 269), but the four sections into which the book is divided, as well as particular poems, emphasize the diverse formative experiences that shape human identity. Among the most important to these poems are childhood, nature, encounters with the divine, music and story, war, and the mystery of suffering and death.

The childhood detailed in the initial section of *Source*, like that portrayed elsewhere in Chappell's writing, is rural, grounded in an agrarian lifestyle. The child's attachment to nature is a key element in defining his sensibility, as is evident in "Nocturne," "A Prayer for the Mountains," "A Prayer for Slowness," "Here," and "Awakening to Music." This last poem focuses, not as the reader might expect, on musical compositions of human origin but rather on memories of "a whiteface heifer" and the daily chore of milking cows. The speaker's memories, however pastoral, are scarcely idyllic. In fact, the poem opens by recounting the boy's efforts to retrieve the escaped heifer in a harsh winter landscape. "I'd curse to melt the snow," he remarks (10). Nevertheless, it is through the activity of milking the cow that the boy comes "to the pulsing green fountain where music is born" (11). "A Prayer for the Mountains," in contrast, does present an idyllic vision of nature as it proceeds through a series of petitions. "Let these peaks have happened. // The hawk-haunted knobs and hollers, / The blind coves . . . ," Chappell writes; "Let these have taken place, let them be place" (5). Elsewhere in the poem he requests:

> In the slow glade where sunlight comes through
> In circlets and moves from leaf to fallen leaf
> Like a tribe of shining bees, let
> The milk-flecked fawn lie unseen, unfearing. (5)

The rhythm and sound effects in these lines offer one effective example of Chappell's artistry. Alliteration and assonance and repetition, together with the weight and pace of the long vowels throughout the passage— especially in the phrases "slow glade" and "tribe of shining bees"—shape the reader's response to this landscape, reinforcing the benison the poem bestows. Many of the poems in the first two-thirds of part 1 convey this sense of peace, of gentle ease, an impression reinforced by images of people and animals at rest and of "the deep Bible" lying open "like a turned-down bed" in "Humility" (9).

In the last few poems in part 1, such tranquillity yields to a darker view of human experience. Part 2, moreover, begins with a nightmare vision of life following a nuclear holocaust, the allegorical "The Evening of the Second Day," a poem in which Chappell reminds his readers that humanity has now developed the power to undo creation, to annihilate the sources that have sustained human beings for millennia. The agrarian landscape so beautifully imaged in part 1 is here transformed, with "*sacred fields in ashes,*" "bat-spattered shell casings [not harvested crops] stacked in the barn loft," "The only green things the scattered bales of money" (17). Instead of the luminous landscape of "A Prayer for the Mountains," the reader encounters an ominously "glowing mountain" irradiated by nuclear warheads (18). The poem is horrifying enough in itself, but read in the context of the earlier poems in *Source,* its impact intensifies. In addition, the poem's narrator thrusts the reader inside this experience of desolation by using "your" and "you": "After your sister on all fours has died fearing water" (17). Preservation of the earth's health, of nature's vitality, is one of humanity's principal responsibilities, Chappell implies.

The third poem in part 2, "Music as a Woman Imperfectly Perceived," marks an abrupt shift in tone, as Chappell revels once again in music's capacity to invigorate human lives. Just as in *Wind Mountain* music is the voice of spirit, one of the ways the transcendent becomes manifest in the temporal world, so here music is linked to the image of a woman as physical being who also represents the poet's muse. Throughout Chappell's work music is a fundamental source of revelation and transformation. Like the woman imperfectly perceived to whom music is compared in this poem, music "sheds such grace / Upon this place / Of darkness, that every flower burns brightly in her face" (22). As Chappell's collection of short stories *Moments of Light* demonstrates, the classical concept of the music of the spheres functions significantly in his writing. For Chappell, music is a "Natural Resource," as the title of a subsequent poem in *Source* indicates, not simply a human artistic creation.

To be aligned with music and nature does not, however, exempt one from mortality, as the poem "Transmogrification of the Diva" reveals, along with the book's title poem, which closes part 2. "An ancient wound troubles the river," the latter poem begins (36), recalling the conventional use of the river as a symbol of temporality. The experience of mortality inspires stories and fables, myths and songs, poems and novels and musical compositions. It also promotes philosophical reflection and religious beliefs. "Source" thus serves as an apt conclusion to part 2, while also introducing readers to the twilight world of part 3 and the terrors and consolations of part 4.

"The Transformed Twilight," the lieder cycle that composes part 3, arises out of the war in Vietnam, as do several of the poems in *The World between the Eyes* and *Midquest*. The poem's central character, a sculptor, is a veteran of that war, haunted by the brutality he witnessed there. The carefully wrought formal structure of "The Transformed Twilight" (seven numbered sections of twelve lines, each divided into unrhymed quatrains) contrasts with the sculptor's emotional turmoil and the poem's at times surrealistic images. Chappell's sculptor labors in vain to recover a vision of wholeness, to reaffirm what Chappell calls the artist's "pact with unbroken eternity" (40). This artist is left instead with his memories of "black terror" in Vietnam and his impression of the contemporary world as "a nebula / Of accident" (45).

Part 4, entitled "Forever Mountain," opens with a poem that extends the bleak mood established in part 3, a poem called "The Capacity for Pain." Five of the six other poems in part 4 likewise address death and suffering, and three of them include the term "terror" or the phrase "the terrors." Like the speaker in "The Capacity for Pain," like the Lucretius portrayed in "Urleid" who "*walked out far to view the Gorgon / Terror*" (54), like the Thomas Hardy who provides the epigraph to part 4, Chappell never dodges or slights pain and anguish. As Ole Fred says in *Midquest*, "Our faith must be earned from terror" (87). It is toward faith, toward affirmation, that part 4 of *Source* moves, as its title poem intimates, yet not without acknowledging the many times when "the prayed-for transformation / remains stone" (50). In "Urleid," a German word suggesting ancient or aboriginal sorrow, Chappell focuses on the Roman philosopher and poet who numbered the soul among material things and thereby sought to liberate people from fear of divine punishment in an afterlife. Chappell lightens the mood of this poem by inserting humorous anachronisms; he has Lucretius deplore, for example, the mysticism of "the detestable Rilke: those angels" and proclaim, "The silliest movie is that empty drawing room farce / They call Olympus" (53). Yet the following poem, "Message," dedicated to fellow poet David Slavitt, whose mother had been murdered in her home by an intruder, uses the very angel image that Lucretius rejects. And although "Message" starts with "The first messenger angel . . . / purely clothed in terror," the poem progresses to a moment of revelation when the message's recipient "is transformed head to foot, taproot to polestar. / He breathes a new universe . . ." (55).

The basis for Chappell's faith in such transformation is implied in the penultimate poem in *Source*, "O Sacred Head Now Wounded," which takes its title from a hymn on which Bach based one of his cantatas. In keeping with the generally somber tone of part 4, Chappell depicts the suffering Christ and the Bosch-like fleering faces that surround Him. This poem consists entirely of sentence fragments, as if to mirror the broken condition of the soon-to-be-executed Jesus. Crucifixion, not resurrection, is the focus of this poem. And yet, Chappell seems to suggest, there is implicit consolation here, for Christianity witnesses to a God who is not remote from human history and human suffering but who has become incarnate, entering the world of time and embracing suffering. Pain and death remain, but so does the promise of resurrection, a promise inextricably bound up, for Christians, with the crucifixion.

It is that promise of resurrection which Chappell highlights in *Source*'s final poem, "Forever Mountain," dedicated to the memory of his father. "Now a lofty smoke has cleansed my vision," the poem opens (57), a clarifying smoke in contrast to the obscuring fog of the book's initial poem, "Child in the Fog." The tranquil mood of the poem and its exquisite images of nature's beauty set it apart from all the other poems in part 4.

The poet envisions his father climbing Pisgah, a mountain not far from Chappell's Canton but also the mountain from which Moses viewed the Promised Land (Deut. 34:1–4). The steady ease with which the poet's father ascends the slope lends an air of assurance, of calm certitude, to this vision. Chappell concludes the poem with the italicized line "*This is a prayer*," and he thus links this poem to the grace-full prayers of part 1 and to the religious conviction that underlies his work, a faith that he repeatedly tests and refines in the fires of suffering and death and doubt.

Chappell's next book of poems, *First and Last Words* (1989), draws its title from the fact that its opening section consists of nine poems conceived as prologues to other works of art while its third section contains nine poems treated as epilogues. Between these two stands a central section of sixteen poems aptly titled "Entr'acte." As if to underscore the centrality of religious vision to the Western artistic tradition, as well as to the poet's own thought, the book begins and ends with poems based upon the Old and New Testaments, the former poem titled "An Old Mountain Woman Reading the Book of Job." A meditation in stately blank verse, this poem links *First and Last Words* to *Source* not only in agrarian setting but also in theme, for Chappell again raises the mystery of suffering that recurs throughout part 4 of *Source*. The widowed mountain woman recalls the suffering of her dead husband, "whom the Lord like a hunting lion / Has carried off" (6). Although, like Job, "she never shall curse God," Chappell also writes of her:

> She will not suffer
> A God Who suffers the suffering of man,
> Who sends the fatherless their broken arms,
> Who sends away the widows empty as faith. (6)

"Tonight's no night for the heartless bedside prayer," the poem concludes, recognizing perhaps, in its use of the word "tonight," that the woman might be reconciled with God some other day. In revising this poem for its subsequent publication in *Spring Garden*, Chappell further muted its pessimism about religious belief by changing the phrase "empty *as* faith" to "empty *of* faith" (67; italics added). But at least at the moment described in the poem, this woman remains adamant, rebelling against humanity's inexplicable burden of pain and loss.

A number of the other poems in *First and Last Words* share the regional

setting of *Midquest* and of such poems in *Source* as "A Prayer for the Mountains" and "Forever Mountain." "The Gift to Be Simple," for example, is a
prologue to Aaron Copland's *Appalachian Spring,* and both "Patience," a
prologue to Vergil's *Georgics,* and "Scarecrow Colloquy," the epilogue to
the Gospels that concludes the book, invoke the agrarian landscape of
Midquest. Chappell is careful, however, to avoid pastoral primitivism. In
"Patience," which employs a hexameter line inspired by Vergil's classical
meter, Chappell undercuts the utopian outlook presented in the poem's
opening section by beginning the second section with the statement, "Always the Poet knew it wasn't that way" (9). The lines following this statement largely translate the final lines of book 1 of the *Georgics,* in which
Vergil describes a world immersed in bloodshed, a violence into which
the farmer is conscripted. In the third section of this three-part poem, the
reader senses Chappell's *im*patience with the marginalizing of the farmer
and of agriculture not only in Vergil's day but also in our own. Like "The
Transformed Twilight," "Patience" might be numbered among Chappell's
political poems.

Many of these prologues address three major themes: the nature of
evil, the often frustrated quest for peace and justice in a world rife with
war, and the varied human responses to suffering and injustice. Such concerns are obvious features of "An Old Mountain Woman" and "Patience"
and of the intervening rhymed poem "The Watchman," a prologue to
Aeschylus's *Oresteia.* While the Book of Job deals with what philosophers
call natural evil, "The Watchman" deals with moral evil, with evil that
originates in human conduct. Like Aeschylus's dramatic trilogy, Chappell's prologue to *The Death of Ivan Ilych,* "Meanwhile," also centers upon
intense conflict, in this case Ivan's confrontation with human finitude. Yet
Chappell attends less to death itself than to the choices people make before death strikes. "A man must get ahead in the world," the poem opens
(13), its neatly ordered unrhymed quatrains contrasting with the loss of
control Ivan experiences. Like Tolstoy, Chappell highlights the tension
between one's career and one's life. "A man must get ahead in the world,"
the poet repeats from Ivan's point of view in the text's penultimate line,
"the world that breaks its first and only promise," the author adds. Yet the
poem, like the Russian novella on which it is based, produces an awareness more of self-betrayal than of external treachery.

Chappell does not, however, simply dismiss Ivan's complaint. Instead he returns to it again in the subsequent poem, "Stoic Poet," a prologue to Thomas Hardy's *The Dynasts*. Hardy's consciousness of human suffering and of the universe's indifference to it leads him to compassion, not to insensitivity. Although "Terrors assail him," he retains "his human sympathies" (14). Like the Lucretius of "Urleid," Hardy represents qualities of courage and endurance amid "the wounds of the world's every crime." Through Hardy's example Chappell affirms the capacity for moral conduct and human values even in a universe that the Victorian author perceives as amoral.

Just as Chappell plays Hardy's personality off against that of Ivan Ilych, so he contrasts Hardy's experience of glacial chill ("our stars implacable and indifferent") with the vision of "A natural transparent Open Harmony" (15) in "The Gift to Be Simple." The tone and meter and exact rhymes of this prologue to *Appalachian Spring*, based on a Shaker hymn tune, differentiate it from all the other poems in the book's opening section. Chappell's frequent anapests create a lilting rhythm that belies Copland's composition of the music in 1943–44, at the height of World War II. At times the rhythm appears to be used for ironic effect, and yet the words of the poem attest to the power of music, imaged as "that Valley of love and delight." Here as elsewhere in Chappell's work, music is linked to "Order" (with a capital O) and is credited with helping us "straiten our Lives." The ability of the arts, both literary and nonliterary, to engender and sustain moral insight, to effect moral change, is one of the principal tenets of Chappell's artistic credo. Nevertheless, the optimism of this poem's closing quatrain is sharply qualified by almost all the other prologues.

The longest and most varied section of *First and Last Words*, "Entr'acte" opens with a three-part poem whose title reflects this cross-fertilization of art and life: "My Hand Placed on a Rubens Drawing." The woman in the artist's drawing is of farmer ancestry, whose own hands have "the smell of earth about them," so that this woman becomes the poet's counterpart— as Rubens himself does too when the poet proclaims, "Rubens sinks the piers of vision deep / Into the earth" (21). Surely the same is true of the author of *Source* and even more so of *Midquest*, with its use of the four elements and its portraits of Virgil Campbell and Uncle Body. "My Hand Placed on a Rubens Drawing" ends with a brief coda consisting of two rhymed quatrains that emphasize the spiritual dimension of Chappell's aesthetic:

> The ages work toward mastery
> Of a single gesture. . . .
>
> Fragments that might still add up
> To compose a figure of the perfected soul . . . (21)

Chappell rhymes "soul" with "whole" in the second quatrain and thus attests to the integrative thrust of his art, his longing to reconcile opposites, to create a unified and unifying vision.

The four poems that cluster at the center of this book are essential to the interpenetration of literature and life—and of past and present texts—that *First and Last Words* posits. The four poems are titled "Word," "Literature," "The Reader," and "The Garden," with "Literature" standing exactly at the midpoint of the volume's thirty-five poems, on a facing page with "The Reader." Far lighter in tone than most of the prologues, these poems fancifully explore the centrality of word and story in defining both self and world. In "The Reader," instead of people opening books, the book opens the reader. "[Books] bring the world—or some outlook of its soul—/ Into her small apartment" (29), the poet observes, again interweaving the physical and the spiritual in his diction. And in "The Garden" Chappell utilizes what has steadily become one of the governing metaphors of his entire body of work, from the Edenic images that *Midquest* invokes at key moments, through the ravaged garden of "The Overspill" (the opening section of *I Am One of You Forever*), to the garden's structural and thematic function in *Spring Garden,* to the rose and garden imagery of *Look Back All the Green Valley,* the concluding volume in the Kirkman tetralogy. Biblical in origin, this garden metaphor is perhaps most directly inspired in Chappell's writing by Dante's mystic Rose in the *Paradiso* and by Eliot's rose garden in *Four Quartets.* It is clearly a metaphor that enables Chappell to embrace both the immanent and the transcendent.

"The Garden" opens by stating, "The garden is a book about the gardener," and continues by elaborating on this initial trope:

> Her thoughts, set down in vivid greenery,
> The green light and the gold light nourish.
> Firm sentences of grapevine, boxwood paragraphs,
> End-stops of peonies and chrysanthemums,
> Cut drowsy shadows on the paper afternoon. (30)

These lush images link nature and art as well as nature and language, but the poem's initial statement may also be read as a version of one of the five classical proofs of God's existence, the argument from design. Such a reading is reinforced by the subtle paradox of Chappell's closing lines: "The book is open once again that was never shut. / What now we do not know we shall never know." These lines anticipate "After Revelation," the final story in *More Shapes Than One*, while functioning here to undercut the invitation to logical proof of God's existence that the argument from design presumes to offer. Between these opening and closing statements Chappell inserts another paradox by reversing the terms of the poem's initial line, declaring instead, "The gardener is a book about her garden." The end-stop in both lines gives each an aura of quiet certitude despite their apparent contradiction. This ability to grasp conflicting or opposing ideas and to hold them in fruitful tension is one of the qualities that Chappell's poetry nurtures in its readers even as it aspires to an ultimate reconciliation of opposites.

The third and last section of the book, "Epilogues," extends Chappell's treatment of the prologues' themes but adds to them an analysis of epistemological questions relating to objectivity versus subjectivity. While Chappell is deeply aware of the complex relationship between the subjective and objective, here as elsewhere in his writing he focuses more on the loss of objective reality presupposed by philosophical idealism and its postmodern variants. "Ideally Grasping the Actual Flower," an epilogue to Kant's *Prolegomena to Any Future Metaphysics*, returns to the images of garden and rose in "Entr'acte." Yet Kantian idealism relegates the "real" flower to a noumenal realm remote from sensory experience, a realm, Chappell notes ironically, "As empiric as the faultless Empyrean" (46). Similarly, the human figure in the poem, whom Chappell has identified not as Kant but as Wallace Stevens (Easa 55), is depicted as "At large in the garden which perhaps he postulates," where he is paradoxically "Determined to picture this *rose* as pictureless" (45). According to Chappell, Stevens shares with Kant philosophical premises that tend to sever humanity from nature, premises that led Stevens to prefer what he called "the planet on the table" (the book) to the natural world. As we have seen, the recovery of the actual, of the concrete physical world, is a recurring theme in Chappell's poetry. In fact, Chappell directs the reader's gaze not toward the "arbitrary starlight" of "Observers" (44), his epilogue to Einstein's *Relativity*, but toward "the cathedral of starlight" in "Slow Harbor" (24), inviting the reader on a pilgrimage "directly to the source / of light, where an endless sheet of stars / burns palpitant and interweaving" (48).

Significantly, the final poem in *First and Last Words*, "Scarecrow Colloquy," presents the title character as a "Sentinel of the Stars" (56). Labeled an epilogue to the Gospels, this closing poem is a companion piece to the book's initial poem on Job. Together these two poems testify to the religious dimension of both Chappell's work and the Western literary and philosophical tradition. Yet like "An Old Mountain Woman," "Scarecrow Colloquy" is a poem of doubt as well as of faith. Indeed, as Makuck has noted, "The poem can easily be read as a dialogue between Faith and Skepticism" (196), with the scarecrow representing faith and his unnamed interlocutor representing skepticism. The latter speaks first, in tercets that alternate with the quatrains assigned to the scarecrow. Chappell thus not only allows the scarecrow to speak at greater length but also assigns him the last word—in fact, the "last words" of the entire collection. The scarecrow's poignant longing for a decisive revelation of the divine is among the most moving elements of this poem. But that revelation never occurs, and the reader may seem to be left with a portrait only of the scarecrow's quixotic fidelity, his patient endurance despite the silence and absence of the God he yearns to hear. Ultimately, however, the scarecrow seems more than a figure of faith; he also appears to be an image of the crucified Christ, Eliot's hanged man. If so, then the "hard farmer" may be less an emblem of an indifferent God and more a symbol of humanity's failure to embrace the possibility of redemption inherent in Christ's self-sacrificial death. As the anonymous interlocutor tells the scarecrow, albeit ironically, "This disaster they call a world might find a pivot / if you but stand outlined within the sunrise" (56).

The ambiguity here is characteristic of Chappell, as is the impulse to allegory that lends this poem its evocative power. The scarecrow's final words, which allude to Isaiah 40 and to the legend that Jesus was crucified on the same spot where Adam lies buried, suggest that more than human fidelity is at stake in the poem:

> *I have spoken in the field till my voice became an owl.*
> *I have surveyed the horizon till I lost my buttons.*
> *The fieldmouse heard my silence and gnawed my flesh of grass.*
> *And still I stand here, guarding the bones of Adam.* (57)

While Isaiah 40:6 avers that "all flesh is grass," that chapter of Isaiah's prophecy also declares, "The word of our God will stand forever" (v. 8), like Chappell's enduring scarecrow-Christ. Moreover, the word that Isaiah 40 proclaims is one of comfort and pardon and divine love even when it appears to Israel that God is absent or unseeing (vs. 1–2, 27–28). Although Chappell's poetry gives voice to doubt, it does so largely within the biblical tradition. Makuck thus errs when he contends that this book's closing poem "endorses a Hardyesque world" in which the scarecrow's "inexhaustible voice [is] still talking to its self-made Other, whistling in the dark" (196). Much of Chappell's poetry, in contrast, presents not a self-made Other but the God manifest in the Judeo-Christian tradition, a divine presence as objectively real for the poet as nature itself—and often equally inscrutable. Makuck correctly perceives, however, the essentially religious outlook of Chappell's poetry. "In the best sense of the word," Makuck writes, "Fred Chappell is an old-fashioned poet, one for whom writing is a spiritual project. . . . Chappell's poems implicitly argue against the current literary/philosophical notion that words are problematically referential, or don't have meaning, or don't mean much. Chappell knows they mean plenty and, skillfully used, are capable of providing sustenance and solace" (197). *First and Last Words* serves to remind the reader of many of the sources of such sustenance throughout the Western tradition, not only in literature and art and music but also in philosophy and religion.

Chappell's book of one hundred epigrams, titled simply *C* (1993), might be thought an unlikely repository of the kinds of philosophical and religious themes that this study has been pursuing, but its fourth poem, "Morning Light," consists of a translation of Giuseppe Ungaretti's "*Mattina*": "Immensity / Illumes me [*M'illumino / d'immenso*]" (2). Thus, early in this book, Chappell posits both a sense of awe in the presence of nature and a sense of nature's didactic dimension, its capacity to instruct, to illuminate, to help people "see" (one meaning of the book's title). In the one-line poem "Coming Home," Chappell uses synesthesia to situate the speaker in nature: "Even the sunlight is a smell you remembered" (31). And in such poems as "Daisy," "White Clover," and "Chipmunk," Chappell personifies the natural phenomena named in these poems' titles and thereby enhances the kinship between nature and humanity. The Daisy remarks, for instance, "Men build Parises and Zions; / I, wide meadows of Orions. / Rome took two thousand years, but in one day / I built a Milky Way" (5). The contrast Chappell draws here between the trimeter closing line and the preceding pentameter line suggests the ease of nature's creative outpourings. Moreover, by linking the Daisy to Orion, Chappell yokes nature to the heavens, creation to Creator, a conflation of images that is repeated in poems XXXVIII (where the snowflake is a "Sugar-star"), XLVI, and XLVII. In "Dodder" the plant offers a prayer (9), anticipating the three graces before meals (14) and the three bedtime prayers (47) that appear later in the book. The simplicity and sincerity of these poems contrast both with the rantings of the televangelists whose "threats of hell" make life a bore in "Rejoinder" (3) and with the pomposity of the preacher in "Televangelist" who envisions himself "reign[ing] equally / With Jesus in eternity" (13).

Again and again Chappell introduces religious terms and concepts and speaks casually of God, whether in the previously mentioned prayer-poems ("Bless us who pray, bless us who can't" [14]) or in such poems as "Blue Law," "El Perfecto," and "Liberal." The first of these invites dancing girls to remove their clothes so that their naked flesh will "Lend spirit to our dwindling hours" (22). This paradoxical claim is reinforced by the poem's insistence that "Spirit [capital S] will at last disclose / The full enormity of its powers" (22). In "El Perfecto" Chappell speaks of this politician's rejection of God's handiwork (23), and in "Liberal" he refers to the doctrine of Original Sin to illustrate this figure's failure of moral insight: "Faced with the problem of Original Sin, / He applies to Science for a sure vaccine" (40). Chappell's capitalization of Science suggests its displacement of God in modern thought—or perhaps only this Liberal's wrongheaded deification of science. Similarly, Chappell's use of slant rhyme in this couplet indicates the insufficiency of the proposed solution to the problem it is intended to cure. The two are not commensurate.

Despite the humor of many of its poems, *C*, like *Earthsleep*, is a book filled with memento mori. The consciousness of time passing is reinforced by the volume's structure, for despite occasional exceptions, the poems move from morning to night, from summer to winter, and from relative youth to old age. The imminence of death is meant to remind the reader that, in inventorying the things that make life blest, Chappell (following Martial) had concluded with "A death not longed for, but without dread" (3). As was noted earlier, to reconcile the reader to the fact of mortality has been one of Chappell's consistent aims. In *C* that intention is particularly evident in the paired poems, "The Moon Regards the Frozen Earth" and "The Earth Replies" (XCVI–XCVII). In these two poems near the book's end, Chappell contrasts two opposing outlooks on life. The recriminatory moon, on the one hand, represents a narrowing of expectations, a retreat from experience into a fruitless asceticism; the earth, on the other hand, speaks for openness to experience, for an expansive celebration of life, including the gains and losses that attend mutability. It is, after all, the moon that is forever frozen, while the earth's winter will yield to spring. Chappell gives the earth almost twice the number of lines allotted to the moon, thus weighting the argument in earth's favor, and the lighter tone of *C*'s last three poems seems meant to imply that the poet has indeed adopted earth's viewpoint. Despite the brevity of its poems, *C* clearly articulates many of Chappell's major themes.

When Chappell published *Spring Garden: New and Selected Poems* in 1995, he included twenty-five of the one hundred epigrams in *C*. The book also reprinted, usually greatly revised and sometimes retitled, ten poems from *The World between the Eyes*, over a third of the poems in *Source*, and just over half the poems in *First and Last Words*. From *Midquest* came only two poems: "Susan's Morning Dream of Her Garden," *Spring Garden*'s opening selection, and "My Grandmother Washes Her Feet." In addition to the selected poems, *Spring Garden* contains nineteen new or previously uncollected poems, together with a general prologue, an epilogue, and separate prologues for the seven sections into which the book is divided: "In the Garden," "The Good Life," "The Garden of Love," "Poems of Character," "Poems of Fantasy," "Epigrams," and "Poems of Memory." The number seven, of course, carries connotations of the sacred because of its association with the account of creation in Genesis, but that number also suggests Chappell's long-standing theme of mutability, the inexorable advance of time as the days of the week unfold.

In the general prologue Chappell compares selecting the poems to the gathering of herbs depicted in French Renaissance poet Pierre de Ronsard's "La Salade":

> We [Fred and Susan] seek out lines still green and with some savor,
> A stanza here and there with a bouquet
> Of sunlight, humus, rain, the virid flavor
> Of fresh-turned earth, perfume of new-mown hay. (4)

While this strategy may strike some readers as highly artificial, it has the benefit not only of providing a structural principle for the book but also of grounding poetry—and human identity—firmly in nature. As David Middleton comments, "Chappell's metaphorical linking of poetry with specimens from the natural order is more than a convenient fancy; it represents a deep understanding of the relationship between the pastoral dream, the agrarian insistence on the binding of culture and agriculture, and the poet's double-rootedness in the eternal ground of being and in a postedenic earth" (xi). On a more mundane level, moreover, *Spring Garden* is an apt title because it is part of the address of the university where Chappell taught for forty years. A spring garden, then, is not only the book's principal setting but also its dominant metaphor, representing fecundity, harmony, and the promise of rebirth while evoking memories both of Eden and of the Earthly Paradise which Dante portrays in the closing cantos of the *Purgatorio*. Early in *Spring Garden* Chappell refers to the book's setting as an "enchanted grove" (10). Yet Chappell's garden, as Middleton notes, is decidedly postlapsarian. Consciousness of time passing and of death's approach pervades the volume. At times that concern with mortality seems excessive, almost morbid, considering the fact that Chappell was not yet sixty years old at the time he published the book. Nonetheless, the *carpe diem* motif is one of this volume's major unifying devices. Significantly, the pleasures the poet urges the reader to seize are not those of body alone; they also embrace the delights of the intellect, the imagination, and the spirit (9). By including both "The Fields" (a heavily revised version of "The Farm" from *The World between the Eyes*) and "Patience" (his homage to Vergil's *Georgics*) in the opening section of *Spring Garden*, Chappell is able to expand the purview of his garden motif so that it encompasses the agrarian experience of his childhood and the agrarian outlook of his mature literary vision.

Like *C* in its overarching temporal structure, *Spring Garden* moves from morning in the general prologue to evening in the epilogue. Yet more than in *C*, Chappell organizes these new and selected poems to highlight, at book's end, his religious concerns. Given the volume's frequently elegiac tone and its pervasive sense of the hurtling passage of time, it is entirely appropriate that the book's final section be devoted to "Poems of Memory." Despite the poet's focus on mortality, however, in the prologue to this final section Chappell speaks of "Fretting little the future present in God" (131). Eight of this section's thirteen poems are reprinted from *Source*, and the opening poem, "Humility," sets a religious tone that is extended by the following poem, "A Prayer for the Mountains," and echoed by the section's final poem, "Forever Mountain," of which the poet says *"this is continually a prayer"* (147; Chappell's italics). The book's epilogue, moreover, again links Chappell's religious vision with that of Dante, whose *Divine Comedy* played such a prominent role in shaping *Midquest*. In that epilogue Chappell remarks that "Pursuit of wisdom" is the poet's true work (153), a wisdom articulated by this garden's "centerpiece medallion with its grave / Beloved quotation from the Florentine" (151). That quotation reads, "L'amor che move il sole e l'altre stelle" (151), the closing line of Dante's *Paradiso*. These words do actually appear on a similar medallion in Chappell's garden in Greensboro, and their appearance there, in the closing lines of *Midquest*, and in the epilogue to *Spring Garden* should again remind readers of the religious sensibility that marks Chappell's writing. That religious perspective is reinforced by the translation that concludes the epilogue, Ronsard's "A son âme" ("To His Soul"), itself a translation of Hadrian's "Animula vagula, blandula."

The first and last translations of *Spring Garden* are thus from Ronsard, both of them emphasizing human finitude. The final poems of sections 4 through 6 also sound this theme, while the seventh section, in contrast, ends with "Forever Mountain" and the hope of resurrection offered by that poem. The references to Dante and the soul in the epilogue make it clear that, for Chappell, the theme of mortality arises in a larger context that includes both the divine love to which the Florentine attests and the power of human love—and of art itself—to transcend death. "Now I lay me down to sleep" is *Spring Garden's* final line, Chappell's translation of Ronsard's "Je dors" (155). But that statement is also the opening line of a well-known children's bedtime prayer. The simple faith evoked by such a conclusion reflects the poet's quiet trust in divine grace, though elsewhere in *Spring Garden* that faith encounters severe challenges, as it generally does in Chappell's poetry and fiction.

When Chappell published his next new collection of poems, *Family Gathering* (2000), he utilized the skillful characterization that is central to the artistry of *Midquest*, especially its portraits of Ole Fred's parents and grandparents and of Virgil Campbell. While the idea of home is clearly implicit in such a family reunion, this book focuses primarily on human traits, not on the Appalachian landscape or on nature's creatures. Religious concerns also play a minimal role in this volume, although Chappell does offer two ironical paired poems, "True Believer" and "Nonbeliever" (30), reminiscent of some of the satirical epigrams in *C*. In "The Rubaiyat of Uncle Hobart," as in *Midquest* and *Spring Garden*, the poet invokes Dante, for Uncle Hobart says, "Midway in this life I paused to think / What Way to choose," but this dipsomaniacal uncle claims only to have "heard / A pleasant Voice exhorting me to drink" (20). And while Aunt Wilma attributes her husband Einar's financial success to God, her vindictiveness toward the philandering Einar leaves readers wondering about her conception of God. In sharp contrast to Wilma stands Aunt Agnes, whose name is linked in Christian iconography about St. Agnes to a lamb, one of the epithets for Christ (*agnus Dei*). Aunt Agnes appears in the book's penultimate poem, "The Strain of Mercy," a title that recalls Portia's famous comment in *The Merchant of Venice* that "The quality of mercy is not strained." After cataloging many of the family members present in earlier poems, Agnes accepts them unconditionally, in an attitude of godlike forgiveness. As Chappell writes, "She recognizes what we are, / Yet holds us in affection / As steadfast as the morning star" (60). In the book of Revelation, Jesus identifies himself as the morning star (Rev. 22:16), but that allusion may be less pertinent here than Chappell's more general association, throughout his work, of the stars with the divine. Ironically but all too humanly, however, the other members of the family resist the absolution Agnes offers; hence the poem's title.

Chappell opens and closes *Family Gathering* with poems that depict eight-year-old Elizabeth's reaction to this reunion. Bored, feeling slighted, she retreats in the opening poem to the porch, where she dances and sings alone. The closing poem finds her in the porch swing, dreaming "vexed dreams," though in the poem's—and book's—final stanzas "her dream gives in to a mockingbird" that Chappell portrays as bringing her words of comfort:

> *"Fear not: The rising of the heedful moon*
> *Signals that nighttime is not the end*
> *Of light, of time. An elegant lagoon*
> *Of space buoys your world up like a balloon.*
> *Fear not, Elizabeth, I am your friend."* (62)

The calm reassurance afforded Elizabeth is also Chappell's benediction on the reader. The mockingbird testifies to the vision of ultimate cosmic order that underlies Chappell's poetry, an order grounded both in nature and the supernatural.

The poems of *Backsass* (2004), as the title indicates, are often satirical and mocking. Among the targets of Chappell's satire, here as in *C*, are those who distort what the poet considers authentic religious impulses. In "Resolution and Independence," for example, a title which echoes that of Wordsworth's well-known poem about the Leech Gatherer, Chappell refers to "the dread Four Horsemen / of Insomnia," one of whom is Religion (along with Politics, Sex, and Literary Critic). Religion is portrayed as "char-black / as the flamesnorting stallion he spurred / bony he was with wild eyes sunken / and flourished a brand of smoking scriptures" (37). The emaciated appearance of this figure suggests an unhealthy rejection of the physical world, while his smoking scriptures seem meant to remind readers of the fire-and-brimstone preaching of too many representatives of Protestant fundamentalism, within and without the mountain South, and of Western Christianity generally, as the Roman Catholic priest's sermon on Hell in chapter 3 of Joyce's *Portrait of the Artist as a Young Man* likewise demonstrates. In "Bringing in the Oaks," with its alteration of the familiar hymn title's *sheaves,* Chappell focuses on the nature of irrational guilt, often the product of excessively judgmental religion, though in this poem such guilt arises from a ludicrous hyper-environmentalism. And in "A Thanksgiving Invitation," one of the two longest poems in the book, both modeled upon satires by Juvenal, the speaker remembers fondly what he calls "*religious times:* when piety was seen / In church and not the television screen; / Village ministers led the heartfelt prayer, / Not teleranters with their bouffant hair" (42).

The playfulness of the poems in *Backsass* and Chappell's frequent creation of speakers from whom the poet distances himself make it difficult to gauge how much weight to give some of these poems' thematic statements, as when in "Down with Democracy" the speaker criticizes politicians because "they strive to eradicate the spiritual" (this in the era of the Christian Coalition and the Moral Majority), or when another poem's speaker contends, "they are gentrifying the Bible too / no more Sodom and Gomorrah but / Gay Land Meadows and Happytyme Acres" (18). But when the speaker of "Agenda" declares his intention to become an ascetic her-

mit, living in a cave or on a pillar like some desert monk, Chappell clearly
undercuts both the speaker's aspiration toward a specious holiness and the
holier-than-thou stance with which the poem concludes (25). As Ole Fred
tells Uncle Body in *Midquest,* "all the world is lit for your delight," words
reminiscent of William Blake's credo: "Every thing that lives is Holy."

Backsass is filled with similar references to religious subject matter,
and it also contains a range of biblical allusions, including poems titled
"Consider the Lilies of the Field" and "Lazarus," as well as the delightful
"No, Said St. Peter," in which the guardian of Heaven's gate explains to a
perpetrator of spouse abuse that his "court-appointed" attorney will come
from "the firm of Steinem Friedan & de Beauvoir" (26). The binary oppositions that help shape *Midquest* are again evident in "We Habitually
Assume the Mind," which also refers, albeit light-heartedly, to "the dark
night of the soul" (17). In this poem the body is portrayed as "sitting here
/ silently plotting one's death" (17), a prospect that should remind readers
of the recurring theme of mortality in Chappell's work, a theme reemphasized in the book's final poem, "Hello Once More," spoken, as is the
opening poem, by the poet's answering machine. Offering to share with
the caller/reader what it terms "the secret / of the universe," this mecha-
nism states, "*a time will come when it is no longer time*" (54). These words
express the mystery and dilemma of human finitude. As Chappell put it
in *Midquest,* "Goodbye I perceive to be a human creature" (156). While
both these statements reflect the *carpe diem* theme that pervades *Spring
Garden,* they also leave open the prospect of eternity, what Chappell in
Midquest calls "the Mountains Outside Time" (169).

In *Backsass,* in *Spring Garden,* in *First and Last Words* and *Source,* and
particularly in *Midquest,* Chappell sustains a view of human nature as
composed of body and spirit, flesh-tree and tree of spirit. Without re-
solving the tension between matter and spirit, body and soul, he rejects
the devaluation of the physical world in much of Western (and Eastern)
philosophy and religion. In an astonishing variety of traditional forms
and free verse, his poetry celebrates nature's vitality and affirms the importance of place—specifically, the agrarian mountain landscape of his
native Appalachia—in determining his fundamental values and beliefs.
Among them is his faith in a creative Power, a sustaining Spirit, whose
love, in Dante's words (as Chappell translates them in *Midquest*), "moves
the sun and other stars."

3

ROBERT MORGAN

"Mountains Speak in Tongues"

LIKE MILLER AND CHAPPELL, Robert Morgan (1944–) was born and raised not far from Asheville in the mountains of western North Carolina. While all three authors share a rural background, Morgan's family lived in significantly poorer financial circumstances and in greater geographic isolation. Morgan spent the first sixteen years of his life on a subsistence farm along the Green River near Zirconia, a farm set on land purchased in 1840 by his great-great-grandfather, Daniel Pace, who had moved to the area from upstate South Carolina. It was literally a one-horse farm, for until the early 1950s the family owned neither tractor nor car or truck. Electricity did not reach the farm until the late 1940s, so the family used kerosene lamps and kept its milk and butter cool in a springhouse. Pole beans were Morgan's father's only cash crop, while butter and eggs were the only consistent year-round source of income on the farm. But Morgan's mother helped to support the family by working in a cotton mill, a beauty shop, and later a General Electric plant. Although Asheville was within thirty miles, Morgan recalls traveling there only about once each year, primarily to buy school clothes or Christmas gifts. "I went off to college," Morgan has said, "to escape the hard work of the mountain farm, the hog killing and wood cutting—so I was surprised, as I began to write more and more poetry and fiction, how often I returned to descriptions of [that] work" (Bizzaro 181). In fact, Morgan has written so extensively about agricultural labor and its implements that Chappell once wryly remarked that "the contents page of a book by Robert Morgan can read like the auction catalogue for a mountain farm going under the hammer" ("Wind-Voices" 65). And Morgan's frequent focus on farm life has led critic William Harmon to assert hyperbolically that "all of Robert Morgan's poems are georgics" (5).

Morgan left his family's farm in 1961 at age sixteen to attend Emory University's campus in Oxford, Georgia, entering college without having finished high school. After a year there he transferred to North Carolina State University to study aerospace engineering and applied mathematics, but he also took a creative writing class from Guy Owen, whose praise for one of Morgan's short stories helped alter the direction of Morgan's college career. As a junior Morgan transferred again, this time to the University of North Carolina at Chapel Hill, from which he graduated with honors in English. In 1968 he earned an M.F.A. from the University of North Carolina at Greensboro, where Fred Chappell was his most important teacher, reinforcing the younger writer's growing interest in poetry. About this mentoring relationship Morgan has written: "Chappell was the best teacher of writing and of poetry I had ever met. . . . I remember thinking that this man knew exactly how these poems were made. I had never encountered that kind of practical critical intelligence before" ("Birth of Music" x).

Morgan's first book, *Zirconia Poems*, dedicated to Chappell, appeared in 1969, by which time Morgan had returned to Green River with a National Endowment for the Arts fellowship, though those funds were quickly depleted. Morgan was farming with his father and supporting himself through part-time work as a house painter when Cornell University offered him a one-year appointment in 1971, the year before his second book of poems, *Red Owl*, was published. That appointment led to a tenure-track position, and Morgan has now taught at Cornell for over thirty-five years. The impact of his move to upstate New York can scarcely be overestimated because, according to Morgan, "it never really occurred to me that I was a southern writer and an Appalachian writer until I left the region" (Harmon, "Imagination" 159). As he remarked to interviewer Sheryl Cornett, "Once I moved away from the South and started teaching at Cornell, out of homesickness I began to go to the library and read about Southern Appalachia" (72). In addition to prompting Morgan to return home via the literary imagination, Cornell offered Morgan an intensely stimulating cultural environment and a sense of community that encouraged the poet to employ more narrative elements in his poetry, a change evident in his 1976 collection *Land Diving*. To date Morgan has published twelve books of poetry, along with a substantial body of fiction, and although some of his poems are set outside Appalachia, "the lodestone of his imagination," in Newton Smith's words, remains "the mountains of his ancestral home" (55). As Morgan writes in *Trunk & Thicket*, "The real word I guess, the / motif, is home. Homecoming. Homing. / How to touch base" (13). For Morgan, that sense of home, of place, largely focuses "on one particular piece of ground," the square mile of land purchased by his great-great-grandfather: "That seems to be the landscape that most nurtures my imagination" (West, "Art of Far and Near" 57).

Yet that imagination is also clearly shaped both by Morgan's interest in the sciences and by American Romanticism, with its celebration of nature and its exploration of the opportunities for spiritual renewal and religious insight to be derived from immersion in nature. The list of Morgan's literary influences is a long one and includes such authors as Thomas Wolfe (whose day of birth, October 3, Morgan shares), Carl Sandburg (who spent his retirement years not far from Zirconia, in Flat Rock), Chinese poetry in translation (especially via Ezra Pound's *Cathay*), the French Symbolists, Thomas Hardy, Gary Snyder, Ernest Hemingway, and Cormac McCarthy. But among Morgan's earliest and most enduring influences are Emerson, Thoreau, Whitman, and Dickinson. In fact, he first read Whitman in his sister Evangeline's American literature anthology before he himself ever left for college, and he was particularly impressed by the opening lines of "Song of Myself": "The lines that really leapt out at me were 'I loafe and invite my soul, / I lean and loafe at my ease observing a spear of summer grass.' It was the contrast between 'soul' and that one 'spear of grass' that really struck me. . . . It was that juxtaposition that first started me thinking about poetry" (Heyen and Rubin 147). Such juxtaposition of the physical and spiritual is characteristic of Morgan's poetry, as is the movement from the abstract to the concrete and from the immanent to the transcendent. Of Whitman Morgan also notes, "The genius of Whitman was to make his body significant. That may be the single great leap of modern poetry" (*Good Measure* 111). In contrast to the metaphysical idealism of Emerson, Whitman insists that he is the poet of both body and soul, an inclusiveness that counteracts the otherworldliness of much fundamentalist Christianity as well. In "The Transfigured Body," the essay in which Morgan voices his tribute to Whitman, Morgan adds, "It is for us to spiritualize the body and nature. . . . We must translate science by recreating the integrity of things, as celebration and praise" (*Good Measure* 112).

This vision of wholeness in nature and this affirmation of the impulse to praise are deeply rooted in Emerson's own writing, which Morgan has said he discovered during his first year at Cornell. "Reading Emerson," he declares, "was like breathing pure oxygen. I was intoxicated . . . by the New Testament rhetoric, by the scientific imagery, by the Neoplatonic metaphors, by the love of the natural world in his sentences" ("Nature" 38). For Morgan, that sense of kinship with Emerson arose in part from his view that the Appalachia of his childhood and early nineteenth-century New England had comparable experiences with religious fundamentalism: "The great genius of American literature, and particularly of American poetry, came out of the collision of New England Puritan zeal with the Enlightenment. So that Emerson in 1832 resigns his pulpit . . . and his first book is not called Salvation or The Soul, it's called *Nature*" (Bizzaro 189). Morgan's resistance to fundamentalist religion, a topic that will be addressed at greater length later in this chapter, is a quintessential feature of his work, and he aligns himself with Emerson by finding in and through nature a language that enables him to articulate spiritual truths, a language that his agrarian childhood had first instilled in him. Although Morgan is far less likely than Emerson to find nature "hint[ing] or thunder[ing] to man the laws of right and wrong, and echo[ing] the Ten Commandments" ("Nature" 1120), he follows Emerson in affirming the interpenetration of the physical and spiritual and the revelatory powers of nature. What Muir Powell, the protagonist of Morgan's novel *This Rock*, calls "twofold" vision, "the natural vision and the spiritual vision" (312), is characteristic of Morgan's poetry, too, as his superb collection *Topsoil Road* (2000) demonstrates.

That Morgan regularly portrays nature as a language, endowing it with powers of speech, is readily apparent throughout this book. He describes various plants, for example, as "the quills and pens of summer" (42), speaks of "the river's variorum" (47), and compares the now-rare wild peavine "curling on a weedstalk" to "some word from a lost language / once flourishing on every tongue" (7). His imagery, moreover, infuses natural objects with human organs of speech, as when he refers to "the lip of ridge" (10) or to a waterfall as the "heavy tongue of river's lip" (32) or claims that lightning has a "blinding tongue," a tongue that speaks a "sentence / of destructive translation" in "Fulgurite" (37). In the closing lines of the book's final poem, he reemphasizes this connection between nature and language by depicting a honeycomb's "crystal-tight arrays" as "rows / and lattices of sweeter latin / from scattered prose of meadow, woods" (53).

As such images indicate, nature for Morgan is rich in texts, rife with potential messages to which poet and reader must remain alert. In the poem "Chicken Scratches," for instance, Morgan says of the chickens' clawing in the dirt, "Some stylus might / have cut the surface and made / a scrawled hand" (33). The chickens' activity is explicitly compared to human writing, the birds' marks "seem[ing] some / funny ogham fading its script / of quest." The flecks of mica turned up by the chickens are said to lie "signaling around the water can," while the birds' "chalks and gritty signs" are imaged, in the poem's closing line, as "the incunabula of morning." The poet's use of the terms "ogham" and "incunabula" not only reinforce the textuality of the chickens' scratching but also suggest the ancient tie between humanity and nature.

That link is highlighted by the strikingly similar situation portrayed in "Besom," where the agent inscribing the marks in the dirt is the poet's grandmother, who uses the implement named in the poem's title, a broom made of twigs. An artist figure involved in "painting neatness on / the ground" (22), the grandmother creates a magical space for the child-poet—until, that is, the passage of chicken and cat across the yard mars the "spell" cast by "the powdery / patterns," "as ordinary circulations / blurred her sandscripts, incidental runes." In this poem Morgan's surprising pun on the word "Sanskrit" and his use of the term "runes" again reinforce, as in "Chicken Scratches," the antiquity of the human quest for order and meaning and revelation. The word "runes," which refers not only to ancient written characters but also to mystery and magic, as well as to Old Norse poems and songs, helps to remind readers of the connection between poetry and the supernatural. This connection is one Morgan underscores by his frequent emphasis on folk superstitions (in such poems as "Thrush Doctor," "Fever Wit," and "Madstone") and by his repeated use of such terms as "ghost" and "haunt," which appear no fewer than eight times in this collection. Morgan's poems delight in transgressing the limits of empiricism, in dissolving the distinction between the human and the natural and between the natural and the supernatural. As he once told an interviewer, "The spirit and the physical world seem to be the same thing; they are located in each other, and poetry reminds us of that connection. It's one of the things the poetic imagination keeps rediscovering" (Elliott 84). For this reason, Morgan adds, "You find very few truly Gnostic poets [that is, poets seeking to escape the world]. . . . [P]oets like Dickinson, Emerson, Whitman are very much interested in experience of this world, at least as analogy and metaphor of experience of the spirit" (84). While poems like "Chicken Scratches" and "Besom" orient the reader to the earth or dirt (as does the book's title), several of the poems in this volume focus on the wind, the most intangible of the four physical elements—earth, air, fire, and water—thought by ancient philosophers to underlie all life. A conventional symbol of the spiritual, of poetic inspiration, and of speech itself, the wind figures prominently in *Topsoil Road*, especially in poems that situate the reader on the verge of revelation or that define the poet's vocation in terms of one of nature's creatures (as in "Wind Rider"). In "Blowing Rock," for example, Morgan imbues one of North Carolina's natural wonders with a spiritual aura through his evocative diction and images, imagery that combines fire and wind to create an impression of sacred space. In Christian symbolism both wind and fire are associated with the descent of the Holy Spirit at Pentecost. Morgan's choice of blank verse in this poem, rather than the book's prevailing syllabics, heightens the dignity of treatment accorded this natural marvel. Such phrases as "blaze / of inspiration" and "gale / of pentecost" reveal the poem's spiritual implications, and Morgan commands the reader's engagement with this experience through the strategically placed imperative in lines 7 and 8. The upward thrust of this "fountain air" leads the reader toward a moment of transcendence:

> What a place to conjure:
> the lip of ridge where breath of deep blue valleys
> ascends and keeps ascending like a prayer
> or song of praise, of supplication, sent
> from busy fields and crossways far below
> to oracle the towering element. (10)

The term "conjure" makes it clear that this is a place of magical possibilities, of entrancement, and the poet's transformation of the noun "oracle" into a verb calls attention to the extraordinary status of this *site*. At the same time, the word "oracle" emphasizes the visionary quality of the *sight* this scene affords, the access to spiritual vision this natural setting provides.

Two other poems present a similar perspective on the wind. In "Wind from a Waterfall" Morgan again yokes wind and the supernatural. Here

the tumbling current of wind resembles the air "above a witch's caul-
dron," darting about wildly before it "whispers, barks in pentecost / and
song" (32). Written in slant-rhymed couplets of iambic tetrameter, this
poem testifies to nature's capacity to thrill and amaze and communicate
through a wind "stirred up / by heavy tongue from river's lip." Likewise in
"Convection," a single-sentence poem employing Morgan's characteristic
eight-syllable line, a natural phenomenon is described in ways that highlight the fundamental mystery of the physical world:

> In the stillest house it startles
> to see the curtains move above
> the radiator, stirred by unseen
> fountains, unseen drafts from warmed sweet
> metal, showing the air alive
> and rising in an oracle. (34)

Here, too, the reader is propelled toward a sense of wonder, the word
"startles" italicized, as it were, by the pattern of alliteration that begins
with "stillest" in line 1 and continues through "stirred" in line 3. Rather
than being cold and impassive, the radiator's metal is itself "warmed
sweet" in an air that is energized, ascending, transformative. The term
"oracle" once again signals the spiritual dimension of this experience, and
to it Morgan adds the terms "ghosts" and "haunt": "the fabric [of the cur-
tains] troubled by ghosts," he writes, the motion of the curtains becoming, in the poem's final line, "the clear trembling flower of haunt" (34).

To draw the reader into such encounters with mystery is one of the
principal aims of Morgan's poetry, as it is of Wendell Berry's. As "Convection" indicates, however, Morgan often uses scientific or mathematical
concepts, not natural phenomena alone, to express this sense of mystery.
In "Π," for instance, he views the transcendental number of the poem's
title as a symbol of the ultimately indefinable but nonetheless knowable,
"transcendental and yet / a commonplace" (40). In its unifying of opposites, this poem celebrates the eternal amid the everyday, finding in the
shape of the letter Π a "gateway" to the infinite and ineffable. As Morgan
notes, for "though / the connection is written / it cannot be written out
/ in full." This confessed gap between insight and full articulation of that
insight helps clarify Morgan's frequent strategy of directing attention to
spiritual mysteries without defining the precise nature of the epiphanies

they offer. In this regard his sensibility is akin to that of the religious mystic or the Emersonian poet-seer who, as Emerson remarks, "re-attaches things to nature and the Whole" ("The Poet" 1182).

It is precisely to such a vision of ultimate wholeness that Morgan witnesses in his poem "The Music of the Spheres." As this title attests, Morgan here returns to the Pythagorean notion of an underlying cosmic harmony, a recurring motif in Chappell's poetry and fiction as well. The poem's single-sentence structure may be meant to parallel the fundamental unity that this philosophical concept posits. In any case, the poem's syntax intensifies the reader's impression of the poet's confidence and control, thus offering assurance of the validity of this poetic intuition. "The first music was don't hear but / know," the poem paradoxically begins, "is inner, the rings around / atoms singing" (39). These lines should remind readers of this book of the many other references to music in *Topsoil Road*. In fact, four of the book's last six poems take music as their subject. And song, along with speech itself, is one of the most frequently cited attributes of nature as Morgan portrays it. Nature's songs prompt the poet's own, as nature's speech provokes his:

> . . . the bright levels
> in matter revealed by colors
> through spectrum scales all up and down
> the quantum ladder in fireworks
> of the inner horizons, each
> zone voicing its wavelength with
> choirs in the tiny stadiums
> of harmony . . . (39)

The resulting vision is one of plenitude—"lit cities / within every speck of substance," in the poem's closing phrase.

This vision of wholeness and light recurs regularly in *Topsoil Road*. According to Emerson in "Nature," "If the Reason [the imagination or intuition] be stimulated to more earnest vision, outlines and surfaces become transparent, and are no longer seen; causes and spirits are seen through them" (1123–24). Emerson relates this idea of transparency to one of the major functions of poetry when he states, "the poet turns the world to glass" ("The Poet" 1183). Just as Emerson finds in poetry such moments of transparency, moments when spiritual realities shine through physical appearances, so Morgan offers what the title of one poem calls "Trans-lumination," occasions of seeing across the customary barriers between time and eternity, matter and spirit. The fine white sand covering a fresh grave in "Translumination" is

> . . . raised like a reef
> or sandbar there to show how shallow
> time's waters are, and how we can
> almost see through earth . . . (27)

"Time is but the stream I go a-fishing in," says Thoreau in *Walden* (1859), and Morgan shares with Emerson's contemporary both a love of nature and a recognition of spiritual realities that transcend nature.

Yet for Morgan, as for Emerson himself, those realities are glimpsed in and through nature and through human interaction with nature, as in Morgan's poem "Bread," which conveys a sense of what might be termed the miraculous mundane, a key idea in the writing of both Emerson and Morgan, as Morgan's *Good Measure: Essays, Interviews, and Notes on Poetry* illustrates. "Bread" traces the process of bread making from "the lushness" of ripened grain, "the gold perfection," through the winnowing of that grain by the wind (which Morgan personifies when he writes, "its eyes do / the fine work") to the mixing of ingredients and the baking itself. In the last seven lines of the poem, Morgan highlights the quasi-magical, decidedly marvelous operation that produces "a cloud of flesh woven / from luminous earth" (45). "Bread" is among the many poems by Morgan that Mary C. Williams says "bless natural processes and invest them with a sacramental quality" (158).

References to such acts of transformation, such rites of renewal, abound in *Topsoil Road* in poems like "Sanghoe," "Polishing the Silver," "Hearth," "Sharpening a Saw," "Fulgurite," and "Manifest." The sang hoe, for instance, a tool used for digging ginseng, provides the title for one of these poems, but Morgan's central focus is on the herb itself and its pre-sumed regenerative powers, which include the ability to "heal the black bruise of blues and send / a torch out through the veins and limbs / many-colored as northern lights" (8). These images of fire and light attest to nature's capacity to illuminate. Crucial to Morgan's larger poetic vision, however, is the poem's final line, which stresses the commonplace ori-gin of this enlightening, restorative power. For these northern lights are "ringing under ordinary dirt," the same dirt that in "Fulgurite" is transformed by lightning's "blinding tongue," by "light's / entry of earth" (37). Morgan's attention both to "ordinary dirt" and to what lies beneath it clearly reflects the twofold vision prevalent in *Topsoil Road*—indeed, throughout Morgan's poetry. In this regard, too, he follows Emerson, who urged people "to see the miraculous in the common," a trait that Emerson termed "the invariable mark of wisdom" ("Nature" 1134). Attuned to nature's texts and to what Emerson called "nature certifying the supernatural" ("The Poet" 1181), Morgan's poems transport the reader from physical to spiritual vision. "All poems," he contends in *Good Measure*, "have the power of mystery, combining two or more worlds of reference at once. . . . [Poetry] sees the otherworldliness in this one" (16, 19).

Early in his life and his career as a poet, however, Morgan found the otherworldly emphasis of the religious traditions in which he was raised something to resist. While Miller and Chappell were brought up as Methodists, Morgan's household was divided between Southern Baptist and Pentecostal Holiness influences, his mother embracing the former denomination, his father—like his father's mother and grandfather—attending Pentecostal services even though he also maintained membership in Green River Baptist Church, which was built by Morgan's great-grandfather on his mother's side immediately following the Civil War. Morgan has said, "I grew up in a very religious family—we read the Bible twice a day, prayed three or four times a day" (Heyen and Rubin 147), and he has cited the King James Version of the Bible and preaching (along with family storytelling) as two of the three major influences on his writing (Cornett 66). "Church was the center of our lives," he also told Cornett; "we went at least three times a week . . . and had a family altar" (65). As a child Morgan attended both Baptist and Pentecostal worship services. Of the latter experience he has remarked, "I was so scared by the services that I wasn't able to write about it until I was beyond forty years old" (Bizzaro 177).

That fear was reinforced by the disputes about the Bible and its prophecies, especially the book of Revelation, that Morgan heard between his father and his Baptist grandfather, with his father predicting that the Rapture would occur by the end of the twentieth century, a prediction that left Morgan "afraid the Rapture would come and I'd be left with the sinners and the moon turned to blood" (Booker 133). As Morgan has shown both in his poetry and in his novel *The Truest Pleasure*, doctrinal disputes within his family and within the Baptist church itself often turned acrimonious, and they are undoubtedly one of the major reasons for Morgan's statement, "I never felt at home in Zirconia, even as a child" (Booker 131). In his teens Morgan turned to science as an alternative explanation of reality. "I was exhilarated to discover science," he comments, "to find that there were other ways of looking at history and the world," and he was drawn to nature precisely because of its indifference, its equanimity, after the emotional turmoil of church services: "I can remember walking out of Bible meetings, where there was so much talk of hell, damnation, and the plan of salvation, and looking at the pine trees and the sunlight on the pasture and thinking, 'This is a very different thing. . . . [N]ature is just going about its business. It has no designs on anyone, no interest in sending us to hell'" (Cornett 66–67).

As this quotation indicates, the religion that Morgan encountered in his mountain community often focused more on the threat of damnation than on the promise of God's grace, leaving Morgan with a profound impression of what he has called "the terror and exclusions of Calvinism" (*Good Measure* 25). "For me just becoming a writer, becoming a poet," he declares, "necessitated a kind of distance from the fundamentalistic Baptist doctrine that I grew up with. . . . And I think this is true not only of me but of many American poets, going all the way back to Emerson and Thoreau and Whitman—coming out from under Calvinism" (Booker 142).

Yet if "emerging from the rapt gloom of fundamentalism into the wide natural daylight" (qtd. in Quillen 50) is one powerful impulse in Morgan's poetry, an even more significant impulse is his celebration of the motif of resurrection, of rebirth, the principal motif in the Christian tradition. "The central figure of our culture is that promise of rebirth," he states; "all tropes are variations on the figure of resurrection" (*Good Measure* 10, 14). Just as Morgan's loving attention to the physical world, to the wide natural daylight, is meant to counteract fundamentalism's otherworldliness, so he seeks to affirm nature's and humanity's capacity for rebirth—physical regeneration within nature, moral and spiritual renewal within the human community.

With few exceptions, the poems in Morgan's first three collections—*Zirconia Poems*, the chapbook *The Voice in the Crosshairs* (1971), and *Red Owl*—contain little material of an explicitly religious nature. When such subject matter does appear, it usually reflects the poet's negative reaction to the religious experiences of his childhood, as in "Prayer Meeting" (*Zirconia* 34) and "Church Pews" (*Red Owl* 49). In the latter, for example, Morgan compares the church to a courtroom "where you touch the wood expecting it to vibrate / with the voices of accuser and condemned." The poems in these collections are highly imagistic, intensely compressed, with only two of the sixty-four poems in *Red Owl* running longer than a page and over half having one-word titles, a trait that heightens the impression that these are texts of elemental definition and description. Written in free verse, they are generally presented in a single stanza or in stanzas of varying lengths. Of these early poems Morgan has said, "I wanted to write poems terse and precise, yet encompassing as mathematical proofs. . . . My dream was to write a maquette-sized poetry, of bonsai complexity and detail. Each poem was a new beginning of perception, an atom of recognition" (*Good Measure* 8, 9).

Many of the poems in *Red Owl* focus on objects and places associated with rural life: "Topsoil" (the book's opening poem), "Woodpile," "Well," "New-plowed Ground," "Planting," "Hog-wire Fence," "Toolshed," and "Milk Gap." Other poems address more general natural phenomena, poems such as "Earthquake," "Wind," and "Aspire." Morgan has noted that one of the significant influences on these early poems was Thoreau, through such poems as "Smoke" and "Haze" in *Walden* (Heyen and Rubin 148). Although rarely explicitly religious in subject matter, some of these poems do anticipate Morgan's later, more extensive treatment of the motif of rebirth and renewal—as his assumption that "each poem was a *new beginning* of perception" might indicate. "Wind," for instance, which opens *The Voice in the Crosshairs* and is reprinted in *Red Owl*, begins "Spirits revive, return from their journeys" and adds in its fourth line, "We are thirsty for the wind," a conventional symbol of the spirit and the spiritual (*Red Owl* 64). Similarly, "Aspire," which deals with the process of evaporation, begins, "The breath of water leaves its body / frantic with ambition / toward the sun" (*Red Owl* 62). Although this water subsequently falls back to earth, Morgan concludes the poem by emphasizing an ongoing cycle of ascent: "Yet sure as Avogadro's number / it rises, purified by the journey." In "Warm Winter Day" Morgan's account of his own activity mirrors his description of the water's breath: "I relax to the ground looking / into space (the great blue seed) like an exile / turning homeward" (65). In these lines the poet depicts himself as positioned in connection with both earth and the heavens; touching the ground does not obscure but rather clarifies his vision of the transcendent, which he considers his ultimate place of origin, its fruitfulness implied by Morgan's metaphoric equation of space with a seed.

Land Diving, the poet's fourth volume, includes many more poems with explicitly religious subjects, in part because in this book Morgan was beginning to draw more heavily on his own and his family's past to strengthen the narrative dimension of his art. The wrathful God he encountered in the Calvinism of his childhood reappears in several of these poems, most notably in "Signs" and "Face." The former is a single-stanza poem that catalogs the dire punishments awaiting those who violate the Sabbath. The latter is in six tercets, a stanza structure that reflects Morgan's increasing interest in traditional poetic forms, including rhyme and meter, in Land Diving. "Face" recounts the religious vision of "an unbeliever" who saw "the Lamb himself, // the face of longhaired Jesus," and snapped a photograph that proved "a perfect likeness / . . . beyond all expectation chilling" (19). But the poem concludes by detailing, in a single stanza, the impact of this experience on the young poet: "For months I kept eyes ahead or to the ground out / of horror, feared looking back I would see / the Tiger clawing through eastern azure." Eliot's Christ the Tiger lurks behind this poem, a vivid emblem of "the terror and exclusions of Calvinism" to which Morgan, as a child, was exposed. The poem that precedes "Face" is entitled "After Church," and it too presents young Morgan's distaste for many of the emotions generated by the church services he attended. In response to the fear of mortality and of divine judgment aroused by the preacher, the poet meditates on the "permanence [that] flared in the pine / grove" and observes that "Even the black coverts of laurel / and bleached pastures said / something comforting" (18).

This recourse to nature as a means not only of consolation but of revelation recurs throughout Morgan's poetry. Like the unorthodox Dickinson and Whitman, Morgan prefers to celebrate divinity out-of-doors, not in the institutional church or in doctrinal statements. Certainly the term "signs" in the poem of that title is meant to suggest, by ironic contrast, the larger typological tradition to which Morgan belongs as well as what he calls "the promise of signs and wonders" implicit in religious sensibility (Good Measure 109). In Land Diving such poems as "Affliction," "Double Springs," "Easter Algae," and "Ice Worm" clearly participate in the Emersonian typological tradition that reads nature symbolically. "Affliction," for example, describes the continuing impact of the chestnut blight, a "curse" in nature whose effects might be said to parallel those of the biblical Fall. The poem's closing lines make explicit the connection between the human and the natural worlds: "Like us straining to ascend, / immortal / only in dirt" (4).

That longing to ascend appears, paradoxically, in this book called *Land Diving*, whose final section opens with a poem titled "Climbing" that uses the phrase "Other / Side" (51). That longing's presence here attests to the dual movement that defines Morgan's worldview. He remains enough of a Calvinist to see the world as fallen or broken; yet he also rejects fundamentalism's earth-renouncing otherworldliness and its excessive emphasis on human depravity. For Morgan, human spirituality is rooted in the soil, and thus the natural objects he depicts often share the human thrust toward rebirth. Their powers of resurrection parallel humanity's own, as in "Easter Algae," a poem that celebrates what Morgan calls "the old impossible blessedness" visible in creation (9), a poem in which sacred and secular renewals coincide. As is true of Chappell's poetry, Morgan's takes seriously the doctrines of creation and incarnation, and this stance helps explain his repeated use of images of dirt, earth, mud, and manure. Body and soul are not at war in his poetry; instead, the body is the instrument, through the senses, of the soul's spiritual awakening. As the title of the final poem in *Land Diving* proclaims, the poet is "Paradise's Fool" (70), living amid an Eden of wonders often overlooked. The poet's impulse, then, as he records it in "Midnight Sun," the book's penultimate poem, is to "strike into the long night of need / a rank garden, an eden" (69). That eden is to be established within the temporal world, in part through a Blakean cleansing of the doors of perception, for many of Morgan's poems, in their praise of natural phenomena, echo Blake's credo that "every thing that lives is Holy." At the same time, Morgan is well aware of nature's destructive potential, its harshness, as in "Cold Friday" (13–14), as well as in several of the poems in the later *Groundwork*, poems such as "Burning the Hornet's Nest," "Milksick Pen," and "Blackberries," which includes the line, "Wade into the snaky weeds as into a minefield" (44). This awareness leads Morgan to conclude "Paradise's Fool" with a stanza that reads, "Neither in surview nor sweet veld / do I escape the terror, / the presence of the comforter" (70). On balance, however, Morgan is more likely to praise than indict nature, for he believes that "the primary business of poetry is delight, complex delight and praise" (*Good Measure* 123), an outlook reflected in the thrice-repeated imperative "praise" in "Volunteer" (58).

Morgan has called *Land Diving* the pivotal volume in his career because of the new possibilities it opened up for him both in subject matter and poetic form, including a more conversational voice that produced some poems of substantially greater length—"Flood" running to six pages, "Climbing" to five. During the period of his next book's composition, he was involved in what he has described as "a new coming to terms with the rhetoric of the New Testament, which I had forgotten since childhood," and he has identified hymns, "readings from the Bible, and the fine rhetoric of pulpit and prayer" as among the most important influences on his sense of language, its rhythms and diction and imagery (Booker 137–38). In addition to engaging in a new reading of Scripture during the mid-1970s, Morgan was also studying both Christopher Smart's *Jubilate Agno* and the religious poetry of Geoffrey Hill. Out of these new and renewed influences came *Trunk & Thicket* (1978).

About this volume Morgan has said, "I wanted to get a new cultural and historical richness and density in my work. At the same time I wanted to recover some of the incantatory power of 'prophesying' as I'd heard it as a child. Suddenly I was able to confront and use that part of myself that had been rejected so long before" (Booker 138–39). That recovery is most apparent in the book's third and final section, entitled "Mockingbird," in which imperatives resembling biblical injunctions predominate. That section is preceded, however, by the book's title section, which combines poetic and prose passages, and by a prose second section titled "Homecoming." That word refers directly to the annual gatherings—now discontinued, the reader is told—of present and past members of the church Morgan's ancestors had helped to establish. The poet's account of this ritual reunion is interspersed with information about the various doctrinal disputes that divided the congregation. Here again Morgan emphasizes the sectarianism and intolerance, the "exclusions" of that church's theology. The vindictiveness bred by such schisms is underscored by the poet's portrait of the distant cousin who rose during worship one Sunday to declare "that in a vision it had been revealed to him my Uncle Robert's death in Europe [during World War II] had been sent as punishment for family sins" (30). Such an attitude helps explain Morgan's negative reaction to the services depicted in poems such as "Prayer Meeting," "Church Pews," and "After Church." More important, though, the sectarian disputes described in "Homecoming" help prepare the reader to receive what might be termed the new commandments set forth in "Mockingbird," which William Harmon has called "one of the most remarkable poems in American literature" ("Pelagian Georgics" 18).

The "good news" Morgan proclaims in this poem directs his readers away from ecclesiastical institutions and toward nature. Yet his diction is suffused with religious terminology. "Believe in the immaculate / conception of matter from energy" is the first of these major pronouncements (36). Others include:

> Interpret literally the eros of detail,
> the saints of wind and water. (37)

> Keep the covenant
> with bottomlands . . . (37)

> . . . Say the statute of
> limitations has run out on original
> sin. (40–41)

> . . . Reject the dryhides and
> take the holy dance. (42)

The flood of language in "Mockingbird" attests to the energy of the poet's vision. Once again, in the image of "the church's talon in the night sky" (37), Morgan expresses his estrangement from the institutional Christianity he encountered as a child. Here too, in contending that "the statute of / limitations has run out on original / sin," he rejects Calvinism's emphasis on human depravity, a rejection that has led Harmon to characterize Morgan's work as "Pelagian," after the fifth-century theologian Pelagius, whose denial of original sin was attacked by St. Augustine and condemned as heresy in 416 C.E. (8). Although Morgan does not ignore evil in either nature or humanity, he does seek to counteract the near obsession with human sinfulness in some Christian denominations. In this poem he also seeks to bridge the presumed gap between this world and the next, time and eternity. "Know time as / magnification," he writes (37), for "Being is fed by time as by / oxygen" (42).

Yet despite his distrust of many of the tenets and practices of religious fundamentalism—as evident, for example, in his reference to "the sermon as firedrill" (41)—Morgan recommends the ecstatic sensibility. "Take the holy dance," he urges. Moreover, he affirms the sense of mystery that underlies all religious consciousness. "See entities beyond / nomination," he declares (37), a statement that insists on the limits of language, that bears witness to the reality and the significance of the ineffable. "Mountains speak in tongues," he adds; "The absent god leaves the forest / and tundra soaked in divinity" (42). And thus Morgan advises the reader to be "in congregation / with mist and rock" (43), to "Play with matches, / correspondences" (37), presumably correspondences between the natural and human worlds and between the realms of matter and spirit. "Where is the man who / would not kill to be reborn," the poet asks (41), announcing the major theme of "Mockingbird" and of many of Morgan's subsequent poems: that of rebirth, of metamorphosis. The poet points the reader toward "the faraway beginning / of your own resurrection," which the reader is instructed to "See / lifting deep in the strata to newplowed fields" (39).

If *Trunk & Thicket* is the volume in which Morgan's prophetic, incantatory voice is most audible, the following four collections—*Groundwork* (1979), *Bronze Age* (1981), *At the Edge of the Orchard Country* (1987), and *Sigodlin* (1990)—continue to address the issues he raises there and in his preceding books. A number of the poems in those volumes extend, for instance, his portrait of the religious practices and beliefs he experienced as a child: such poems as "Death Crown" and "Baptism of Fire" in *Groundwork*, "Earache" (a rare terza rima sonnet) in *Bronze Age*, "The Gift of Tongues" in *Orchard Country*, and "Baptizing Trough" in *Sigodlin*. At times, as in "Death Crown," he adopts the stance of objective informant, documenting an example of folk belief. Typically, however, Morgan's response to these experiences is tinged with irony, as is evident in his use of the word "trough" and in his character sketch of the contentious Gondan in "Baptism of Fire."

Crucial in this regard is "The Gift of Tongues," which focuses on young Morgan's discomfort with his father's Pentecostalism:

> The whole church got hot and vivid
> with the rush of unhuman chatter
> above the congregation,

and I saw my father looking at
the altar as though electrocuted.
It was a voice I'd never heard
but knew as from other centuries.
It was the voice of awful fire.

. . . .

And we sang and sang again, but
no one rose as if from sleep to
be interpreter, explain the writing
on the air that still shone there like
blindness. None volunteered a gloss
or translation or receiver
of the message. My hands hurt
when pulled from the pew's varnish
they'd gripped and sweated so. Later,
standing under the high and plain-
sung pines on the mountain I clenched
my jaws like pliers, holding in
and savoring the gift of silence. (29)

While the child's largely negative emotions are apparent in such terms
as "unhuman," "electrocuted," and "blindness," in his clenched jaws at
poem's end, and in the carefully balanced contrast of title and closing
phrase, as well as in the contrasting sound effects of the plosive *p*'s of
"pulled," "pew's," and "gripped" and the sibilant *s*'s of "savoring" and "silence," the adult poet also presents the father's "flare of / higher language"
as "sentences of light." For Morgan "The Gift of Tongues" was a break-
through poem. Written after he turned forty, it enabled him to see "that
I didn't have to be ashamed of it [the world of his childhood religious
experience], that I could write vivid, honest descriptions of my own experience" (Cornett 69). It was this recognition, he adds, that enabled him
to write fiction about that world, including his novel *The Truest Pleasure*,
told from the point of view of Ginny, who participates in Pentecostal Holiness services.

Morgan's later poem "Heaven" (*Sigodlin* 30), like such novels as *The
Truest Pleasure, This Rock,* and *Brave Enemies*, reflects an increasing engagement with Christian belief. Although the poem expresses skepticism

about traditional views of the afterlife, Morgan's initial tone is clearly one
of regret:

> And yet I don't want not to believe in,
> little as I can, the big whoosh of souls
> upward at the Rapture, when clay and ocean,
> dust and pit, yield up their dead, when all
>
> elements reassemble into the forms
> of the living from the eight winds and flung
> petals of the compass. And I won't assume,
> much as I've known it certain all along,
>
> that I'll never see Grandma again, nor
> Uncle Vol with his fabulations,
> nor see Uncle Robert plain with no scar
> from earth and the bomber explosions.
>
> I don't want to think how empty and cold
> the sky is, how distant the family,
> but of winged seeds blown from a milkweed field
> in the opalescent smokes of early
>
> winter ascending toward heaven's blue,
> each self orchestrated in one aria
> of river and light. And those behind the blue
> are watching even now us on the long way.

Here the poet both acknowledges and resists his doubts. The unlikelihood
of Christ's Second Coming, with its general resurrection, is underscored
by the phrase "big whoosh of souls." Yet the poem's speaker inclines toward a species of agnosticism, however intense, rather than outright disbelief. Through the first four stanzas "Heaven" is built on negatives—and
on denials of denial: "And yet I don't want not to believe in," "And I won't
assume," and "I don't want to think."

Shifting to what the speaker *does* want to think in the middle of the
fourth stanza, the poem changes from its predominantly optative mood
to the indicative. Its closing sentence, preceded by the great beauty of the
natural images in lines 15–19, stands in sharp opposition to the earlier

skepticism: "And those behind the blue / are watching even now us on the long way." The conviction of that claim is somewhat diminished, however, by the poet's deliberately awkward syntax, his unidiomatic phrasing. Nevertheless, Morgan's poem, in its structuring of its ideas, clearly reverses the pattern common to many of Dickinson's religious poems. Whereas Dickinson often begins with certitude ("I know that He exists," "This World is not Conclusion") and moves toward radical doubt, Morgan begins "Heaven" with skeptical detachment and moves toward what he has called "the triumph of aspiration and hope over ordinary skepticism" (letter to the author, March 31, 1991). The carefully patterned, primarily slant-rhymed quatrains that Morgan employs in this poem demonstrate his increasing interest in traditional verse forms.

As already indicated, Morgan's poems return again and again to images of transformation, renewal, and rebirth, with the movement toward rebirth frequently involving descent into a pit of some kind and reemergence from it. This motif is present in "Zircon Pit" (*Groundwork* 49) and in "Potato Hole" (*Orchard Country* 32), both poems in which the poet himself is the central figure. In the latter poem Morgan states, "I'll rise with the first shoots / of Lazarus green," alluding to Jesus's miraculous resurrection of his friend. Such poems of human rebirth are complemented by similar poems focusing on creatures from the natural world—for example, "Wallowing" and "Den Tree" (*Groundwork* 38, 51). The former describes, in lovingly detailed, sensuous imagery, a horse's "emery submersion salving / harness galls and currying off sweat," a wallowing from which the horse arises "pure and free / as if new-born in the depression." The latter poem describes a bear's hibernation but looks toward the animal's spring awakening, when "He will hear that lovesong [a dove's] / lighting his new hunger." Similar transformations also occur when human beings and nature interact, as in "Man and Machine," in which the poet's cousin Luther plows all night, becoming a mythic figure of renewal. The resurrection motif is most prominent here in Morgan's concluding statement, the poem's only single-sentence line: "And by morning the fields were new" (*Orchard Country* 51). A variant of this motif likewise appears in the same volume's "Hay Scuttle," although here the movement does not involve descent into a depression in the ground but rather a return to the barn's floor. That descent is imaged in ways characteristic of Morgan's commitment to the earth: "Only way out to the sun is down, / through the exquisite filth" (36).

In all these poems immersion in the physical world is necessary and illuminating—even purifying. As Roger Jones observes, "[Morgan's] poetry provides proof that spiritual and metaphysical moorings are to be drawn first, and most powerfully, from the ground itself" (219). In opposition to the lesson taught by the Protestant fundamentalism of Morgan's youth— "how little this world had to do / with the next except as staging ground" (*Orchard Country* 59)—the poet stresses the importance of "land diving," of "groundwork," of realizing that, here and now, we dwell "at the edge of the orchard country," to cite just three of his book's titles. In a journal entry from the early 1970s, Morgan refers to himself as "the elohist of topsoil" (*Good Measure* 114), a phrase doubly significant in this context. Not only does that phrase emphasize the spiritual potential of the material world; it also implies Morgan's rejection of Calvinist exclusivity in religious matters. In biblical criticism, the term "elohist" contrasts with the term "yahwist," each derived from a different Hebrew name for God. The word "Elohim" is the more inclusive of the two, for it refers to God in God's role as creator and ruler of all humanity, whereas the name "Yahweh" refers to the God who enters into a covenant with the chosen people, the Israelites. It is not the elect, not even the entire human community, but the whole of creation for which Morgan chooses to speak. As the poet says in one of the interviews reprinted in *Good Measure*, "I have tried to create verbal spaces in which other *things* and animals, not just people, can be heard" (130). In other interviews Morgan speaks of poetry itself as involving "holistic animism" (Cornett 72) and claims, "Through poetry . . . we recover a sense of animism . . . when you get back into a world that's spirited, where things are spirits, alive and connected" (West, "Art of Far and Near" 51).

In the vicinity of Eden, then, Morgan sets out to read the "signs and wonders" that surround him. Like the pioneer settler of "Feather Bed," he is drawn "back / over the hills and piedmont and tidewater, / across the troubled Atlantic and centuries / toward a white immaculate garden" (*Orchard Country* 7), an image of primordial innocence and unity. That mythic garden is an important symbol in a number of his poems, as it is in Chappell's work. More often, however, Morgan discovers spiritual presences and possibilities in the commonplace, the close-at-hand, rather than in the remoter realms of mythic gardens. He examines what one poem calls "the scripture / of signs" (*Orchard Country* 9) in such unlikely places and objects as manure piles, lightning bugs, and his aunt Florrie's parlor, as well as in such natural phenomena as Brownian motion and inertia. Morgan's poems insist that such interpretation of "the written characters of all creation"—a phrase used twice in the poem "Jutaculla Rock" (*Orchard Country* 63)—is one major responsibility of human beings. Yet he acknowledges the difficulty of this interpretive process "without / a key to its [creation's] whorls and wisps / of scripture." Moreover, in "Writing Spider" (*Sigodlin* 49), he warns against the extreme subjectivity to which that process can lead. But what he calls "a lifetime's work" remains: the demand that people "read" the world's manifold objects, name them, and accept responsibility for that naming.

The readings embodied in Morgan's poems typically highlight the mystery and plenitude of existence. Amid even the inanimate dust of "Brownian Motion" Morgan discerns a universe of endless vitality:

> The air is an aquarium where
> every mote spins wild
> and prisms the morning light.
> Lint climbs sparkling on
> convection's fountain,
> and magnetic storms boil away
> like gnats bumped by molecules.
> Every breath swarms
> the clear spores, ion seethe,
> magnified in playful flight.
> Look at the dust panic
> off a fingertip. Each
> particle is an opal angel
> too small to see but in the glare
> of this annunciation. (*Orchard Country* 23)

In a poem like this one Morgan's scientific training and interests complement his poetic vision. Rather than seeing science and religion as foes, after the fashion of much of fundamentalist Christianity, Morgan employs the perspectives of both to convey the wonder of creation. In fact, he speaks of "the counterpoint and harmony of the scientific and the spiritual," not of their antagonism, and he notes that "some of the true mystics of the century are the physicists" (letter to the author, February 10, 1991).

In "Brownian Motion" Morgan again combines careful scientific observation with the insight of a visionary like Blake. Morgan's poems often create a Brownian motion of their own, as they become annunciations of a
power in nature that radiates supernatural light.

Perhaps the best example of this quality in Morgan's work occurs in
"Lightning Bug," the poem that follows "Brownian Motion" in *Orchard
Country* and the poem that gives the collection its title phrase:

> Carat of the first radiance,
> you navigate like a creature
> of the deep. I wish I could read
> your morse across the night yard.
> Your body is a piece of star
> but your head is obscure. What small
> photography! What instrument
> panel is on? You are winnowed
> through the hanging gardens of night.
> Your noctilucent syllables
> sing in the millennium of
> the southern night with star-talking
> dew, like the thinker sending nous
> into the outerstillness from
> the edge of the orchard country.

The profusion of metaphors here, the care the poet has given to rhythm
and phrasing and sound effects, the suggestiveness of the diction as it
echoes and alludes to the Bible and classical culture, the poet's appropriation of the Emersonian tradition of reading nature symbolically—all
contribute to the strength and beauty of this poem. The poet longs to in-
terpret the insect's apparent message, its morse (with a pun on morris
as a dance), a message that is linked to the process of illumination and
perhaps to the *fiat lux* (that "first radiance") of Genesis 1:3. The insect
is not merely addressed in this poem; its "noctilucent syllables / sing."
Here the reader encounters not a Calvinist Outer Dark, where sinners
weep and gnash their teeth, but an "outerstillness" of immense tranquillity. Moreover, Morgan's reference to "the thinker sending nous" into that
outerstillness, while punning on the word "news," invokes a long philosophical and religious tradition for which the Greek word *nous*, literally

meaning mind or intelligence, also suggested the Mind that gave rise to the universe. While Morgan does not capitalize the word "thinker" in this poem, he seems to invite, at least on one level, a theological reading of that figure's identity.

Despite his early rebellion against the religious traditions in which he was raised, Morgan considers himself a Christian, albeit an unorthodox one (Schurer 258), and reads the Bible "virtually daily" (Cornett 67). In his poetry he strives to be "true to / spirit level," a phrase that appears in the title poem of *Sigodlin* (3). "I can't imagine poetry without some sense of worlds beyond the merely physical," he has said; "perhaps poetry is the unifier, seeing at once the spiritual and the physical" (Harmon, "Imagination" 169). The term "sigodlin" means out of plumb, askew, and thus captures Morgan's sense of living in a flawed, fallen world. But Morgan locates human beings in far greater proximity to Eden than did his Calvinist ancestors. As he remarks of "Sigodlin" in an interview, "What's the quote Emerson likes, 'God writes straight in crooked lines'?" (Elliott 94). For the Morgan of "Sigodlin," the impulse to uprightness in a broken world reflects humanity's "love of geometry's power to say / . . . / the power whose center is everywhere" (3). According to St. Augustine, that power—which he described as a circle whose center is everywhere and circumference nowhere—is God. For American readers, Augustine's definition of God is perhaps most readily available in the opening paragraph of Emerson's essay "Circles," an essay with which Morgan is most certainly familiar.

"The power whose center is everywhere." Surely this conception of divinity fuels Morgan's imagination, intensifying its exploration of nature. Though he rejects the otherworldly religion of his childhood, he continues to affirm humanity's spiritual potential, as two paired poems in *Sigodlin* will help to show. Initially, these two poems, "Inertia" and "Stretching," appear to focus on physical phenomena. In both poems, however, Morgan evokes the spiritual. "There is such a languor to matter," the former begins. But as the poem progresses Morgan challenges "the reverie of substance, the / immobility and dream of / the body's authority," by describing such inertia as seeming "reluctant as a bear to wake / from the immanence and ponder" (8). Morgan's poems, I would argue, are largely exercises in just such awakening to wonder, to what "Stretching" calls "the savor of being" (9). In "the sweet mobility of used / muscle," Morgan writes in the latter poem, "you are more than you remembered." This recovery of an enlarged identity once more reveals the underlying motif of rebirth and renewal in Morgan's poetry. Their initial focus on the physical notwithstanding, both poems testify to their author's assumption that "the major subject of poetry is the recovery of spiritual desire" (*Good Measure* 16).

Morgan comes out from under Calvinism, then, by distancing himself, as Miller and Chappell do, from the excessive otherworldliness of such religion, from its wrathful God, and from its vision of a depraved humanity of which only an elect few will be saved. He retains, however, the sense of wonder and mystery so integral to authentic religious consciousness. Rather than assuming with Miller that Appalachian literature is radically secular, Morgan makes his poetry and fiction, in great measure, instruments of spiritual quest. What he calls "the fierce aspiration of the brush arbor" is one major source of his poetic impulse (*Good Measure* 112), and for him as for Emerson, nature is "an image or a language of the soul" (Heyen and Rubin 157). Morgan, more than any of the other poets examined in this book, draws on the theories and discoveries of contemporary science to limn his sense of religious mystery, as poems like "Radiation Pressure" and "Shadow Matter" in *Sigodlin* indicate. As Louis Bourne wrote more than thirty years ago in the Robert Morgan issue of *The Small Farm*, "Morgan seems to feel that science awakens an open-ended exploration into the mystery and spiritual majesty of natural phenomena" (73). Bourne's remark is strikingly illustrated in the poem that gives Morgan's most recent new and selected poems, *The Strange Attractor*, its title, for that poem revolves around physics' positing of a "great mass" as yet "unseen, . . . unheard, unplaced" that accounts for the observable effects of gravitation. For Morgan, the poem implies, a similar spiritual hypothesis is necessary to account for the wonders of nature itself. Morgan's description of that "great mass" speaks not just of physical data but of movement "toward a heart that holds the spinning / bits of glitter of the seen in / their coherent scatter" (12). This sense of ultimate coherence, of Emersonian wholeness, underlies the poet's religious vision.

Among the various "powers" that Morgan associates with poetry—the power of naming, of remembering, and of honoring the dead—the one he calls "perhaps the most important of all" is "the power of praise." "And all praise ultimately is praise of God," he says, "whatever the names and terms we use" (letter to the author, February 10, 1991). In addition to that power of praise, his poems witness to both the need for and the experi-ence of rebirth, of resurrection, and they thus incorporate Christianity's principal metaphor and promise. To read Robert Morgan is to stand again at the edge of the orchard country, to gaze upon and move toward what he calls in the final lines of "Land Bridge," with its superb concluding pun, "the tip of some unfolding / giant land of our new being, / the bridge to the original / now buried beyond the littoral" (*Sigodlin* 15).

4
JEFF DANIEL MARION
"Measures of Grace"

AT ALMOST THE SAME TIME that Jim Wayne Miller published his poem "Small Farms Disappearing in Tennessee," Jeff Daniel Marion began planning a new poetry journal that he named *The Small Farm*. Miller and Marion would later serve together as poets-in-the-schools in southwest Virginia and east Tennessee, and Miller was among the many poets whose work appeared in *The Small Farm* between 1975 and 1980, the year the journal ceased publication. In founding this literary journal, Marion has said, he did not intend to limit its scope to writers from the Appalachian region; instead, he aimed to create a community of writers and readers from around the nation who were interested in "a poetry coming from and committed to specific places" ("Poetry Magazines" 384). Although the journal itself contained no literary manifesto, Marion wrote of *The Small Farm* in the same essay, "We want a poetry that speaks to us now in a language that renews earth realities and possibilities" (384), "poems that take our earth consciousness in new directions" (383). Implicit here is Marion's criticism both of modernist deracination and estrangement from nature and of the excessive otherworldliness of the Southern Baptist denomination in which he was raised. Among the major poets from outside Appalachia whose work appeared in *The Small Farm* were Wendell Berry, Rodney Jones, Ted Kooser, and William Stafford. In fact, Marion devoted a double issue of the journal to Stafford's poetry. In addition to Miller, *The Small Farm* published such prominent (or soon to be prominent) authors from within the region as Robert Morgan, Fred Chappell, George Scarbrough, George Ella Lyon, and Michael McFee, with Morgan and Chappell contributing essays as well as poems and Marion doing a special Morgan issue in 1976.

The name Marion gave this journal testifies to the enduring impact of his childhood experiences in an agrarian setting. Born in 1940 in Rogersville, Tennessee, that state's second oldest town, where his father was employed in the ink room of a card and label company, Marion spent most Saturdays on his maternal grandmother's 140-acre farm located less than ten miles from Rogersville. His uncle Gene also farmed nearby. During the time Marion was editing *The Small Farm,* he himself lived on a farm near Dandridge, Tennessee, where he raised chickens and cattle and planted a large garden (Coward 313). The regular contact with the natural world that these settings insured rooted Marion deep in the landscape of rural east Tennessee. In fact, he first began writing poetry seriously during the 1968–69 academic year, which he spent in southern Mississippi feeling intensely homesick. "The first poems that came," he reports, "were the ones that touched base with the place that I knew best growing up—my grandmother's farm" (S. Marion 179). Not surprisingly, then, when his first two poetry chapbooks and his first full-length collection appeared—all three in 1976—they bore titles that reflect their grounding in rural life: *Almanac, Watering Places,* and *Out in the Country, Back Home.*

About the title of this first book, *Out in the Country,* Marion wrote to his publisher, "it is a directional title and so much of the book attempts to locate, to map, to *place* the reader within a certain environment. . . . This placing . . . is also a kind of homing signal, a searching for that which is fundamental and sustaining" (Wood 40–41). This statement helps explain the poet's use of a late eighteenth-century map of Tennessee as the cover illustration for the book, a map that highlights the area's rivers and mountains. This statement also accounts for Marion's decision to open the book with a "directional" poem, "In a Southerly Direction," with a markedly colloquial speaker and tone. Yet the directions given assume a familiarity with the place that the person addressed as "you" may not possess—and that most readers of the poem assuredly lack. Thus the directions create an element of uncertainty, however friendly and well-intentioned the speaker may be. That speaker's closing words, "Why hell, son, / you can't miss it" (13), ring with both intimacy and implicit irony, for Marion knows how many people do indeed overlook their dependence on nature, their need for renewed "earth consciousness." Similarly, the "you" addressed in the volume's title poem is depicted as "passing" the seemingly unpromising "shack of tarpaper / and bare planks" that "wobbles" on a hillside (17), although the poet clearly invites his readers not to pass quickly but to stay to ponder the import of this homestead and its surrounding landscape, as the poet himself does in the book's central poem "Lines." In this poem, the twenty-fourth of forty-seven and the one that concludes part 2, Marion closes the poem by referring to his mind's "rooting itself deep in this place" (38), a stance his poems regularly enact.

Marion divides the poems of *Out in the Country* into four parts under the titles "Farm," "Wintering," "Rural Route," and "Beginnings." The book's first section establishes the farm as locus of origin, as do the woodcuts by Thomas Bewick that appear on the title page of all four sections. As in many of Jim Wayne Miller's poems, however, the farmhouses and barns and agricultural implements depicted here are often dilapidated if not outright abandoned. In "Loft," for instance, Marion has this physical setting resonate with the "silence of chapel bells / unrung" (21), a passage that illustrates his characteristic skill with line breaks. "Deserted Barn" also conveys this sense of emptiness. The final poem in part 1, "Song for Gene," likewise describes the poet visiting his uncle's farm long after Gene has stopped farming there; yet here the poet rejoices that heartleaf, an aptly chosen wildflower, still "arrowheads its way in the woods / evergreen" (24). Despite the farm's decay, the environing natural world that sustained it survives and continues to offer its wonders. The striking verb "arrowheads" may be meant to suggest continuity between past and present, between the original Native American inhabitants of the region and its European settlers (and their descendants), for such historical consciousness is a major feature of Marion's poetry.

At poem's end, however, Marion emphasizes a different source of continuity when he writes:

> today a song rises like
> smoke from this woods-hearth:
> homestead
> where all our words grow warm. (24)

As is frequently the case in Marion's work, these lines refer to the nature and function of poetry itself because it is the poem that preserves what might otherwise be lost. The song that rises is Marion's own, which becomes, through the alchemy of language, the "homestead" now lost to human habitation, yet a homestead revivified through the poet's and reader's shared vision: "our words." Marion's subtle use of "you" and "we" in many of the poems in part 1 invites the reader into this community of vision.

The title of section 2, "Wintering," seems intended, at least in part, to deflect charges of sentimentality and nostalgia. Here Marion chooses to detail not springtime but the harshest of the seasons, setting its chill in opposition to the warmth of words. As Don Johnson remarks of this dimension of Marion's poetry, "In a totally benign world the notion of home as refuge lacks resonance" (18). Throughout these poems and his work as a whole, Marion acknowledges the power of cold and darkness. "Unnamed," for example, begins with the lines, "Dark, darker: waves coming, / rising within to wash our lives" and closes with a stanza that reads, "its [earth's] waves touch us still and our words / like snowflakes go out searching that home / so far and cold in this darkness we move through" (30). Significantly, this darkness is both within and without, psychological as well as physical, and Marion's simile, "like snowflakes," may indicate something of the evanescence, as well as the beauty, of words. Earlier in this poem, however, the poet also says, "each snowflake locks in light," and thus this simile can serve to counteract the darkness. Other poems also attest to the negative forces at work in human experience. In "Orpha" Marion underscores not only the title character's loneliness but also human mortality generally in the poem's closing lines: "a grave, mound of earth, / loaf, / our daily bread" (28). And in "Going Back for J.L.," a title that echoes—in the word "back"—one of the key terms in this book's title, the poet concludes, "some things are never rescued" (34).

Mutability, decay, loss, and death—all are perennial concerns of this poet, for whom the "Rural Route" affords no automatic panacea, as the poem "Rambling Rose" of part 3 demonstrates because the title character and her husband support themselves by selling their children. "I could give you a cameo," the poet announces in the poem's opening line, suggesting that he could devise the kind of polished portrait readers might expect from an agrarian sentimentalist, but instead Marion presents the haunting facts of this woman's life and ends the poem by stating, "from this heirloom / there is no relief" (46). And yet Marion also insists that rural routes put people in touch with the "fundamental and sustaining." The water imagery in the last three poems of part 3 reinforces the image of "tapping / hidden springs" in the central poem in this section, "Razing the Well House" (47). "J.D.M.," for example, a tribute to the poet's father, concludes with his father's credo, "There are some springs that never go dry" (52). The following poem, "Brakeshoe Spring," describes an act of human intervention in the natural world that enhances nature's life-giving resources, as skilled farming likewise does. Moreover, this poem opens out onto vistas universal as well as regional, for Brakeshoe Spring "nourishes the names / of galax & laurel // earth & sea" (53). Surely, Marion wants his readers to hear overtones of "galaxy" in the name "galax," an evergreen herb found only in the southern Appalachians, one that takes its name from the Greek word for milk because of its white blossoms, milk itself being a fundamental source of sustenance.

The final section of *Out in the Country* bids the reader to "Beginnings," to what an earlier poem called "the long flow / toward a new world" (23). In this section's second poem Marion invokes "Wintering" when he writes of "paring winter / into a harvest / of vision" (58) and declares, in the section's title poem, set in midwinter, that "Possibilities brim across fields" (63). The book's penultimate poem, "Ebbing & Flowing Spring" (which, in the plural, became the title of Marion's 2002 collection of new and selected poems and prose), returns to the water imagery that closed part 3. In its ebbing and flowing this spring reminds readers of the duality of darkness and light, of cold and warmth, that attends human experience in time, for the word "spring" also invokes the cycle of the seasons. A poem reminiscent of Robert Frost's "Directive," "Ebbing & Flowing Spring" concludes with the simple imperative "Drink," while omitting the remainder of Frost's final line, "and be whole again beyond confusion" (521). That omission may indicate Marion's reluctance to adopt Frost's oracular stance, which verges on the sententious in "Directive," but Marion might also be eliding Frost's statement and hoping that the reader will supply the missing prophetic element. In any case, Marion has acknowledged Frost as one of his early important influences (Christianson 22), an influence also evident in the title of Marion's chapbook *Watering Places*, which derives from the penultimate line of "Directive."

It is in "Boundaries," the final poem in *Out in the Country*, that Marion presents readers with his poetic credo, reaffirming his commitment to a clearly delineated and delimited rural mountain landscape:

> Yoked in these lines
> I mean to work this land.
> . . . .
> I'm always at home here
> still believing

the reward of this labor
is vision
honed to the blue sharpness
of ridges. (66)

This passage links the poet to the farmer, though Marion cultivates vision, not corn or tobacco, and these lines emphasize the interrelationship between the poet and his place, this soil, these mountains. Above all, these lines reiterate Marion's sense of being at home, both within the Appalachian region and within the much broader landscape of the natural world itself. *Out in the Country* is dedicated to the memory of the poet's maternal grandmother, "who taught me to love the rural parts," he says (9), phrasing that suggests a larger whole of which the rural is one major—though not all-inclusive—dimension. That Marion anticipated a more comprehensive perspective as early as this first book is evident in the title of one of its poems, "At the Railway Station Back Home" (48), a poem set not out in the country but in Rogersville, one of the major foci of the poet's memories and a major source of his sense of history, of continuity with the past, for walking home from school every day, he passed the cemetery in which Davy Crockett's grandparents were buried. Grounding himself in the landscape of east Tennessee, Marion also positions himself to reach out beyond it, as subsequent volumes will do once Marion develops his own version of Miller's cosmopolitan regionalism through his persona of the Chinese poet.

What Robert Morgan calls, in his Introduction to *Out in the Country,* "the act of homing" has persisted throughout Marion's poetic career (8). At his farewell reading at Carson-Newman College on the occasion of his retirement after thirty-five years of teaching there, Marion said that "home" had been his "obsessive theme," his "metaphor for a life's work" (Worthington 16). Likewise, speaking to Lynne Shackelford, Marion commented, "Much of my writing has been a process of trying to seek out the elements of home. . . . And the moments when I feel best are the moments when I have touched that resonating spirit" (322). At least fourteen of Marion's poems end with the word "home" or include that word or a variant (for example, "homecall") in their final lines. Yet Marion speaks of home in a variety of ways, both literal and figurative. In his essay "Appalachia," for instance, the term has a geographical reference: "I've come

to love East Tennessee like no other place. This is my home, the shaper
of my consciousness. Ours is a sacred landscape" (114). Home is in part
the mountains themselves, with which Marion says he feels "almost a
spiritual harmony" (Hatch 212). It is also the Holston River, which runs
through Rogersville and near his grandmother's farm and beside which
Marion lived in his house on Old River Road outside of New Market, Tennessee, during much of his teaching career. Yet for Marion "Circling Back
Home" is also "a metaphor for writing" itself ("The Long Way" 214), with
home thus becoming, to varying degrees, an imaginative construct articulated by the poem. As he notes in an interview titled "Listening for the
Hello of Home," "The poem and home can become one and the same"
(187), a statement that helps explain his lifelong commitment to his art.
For it is through his poems that he has defined both home and self, the
discovery of his identity developing out of his sense of place and of family
ties. "The quintessential means of seeking home for Marion," as Shackelford observes, "is through a strong sense of one's heritage preserved by
memory" (323).

The six volumes of poems that Marion has published since his first
book continue to limn that heritage. *Tight Lines* (1981) and *Vigils* (1990),
along with *Out in the Country*, form what Marion has described as "essentially one book" dealing with "my particular roots in East Tennessee" (Lee
210). *Vigils* reprints many of the poems from his first two books and adds
twenty-three other poems, two of them from *Watering Places* and seven
from Marion's exquisite chapbook *Miracles of Air*, privately printed in
1987. Most of these poems are written in highly imagistic, compact free-
verse lines that pay careful attention to sound effects and utilize striking
figurative language. In "Old Mason Jars" the jars become "bone's breath
sealing / garden marrow" and are imaged as "sand's blue ice" (*Vigils* 54).
In "Riving," a poem about making shingles with a froe, the shingles become animate in the closing stanza:

> these white oak wings
> lapped across rafters
> weave their nest here
> sheltering home[.] (*Vigils* 14)

Marion's skillful use of alliteration and assonance, especially in the careful balancing of long vowel sounds (the long *e* of the initial syllable in

the first and third lines, the long *o* of "oak" and "home"), is a constant throughout his career. The poems of *Tight Lines* and *Vigils* present the poet "turning this local soil / in search / of tongue's delight," as Marion says in "The Garden" (*Tight Lines* unpaged); singing hosannas in "By the Banks of the Holston" (*Vigils* 26); feeding winter birds, those "miracles of air," in "Gifts" (*Vigils* 61); and observing "January Thaw," a time when "morning is a flame / set to the taper / of icicles" (*Vigils* 62).

In collecting the poems in *Vigils*, Marion divided them into three sections whose titles suggest his ongoing concerns: "Making Believe," "Listening to the Land," and "Simple Gifts." The first title invokes the power of the imagination but also implies the poet's capacity to shape his readers' response to the subject matter of the poems, his ability to re-create convincingly often-vanished scenes and people. Part 1's opening poem, "Nocturne: Rogersville, Tennessee, 1947," returns to the poet's childhood and uses the figure of Ned, a harmonica player, as an emblem of the poet himself, "calling us home into the circle of his song" (3). The image of the circle, a conventional symbol of completion or perfection, here represents connection and community. Ned creates "melody liquid as the meadowlark's" (3), a simile that links art and nature. The spirit of Walt Whitman presides over this poem, for Ned is described as "loafing at ease" as he prepares to play for the gathered boys, and his music, like the poet's song, offers a moment of transcendence: "the lift of wing over wing, / . . . rising above wires thrumming / with talk, over house & barn, beyond yard & field" (3). Being in motion is among the most prominent stances of this poet, as in "Crossing Clinch Mountain in February," in which the poet says, "I take the long road to arrival" (22). Despite its winter setting this poem voices an idealized vision of agrarian life: "Fields lying fallow along the way / sow dreams of a small farm / washed in creek-light," and cattle arrive at the barn "to be stabled at last / beneath a dark / vaulted & hushed as cathedrals" (22).

The final poem of part 1, "Waning," also depicts the poet in motion, "coming home along the old river road" (27). Despite the isolation experienced by the poem's speaker, Marion ends part 1 on a note of affirmation:

> O empty and alone
> among stars riding a dark river of sky:
> endless, endless, this zodiac.
> I breathe my grief on the world
> and it shines. (27)

In these lines Pascal's immense abyss of the heavens, which dwarfs the human, is transformed into something gleaming with possibilities even amid sorrow, its endlessness teeming with promise, not futility. The speaker of "Waning" and the stars in this passage both dwell beside rivers, whether literal or metaphorical, and rivers are one of the natural phenomena that make "Listening to the Land" a crucial activity and make rivers themselves one of the "Simple Gifts" for which Marion gives thanks. Those simple gifts include many other features of nature: assorted birds, lichen, buckeyes, jonquils (as harbingers of spring), a panther long thought to be extinct in southern Appalachia, the cycle of the seasons. But among those simple gifts is also song itself, as the Shaker hymn title that gives this final section of *Vigils* its name suggests. At the time this book was published, Marion had a framed copy of that hymn on his desk (Richman 20), and that text's "valley of love and delight" clearly confirmed Marion's own conception of nature's plenitude and of the power of poetry, as song, to communicate that vision. Marion concludes *Vigils* with "Song for Gene," a poem discussed earlier. Thus, just as Ned's songs in "Nocturne" invite the reader into *Vigils*, so Marion's own song brings the book to a close, recollecting Gene's farm and envisioning a renewed "homestead / where all our words grow warm" (72).

By the time Marion published his next book, *Lost & Found* (1994), his poetry had changed in several significant ways, although his underlying vision of humanity's relationship to nature had not altered. The poems of *Lost & Found* grow more expansive, both in individual lines and in overall length. Whereas only a handful of the poems in *Vigils* extended beyond a single page—and only one poem in *Out in the Country, Back Home* did so—*Lost & Found* contains half a dozen such poems in the first of its three sections. The poems also have a more conversational tone and draw more regularly on the poet's personal experiences with family members, including the death of his father. Many of the poems employ a formal structure that Marion adapted from William Carlos Williams: a three-line stanza with the second and third lines each indented one additional tab beyond its predecessor. About this stanza structure Marion comments in an interview with Larry Richman, "That kind of stair-step, reversed stair-step, . . . I find very satisfying, because it's much like the landscape around here, a tiered, layered effect" (20). *Lost & Found* is also noteworthy for giving prominence to Marion's persona of the Chinese poet, who first appeared in a single poem in *Tight Lines*, with a second poem about him added to

Vigils. In the closing section of *Lost & Found*, six of the twelve poems are devoted to this persona, including the first two, the sixth, and the final three. These positions of emphasis make the Chinese poet as significant a figure in Marion's work as the Brier is in Miller's, especially since Marion's next book, *The Chinese Poet Awakens* (1999), would assemble thirty-five poems that use this persona.

Although *Lost & Found* incorporates several new features into Marion's poetry, the book also seeks to establish continuity in Marion's writing career, for the volume's epigraph, *"Leaf by leaf I learn my life,"* served as the final line of his chapbook *Almanac.* This epigraph recalls Whitman's *Leaves of Grass,* another poetic project that grounds itself in the natural world and that makes the connection between nature's leaves and the printed page as leaf. In *Lost & Found* that connection is reinforced by the drawings of leaves that appear on the book's cover and on the title page of each of its three sections. The book's title itself functions on several levels. It suggests the activity of searching or questing, and it implies the successful resolution of such ventures. It also suggests, through poetry's acts of memory and of imaginative re-creation, the retrieval of what has vanished. And of course the title has obvious religious connotations, recalling the parables of the lost sheep and the lost coin as well as the famous hymn "Amazing Grace," the first stanza of which concludes, "I once was lost, but now am found; / was blind, but now I see." Given Marion's identification in "Boundaries" of *vision* as the reward of his poetic labors, both of these hymn's lines seem strikingly apropos because he clearly aims to enhance his readers' vision and to enlarge his readers' memory. In his interview with Linda Parsons Marion, he notes, "By remembering the past, we make those things visible and memorable, things at risk of disappearing" ("Listening" 189). Similarly, speaking in terms of place in another interview, he states, "To try to get the details, the essence, the experience of a place in writing is one way to help another person to come to love it" (Lee 204).

The most significant loss recorded in *Lost & Found* is that of the poet's father, to whose memory Marion dedicates the book. Part 1, "In My Father's House," closes with five poems devoted to this man, and Marion focuses on or mentions his father in several earlier poems in that section, too. Of part 1 Don Johnson claims that "the title notwithstanding, this section contains none of the comforting images of home so familiar in Marion's early work" (19). While Johnson overstates the case here, particularly when he adds, "'In My Father's House' mentions home in only one poem" ("Coming the Long Way" 19), the most prominent use of that term, as Johnson observes, occurs in the phrase "the hope of home," which Marion goes on to describe as "but a thin path to walk / above the empty and / cradled dark" (12). Marion's father's death confronts the poet with the inexorable fact of mortality, personalizing it, making it more visceral.

In the second part of the book, a section entitled "Along the Back Roads," Marion exhibits his characteristic tendency to situate himself out in the country, amid natural phenomena, whether in delighted praise of the tang of barbecue, of "jowl and hock, fatback and sowbelly" (26), or in praise of the beauty of October leaves making "their lonely pilgrimage / home" (35). The final poem in part 2, "In Passing," returns to the fact of mortality as a neighbor's death is reported, a neighbor who had been seen outside working on the preceding day. A cobalt blue water glass left standing atop a fencepost signals this man's former presence now transformed into absence. Yet Marion makes this passing seem a natural part of time's passage by linking the glass's color to the blue of both the river and the surrounding hills. Although this death has occurred unexpectedly, it does not cause the poet anguish or distress. The poem's measured tone is one of acceptance, and what the speaker emphasizes, in addition to the blue glass, is the "neighborly wave" he received the day before, a wave he calls the "final gesture" of the deceased (37).

The appearance of the Chinese poet in part 3 of *Lost & Found*, while it highlights a major new persona, does not change Marion's long-standing intention to pursue what is "fundamental and sustaining," particularly in terms of humanity's interaction with the natural world. Chinese poetry is renowned for its loving attention to nature, especially rivers and mountains, birds and flowers, subjects much beloved by Marion too. As an undergraduate Marion had bought a copy of Robert Payne's *The White Pony: An Anthology of Chinese Poetry* (S. Marion 189), and Marion's early chapbook *Watering Places* includes a four-part sequence on the seasons entitled "Four Poems in the Manner of Lin Pu," a poet of the Sung dynasty. Chinese poetry's clarity and simplicity of style, its highly imagistic qualities, and its sense of the sacred in nature—all appeal strongly to Marion's sensibility. As he remarks in an interview, "I read Chinese poets because I'm startled by somebody in the year 600 having the same feelings that I'm having . . . nearly 1400 years later. And yet there is the same emotional response to certain elemental things in the world" (S. Marion 182). What Payne in his introduction to *The White Pony* identifies as principal traits of Chinese poetry—"delighted awareness of the physical universe" (ix), "find[ing] the simplest things of life and celebrat[ing] them" (xvi)—is amply evident in Marion's work as well. Moreover, as David Hinton states in his anthology *Mountain Home: The Wilderness Poetry of Ancient China,* in this "rivers-and-mountains poetic tradition," "the universe is experienced in its fundamental dimensions as home in the most profound and organic sense" (xvi). According to Hinton, the worldview on which this poetic tradition is based "is secular, and yet profoundly spiritual" (xvi). The same can be said of Marion's worldview as he articulates it in his poems. Though readers need to remember that Marion and his persona are not one and the same, the two share many characteristics. Like Marion, the Chinese poet walks "the river road" (41), fishes with the Brier (42), has a dog (48), adopts a seemingly apolitical stance (52), and wears a white beard (54). And both poets relish contact with the natural world, in which they feel at home. The voice of the Chinese poet is, then, often indistinguishable from Marion's own, and yet this persona serves to remind readers of the global reach of Marion's concerns, though Marion situates this figure geographically not in China but in east Tennessee. Nonetheless, as Johnson rightly points out, "the Chinese poet's roots . . . connect him not to East Tennessee, not to the United States or even to China, but to rivers and mountains and stones, elemental forms" ("Coming the Long Way" 22). Thus, in the six poems in which this persona appears in *Lost & Found,* the Chinese poet refers to both the wind and the river as "friend" (41, 53) and apostrophizes the earth in the following passage, which owes as much to Whitman (in its echo of section 21 of "Song of Myself") as to Asian poetry:

> O prodigal earth, receive us
> in our journey!
> O friendly waste of color,
> welcome us on your path! (48)

According to Johnson, the persona of the Chinese poet "rescued his creator from the threat of insularity and restrictive regionalism, broadening the poet's vision" (22). Of the Chinese poet poems in *Lost & Found* Johnson also writes, "the Chinese poet guides Marion out of the dislocation and despair resulting from his father's death by connecting him to a world at large in which he is 'at home'" (22).

In this respect it should be noted that reconciliation with the fact of mortality is likewise the subject of the very first poem Marion wrote about this persona: "The Chinese Poet Awakens to Find Himself Abruptly in East Tennessee," the third poem in *Tight Lines*. In that poem, having come home "heavy from the day's labor," the poet thinks, "No escape: everything settles into dust," only to have this spirit of dejection promptly dispelled:

> Suddenly from behind
> the goat who has waited
> all day to be fed,
> charges—butts me forward.
>
> I am moved.
> The old bearded one knows his master. (unpaged)

The humor of this situation contributes to the change in the speaker's outlook, and that element of humor leavens other Chinese poet poems, a humor evident in the whimsicality of such titles as "In Early Fall the Chinese Poet and His Dog Decide to Take a Stroll along the River Road" and "The Chinese Poet Discovers His Roots While Walking along the Abandoned Roadbed." The intriguing ambiguity of the closing line in the stanza quoted above allows the reader to consider, among other possible interpretations, both the poet's recognition and acceptance of his subordination to nature (as "his master") and the poet's awareness that nature, in the figure of the goat, is at best an unruly servant in its human "master's" hands.

The closing section of *Lost & Found* contains as many poems from which the Chinese poet is absent as poems in which he appears. But the former set of poems, most of which focus on natural phenomena (wild geese, egrets, a muskrat, a blacksnake) certainly coincide with the temperament of the Chinese poet, whose principal setting is the outdoors and who is regularly depicted as walking. To some extent, then, the Chinese poet counterbalances other poems' emphasis on home as a particular dwelling or distinct place, whether farm or small town—although Marion's books also provide many examples of the poet himself wander-

ing through nature or traveling toward home rather than being ensconced
there. Perhaps it would be more accurate to say that the Chinese poet's
peripatetic lifestyle confirms and extends Marion's use of the journey or
pilgrimage motif. Among Marion's important influences, I would argue,
is A. R. Ammons, for not only in the Chinese poet poems but throughout
Marion's work, there is a notable affinity between Marion's stance and
Ammons's notion that "A Poem Is a Walk," the title of one of Ammons's
best-known essays. Marion's extensive use of colons rather than periods
as his principal punctuation in many of his early poems also points to
Ammons's influence.

The Chinese Poet Awakens reprints all eight of Marion's previously published poems employing this persona and adds twenty-seven new poems
featuring this figure. The poems are divided among four numbered but
untitled sections, the number four clearly meant to suggest the cycle of
the seasons. The increasing convergence of author's and persona's perspectives is evident in Marion's associating the Chinese poet not only
with a public literary figure like Miller's Brier (whom Marion memorial-
izes in a poignant farewell poem) but also with Marion's close personal
friend Daniel Leidig of Emory & Henry College, who is referred to as Old
Cricket in the titles of two of these poems and as Old Hippycricket in a
third. Many of the new poems have a more explicitly religious or mystical aura than the eight initial Chinese poet poems, an aura that owes as
much to St. Francis as to Buddha, though it is also indebted to Whitman,
as the book's closing poem, "The Chinese Poet Writes His Last Will and
Testament," reveals. The equanimity these poems achieve arises not by ignoring "the hard blue / cold of December" (6) but by affirming "the grace
/ of this day" (31), however fleeting, in a natural world where "The air
whispers in wings lifting / toward a sky filled with promise" (3). Images
of ascent suffuse these poems, but so do images of descent into the earth.
"If I dig deep enough in earth, / will I come home again?" the poet asks
(5), a question to which Marion's poetic career answers in the affirmative.
Although living things wane and flow and vanish, "brief as a snowflake"
(8), the pumpkin's seeds hold the promise of new life: "the hope of harvest / to return again and again" (7). Similarly, the poet's "river / of words"
(9) preserves what is borne along by "the long river of time" (37), making
individual and collective memory—and the poem that houses memory—
tributaries to what Marion calls "forever's river" in the closing line of his
elegy for Jim Wayne Miller (20).

In overtly Eucharistic images, the Chinese poet urges his friends/readers to "sip the wine / of memory" (16):

> The words I would give you are already there:
> in the cup that remembers the potter's hands,
> in the wine redolent with the scent
> of fresh-turned soil,
> in the bread broken on family tables. (17)

Marion's sacramental vision is readily apparent in such a passage, and among the most important things he wishes his readers to remember are the wonders of nature itself, fragile wonders susceptible to human destruction, like the wildflowers and trees of a clear-cut hillside in the poem "Wandering Alone on the Hillside at Midnight the Chinese Poet Meets Despair." In the presence of such devastation, the Chinese poet experiences a dark night of the soul, acknowledging that "the loops and swirls of my words, / rooted in this patch of earth's memory, / cannot bring them back, those blossoms of delight" (21). Yet he hopes to prevent further degradation of nature by moving the reader to deepened appreciation of its beauty.

Near the end of *The Chinese Poet Awakens*, Marion's persona proclaims, "I have spent my days turning the soil / of memory" (52), a declaration that applies equally to Marion himself. In *Letters Home* (2001), which Marion has labeled "the most personal of my books," those memories focus not on the natural world or human interaction with it, but on people, primarily family members, and the experiences that shape them. The book grew out of his family's move to Detroit during World War II, where he and his parents lived from 1942 to 1945 while his father worked in an Alcoa plant. (A similar move is dramatized in Harriette Arnow's novel *The Dollmaker*.) *Letters Home* also arose from Marion's unusual family circumstances in which his father and two of the father's brothers married three Gladson sisters, with the poet being the only child produced by those three marriages. Given such a lineage, Marion feels a special responsibility to serve as the repository and conveyer of family memory. Born in 1940, Marion was too young to remember most of the events of those Detroit years, and so he becomes the spokesperson for his family's collective memory. Even though *Letters Home* deals, then, with highly personal experiences, Marion also views the book as representative of the out-migration of many Appalachians during World War II and other periods of economic hardship, of people displaced from their homes who long to return (Lee

207–8). Thus in this collection the term "home" becomes much more place specific and less metaphorical in scope.

The first of the book's four numbered sections consists of just two poems, the volume's title poem and "Sign, South Pacific, 1943." Both revolve around Uncle Gene's experiences in the Navy during World War II, and both invoke what the latter poem calls "the anchor / of home" (4). Section 2 features a twelve-part sequence under the title "Detroit Days" and a six-part sequence, "My Mother Remembers." The term "home" recurs frequently in the former sequence, especially in "Night Train, 1944" with its lines "traveler dreaming to wake / in some station called home" and its reference to the "conductor's arrival chant, / homecall, *Knoxville, Tennessee*" (16). Likewise, "A Saturday Night, 1944" portrays the family in Detroit trying to tune in the Grand Ole Opry on the radio:

> . . . signal calling over
> mountains to the blue valleys,
> curling smoke from the homefires,
> wings of song settled down there. (18)

Sections 3 and 4 each contain seventeen poems that are more varied in subject, with a larger cast of characters, although the majority of the poems continue to deal with childhood or family memories. According to Marianne Worthington, time itself and its passage become the central concern of many of these poems, whose titles—"My Grandmother Tends the Time," "My Father's Watch, 1950," "Saving Time"—reflect this theme (412). For Marion the book's poems themselves become letters home, preserving precious memories but also offering resources from the past that remain available to present and future generations. As Marion comments in an interview with Ernest Lee, "One of the dangers of our age is a disconnectedness from the lives of the past" (208). *Letters Home* is clearly meant as an antidote to such historical discontinuity. Like the flea market the poet visits in a poem of that title, the past affords "an alphabet of abundance" for those with discerning minds and memoried vision (75). Yet Marion does not simply idealize the past or family relationships, as a poem like "Up This Crooked Way" indicates in its chronicling of Great Aunt Mollie's grudge against her brother.

In its extensive reliance on family memory, this volume is a new departure for Marion, though one that builds on impulses evident as early as his first book. *Letters Home* is also a new departure in its use of syllabics; most of the poems are written in seven-syllable lines, a structure that enables Marion to impose some discipline on the narrative flow of these memories. That narrative flow is heightened, as Worthington aptly observes (406), by Marion's decision to present most of the poems in a single-stanza format, the most striking exceptions occurring in "She's Solid Gone," which returns to the reverse stair-step stanzas of *Lost & Found*, and in the poems that conclude sections 3 and 4. Despite the book's title, none of the poems in *Letters Home* adopts an epistolary structure, even though Marion had used that device in earlier collections. Here the title refers to Marion's words themselves and to the letters of the alphabet that make communication—and human communion—possible. Moreover, by calling these poems *Letters Home*, Marion grants himself the privilege of speaking more conversationally, more intimately, to his readers, with a greater degree of self-revelation, a stance whose success he attributes to the emotional openness he cultivated in *The Chinese Poet Awakens*. "I don't think I could have written *Letters Home*," he told Lee, "without having first written those *Chinese Poet* poems" (210).

Marion's *Ebbing & Flowing Springs: New and Selected Poems and Prose, 1976–2001*, reprints many otherwise unavailable poems from out-of-print volumes, along with twenty new poems. It also includes four short stories and three essays, among the latter "On the Banks of the Holston," an essay first published in 1984 in a special issue of *The Iron Mountain Review* that Marion guest-edited. The new poems present an array of Marion's familiar subjects, some related to country life ("Rainbarrels," "Silo"), some focusing on family members and childhood memories ("Breaking Up Housekeeping," "Ink Buckets," "Aunt Clara's Credo"). Others address nature's creatures ("Lightning Bugs," "Trio"), while additional poems ("78 RPM," for example) meditate on mutability: "dance / of then to dust of now" (132). In a brief preface to the book, "Looking Back, Looking Forward," Marion speaks of his need "to work at a craft that can give lasting body to the love I feel for my world fast fading and too soon gone" (xvi). The silo of that poem's title thus stands as a "grave marker," rising midway above an artificial lake that covers the surrounding farmland.

In contrast to such erasure of humanity's dependence on nature, Marion's poetry gives voice to a spiritual vision of nature's sacramental identity. His essay "On the Banks of the Holston" begins with what amounts to a prayer of invocation in nature's behalf, a passage that later became the prose poem that opens the chapbook *Miracles of Air:* "Damselfly, caddis, and dragonfly; for what rises from and enters into the river, winged or wingless, named in song or praised with silence" (191). This river, which becomes an emblem of time itself, is later linked to poetry: "praise for the word that yearns to be water, mystery held in a single bead, touching your tongue at last, sacrament for the long, long thirst" (191). Marion here makes poetry an elemental force, essential to human survival, as he does elsewhere when he refers to poetry as "our daily bread" in an essay of that title. In his interview with Lee, he remarks, "It's as though the very saying of the poem is a form of prayer, which is a kind of communion. To pray is to commune with something outside yourself, with a power that moves through all things" (207). The qualifying terms Marion uses in this statement ("It's as though," "a form of," "a kind of") indicate a desire to distance himself from orthodox religious language. Yet to Shackelford he declares, "I am trying to commune with some spirit that is much greater than I could ever be and that nourishes me, that feeds me, that gives me this great gift of the world" (323). At the very least, this is the language of religious mysticism.

Most published commentary on Marion's poetry finds in it a marked religious consciousness. Dan Leidig, for instance, the first critic to offer an extended analysis of Marion's work, writes, "The places Marion recovers in his poetry are hallowed places, reverentially and lovingly arranged, not merely as matters of record, but as intercessions for the human quest" (155). Gerald Wood, one of the poet's colleagues at Carson-Newman College, says of Marion's own quest that it "is essentially a religious one" and remarks of the changes in Marion's poetry over his first two books, "the poetry . . . has become more religious in the existential sense. The poet is like a priest who makes an endless quest toward meaning and order in a world rimmed by darkness" (40, 42). Reviewing *Vigils,* Larry Richman notes that the book's final section, "Simple Gifts," reflects "the tight interweave of time and eternity, Below and Above" (14). Richman's review provides nuanced, insightful explications of the religious themes and imagery in "Loft" and "Fall Passage." Both Rita Quillen and Lynn Powell refer to Marion as a "mystic" (41; 14), while Shackelford links Marion to American Transcendentalism and, more specifically, to Emerson's claim that "Nature is the symbol of spirit" (323). "In his work," writes Shackelford, "Marion constantly moves from physical reality to spiritual insight through metaphor" (323).

Yet anyone who has read widely both in Marion's work and in that of his contemporaries among the region's poets is likely to be struck by what is absent from Marion's poems in terms of religious subject matter. There is, for example, virtually no God-talk in these poems, almost no direct reference to the deity, in sharp contrast to the poetry of Charles Wright, with its anguished exploration of the problem of belief in the modern—or postmodern—world. Nor is there any elaborate Dantean schema like that in Fred Chappell's *Midquest,* nor does one find a profusion of explicitly religious poems like Chappell's "An Old Mountain Woman Reading the Book of Job" or "O Sacred Head Now Wounded" or "Scarecrow Colloquy." And despite Marion's tacit rejection of what Shackelford calls the "narrow-minded denominationalism and aggressive proselytizing" of the Southern Baptist tradition in which the poet was raised (320), Marion's poems generally omit any references to childhood experiences of churchgoing of the sort that recur regularly in Robert Morgan's poetry: in "Prayer Meeting," "Church Pews," "After Church," and "The Gift of Tongues," among many others. Nor does Marion evince the anxiety about salvation and damnation apparent in Morgan's "Signs" and "Face," although "Graven Image" of *Letters Home* is a notable exception to his usual silence about such matters. In comparison to the poetry of Chappell and Morgan and Wright, Marion's work may at first seem almost secular. What, then, are the qualities or features of his poetry that have led so many critics to identify him as a poet with religious concerns?

One way to approach this question is to consider what is meant by the term "religion" in its broadest sense. Etymologically, the term implies a kind of restraint or tying back, from Latin *religare* (also the root of the English word "rely"). The Latin root *ligare* is likewise the source of the English words "ligament" and "ligature," both of which suggest bonds or connections. Religious consciousness implies connection to something beyond the self or beneath the surface of the everyday, precisely the sort of connection that Marion acknowledges in his remarks to Lee and Shackelford quoted above. Winston L. King, writing in the sixteen-volume *Encyclopedia of Religion,* concedes the difficulty of defining the essence of the term "religion" but nevertheless offers readers several traditional definitions, along with his own, that help to illuminate the religious dimension of Marion's poetry. These include Friedrich Schleiermacher's view that religion is a "feeling of absolute dependence," Rudolf Otto's emphasis on awe in the presence of the holy, and Mircea Eliade's conception of religion as involving an awareness of "sacred space" (including rivers and trees and mountains), not just encounters between human beings and God (283–85). King's own definition, intended to encompass as many religious traditions as possible, reads as follows: "Religion is the organization of life around the depth dimensions of experience" (286), a definition that is strikingly relevant to some of Marion's most evocative poems.

Consider, for example, the title poem of *Tight Lines*. This poem originally appeared in *Watering Places*, where it concludes the chapbook, and it thus represents the earliest period in Marion's poetic career. As the opening poem in the 1981 collection, it sets the tone for the remainder of the book, urging the reader to look beneath surfaces, to plumb the depths. It functions on at least three levels—as a poem about fishing, as a poem about poetry and the discoveries it affords, and as a poem about religious mystery:

> First read the water,
> then cast toward pockets,
> the deep spaces between
> the cold print of rocks.
>
> It's the flow that beguiles—
> what's beneath that lures.
>
> But when the line goes
> taut,
> a dark, waiting presence
> will flash
> and weave its way,
> throbbing, into your pulse.

This sense of mystery at work in the world is definitive of religious consciousness, and it permeates Marion's poetry. In his essay "Try to Picture It" Marion speaks of "the haunting power of mystery, a force that pulls you toward it, keeps you in a state of wonder" (23).

The reference to water at the beginning of "Tight Lines" invokes Marion's principal image for life itself—rivers and springs. Water is undoubtedly the most prominent image in his writing. From the chapbook *Watering Places* to *Ebbing & Flowing Springs*, water repeatedly elicits from him both a sense of wonder and the impulse to praise. In "Sycamores" in *Watering Places* he speaks of the "grace of water's flow," and in another poem he refers to himself as "drawn by waters / I cannot fathom" (*Lost & Found* 43). He concludes the poem "By the Banks of the Holston" with an outpouring of praise:

> for the dark loam of hidden coves,
> for the river's shifting eddies & shoals,
> let there be hosannas,
> hosannas forever,
> hosannas forever & ever. (*Vigils* 26)

The biblical rhythms of the repetition in these lines help to instill in readers the sense of the sacred that Marion's poems often mediate. Marion doesn't define the sacred in sectarian terms, certainly not the terms of any particular orthodoxy; he simply witnesses to its presence in and beneath the beguiling flow of time itself.

As the mention of "dark loam" in the preceding quotation indicates, Marion's sacramental vision is not limited to water. Indeed, the poet imbues the whole earth with an aura of the sacred. Rather than positing a sharp distinction between God and the creation, between the transcendent and the immanent, Marion finds the sacred in the temporal. This attitude, as King points out, is more characteristic of Buddhism and Hinduism than of traditional Western theism (282, 284) and thus may partially account for Marion's interest in Chinese poetry and the persona of the Chinese poet. It should be noted, however, that the Judeo-Christian creation story and the Christian doctrine of the Incarnation both affirm the goodness of the physical world, for, as Richard Wilbur testifies in the title of one of his best-known poems, "Love Calls Us to the Things of This World." Marion echoes Wilbur's stance in "The Farm Wife's Aubade" when he writes, "Let my song be a kitchen window, / . . . / filling with the world outside" (*Vigils* 23). Yet what Marion has called a marked family trait of "attentiveness to the world" (Richman 13) is likely to have developed, in part at least, in reaction to the pronounced otherworldliness of his formal religious upbringing.

Such attentiveness, as has been noted previously in this chapter, pervades Marion's poetry, with its lovingly inscribed portraits of the natural world, and that attentiveness is made explicit in the title *Vigils*, a term freighted with religious meaning. The word suggests a prayerful watchfulness or alertness, a wakefulness that involves spiritual preparation, as for a religious feast or festival. Marion's poems invite the reader to share the poet's sacramental vision, to appreciate nature's "vocabulary / of wonders" (*Lost & Found* 34). Here on earth we are "sheltered on the oldest ark we know," says the poet (*Out in the Country* 30), using a metaphor that aptly combines images of water and land amid a biblical context that promises divine protection. Like the Robert Morgan of such titles as *Groundwork* and *Topsoil Road*, Marion is a poet of the earthly, of the soil and dirt as well as of water, and his attentiveness to local soil is both an affirmation of his region and a reminder to his readers that nature is not a product of human making but rather one of the many "gifts" his poetry gratefully acknowledges.

Not surprisingly, the patron saint of this poet is St. Francis, who appears by name in the poem entitled "Gifts" but who is alluded to as well in some of the Chinese poet poems through such phrases as "brother Cushaw, / . . . sister Squash" and "Sister Sky, Brother Rock" (6, 16), the latter pair spoken of as "our ancestors." In "Gifts" itself, a frigid winter morning ("–24° last night") finds the poet refilling his birdfeeder and scattering seeds upon the ground. The final two stanzas illustrate both Marion's careful crafting of imagery and sound effects and his fundamentally religious vision:

> what I sow here will soon blossom
> in a flush of wings, flash
> of brown in towhee, quick
> flick of flint black eyes
> in titmice, twirl of chickadee:
>
> O St. Francis of Assisi, I lift
> my cupped hand of seeds in praise
> & reap your miracles of air. (*Vigils* 61)

The bird imagery so central to this poem recurs often in Marion's writing (Richman identifies nineteen different species of birds in *Vigils* alone [21]), functioning symbolically on several different levels. As creatures of nature, birds represent the physical world, of course, but they are also conventional emblems of the poet and the poet's song. In *Ebbing & Flowing Springs*, for example, Marion refers to "my words, / those black birds gathering on this field / of white" (139). As *winged* creatures, moreover, birds symbolize humanity's capacity to soar above the merely physical. Like the butterfly, birds frequently become emblems of the soul or of spiritual aspiration. In "Gifts," however, Marion uses the birds primarily to call attention to nature's wonders—and to nature itself as a gift of grace. But elsewhere in Marion's poetry, images of birds and wings attest to the dual impulse in his writing: an impulse toward rootedness versus an impulse toward ascent. This dual impulse is also evident in the contrasting motifs of being at home and being on a journey or simply on a walk.

Two of the poems about birds in *Lost & Found* help to demonstrate the poet's perception of the transcendent amid the things of this world. Set in autumn, "The Wild Geese," one of the two longest poems in the book, describes the birds' cries as "awakening an unnamed yearning" (43), a yearning seemingly linked to the geese's migratory passage, although the poem's fifth and final section notes the speaker's uncertainty about how to respond to what an earlier section calls "this blessing // of geese" (44). The succeeding poem, "The Egrets," which Fred Chappell in a review of *Lost & Found* terms "a poem about desire for transcendental experience" (34), also focuses on the birds' migratory flight. In this poem, too, such flight exceeds the poet's powers: "But they were beyond me, / measures of grace," he laments (46). Despite the poet's failure to soar on these occasions, Marion continues to affirm such longings as definitive of human identity. He speaks variously of "the long flow / toward a new world" (*Out in the Country* 23), of "the long, long thirst" (*Ebbing & Flowing Springs* 191), "the long ascent" (*Lost & Found* 54), "the long, long journey" (*Chinese Poet Awakens* 50), and "the long flight" (*Ebbing & Flowing Springs* 139)—all phrases indicative of enduring spiritual questing.

Such spiritual aspiration has been present in Marion's work from the beginning, as the following lines from "On the Trail to Mt. LeConte," a poem first published in *Watering Places*, reveal:

> these songs pulse
> dreaming of wings
> that will map roots
> across the sky[.] (*Vigils* 41)

In this stanza the poet links earth and heaven through his image of roots that fill the sky while at the same time he connects his own poems with birds in their ability to soar. A similar juxtaposition or intermingling of earth and heaven occurs in *Tight Lines* in Marion's depiction of the earth as "a zodiac of the dirt / where we reap / our lives."

The preceding lines appear in a poem titled "The Garden," which Marion places at the exact center of *Tight Lines*. Gardens are a major site, obviously, of the interaction between humanity and nature, but in Western culture they are also, as with the Garden of Eden, a mythic locus of interaction between humanity and the divine. Marion recalls that linkage in one of the new poems in *Ebbing & Flowing Springs*, a poem entitled "Aunt Clara's Credo," a credo aligned with the poet's own. As with "The Farm Wife's Aubade," the poem is presented in the form of a petition or prayer:

> Let elms spread wide their branches,
> cast a cathedral of shade
> over all our days; let rocks
> end their journey here beside
> primrose and the quiet tongues
> of hosta, vowels of rain
> tapping a steady drumroll
> on my tin roof, a bright splash
> of syllables evergreen,
> my hand abloom with flutter
> of the wren's wings come to peck
> thistle seed from my palm; let
> the trill of birdsong be choir
> to sing summer's lush pages,
> and let me scribble my time
> in this home dirt, seeds like words
> sown, praise for each season; when
> the lean sentence of winter
> asks for my ashes, scatter
> them here in this garden, my
> home, this perennial poem. (141)

Several features of this poem deserve comment in light of the analysis of Marion's themes offered in this chapter. Readers should observe, for example, the religious aura with which the poet endows nature through his use of the terms "cathedral" in line 2 and "choir" in line 13. Aunt Clara's stance in feeding the birds clearly mirrors the poet's own in "Gifts," and both figures are predisposed to praise. Like Marion and Morgan (and like Emerson before them), Aunt Clara tends to conjoin natural phenomena and human speech in such phrases as "the quiet tongues / of hosta," the "vowels of rain" with their "bright splash of syllables," and "summer's lush pages." Such images assert the poet's sense of identification with nature, an identification made explicit in Marion's closing lines, where the garden becomes a "perennial poem" that is simultaneously Aunt Clara's "home"—the most resonant word in Marion's poetic vocabulary. Through Aunt Clara, whose name suggests lucidity of vision, the poet voices his desire to "scribble my time / in this home dirt," a dirt (or dust) to which he seems content to return whenever "the lean sentence [a striking pun] of winter" (that is, death) should require his life. The tranquillity that marks the speaker's tone here is characteristic of Marion, who seems to subscribe to the admonitions of both the Sermon on the Mount—"do not be anxious about tomorrow" (Matthew 6:34)—and of section 48 of Whitman's "Song of Myself": "Be not curious about God. / . . . // Why should I wish to see God better than this day?"

But "Aunt Clara's Credo" is not the final word on gardens in *Ebbing & Flowing Springs*. The selection of new poems in it ends instead with one titled "The Arbor," whose closing lines hold out the possibility of "passage through / time to new gardens beyond" (150). Marion's allegiance to earth and to the flowing river of time does not prevent him from longing for more, does not preclude his glimpsing the presence of the eternal. As the final poem in *Tight Lines* likewise attests,

> Somewhere beyond this drift
> stars chart their courses,
> shards of light
> buoyed on dark waves.

In and through his poetry Marion both sanctifies the physical world and aligns himself with those "shards of light," the stars to which both Dante and Chappell allude at the end of each section of their epics. As he states in "Crossing Clinch Mountain in February,"

> In this dusk
> I am your single candle,
> faint echo of starlight

on far mountain roads
singing the way
home. (*Vigils* 22)

While that home is grounded in the temporal world, it also looks out upon eternity, for Marion sings both the luminous and the numinous, celebrating "this wedlock in earth / tapping / hidden springs" (*Out in the Country* 47). For Marion, those springs have their ultimate source in religious mystery. Like the egrets in *Lost & Found*, they are measures of grace.

5

KATHRYN STRIPLING BYER

"Laying up Treasures on Earth"

"IN AN IDEAL WORLD," Kathryn Stripling Byer has said, "our poets would through their poems urge us to . . . fall in love again and again with the things of this world" (Woloch 60). Such a statement clearly aligns Byer with Jim Wayne Miller's assumption that Appalachian literature is decidedly this-worldly, and in many respects the two poets' views do tend to coincide. Like Miller, Byer combats the problem of "amnesia" in American culture. "With each passing year," she laments to another interviewer, "our connections with the past, with family, with the land itself, become weaker and weaker. I see my poetry, all poetry, as a struggle against amnesia" (Johnson and Walden 29). Yet unlike Miller, Byer also contends with the sexism, both explicit and implicit, that afflicts the Judeo-Christian tradition, for she recognizes, as have feminist theologians, that the otherworldly impulse in Christianity that demeans the physical world has likewise demeaned women, whom male theologians have regularly identified with nature and the body, as well as with sin itself. Over the course of her career, Byer's poetry has rejected that otherworldliness in favor of celebrating the natural world and the depths of human love. Native American spirituality, with its affirmation of the sacredness of the earth, has played an increasingly important role in her poems, as has her insistence on laying up treasures on earth, in direct contrast to Jesus's advice in Matthew 6:19–21. What Miller simply takes for granted, a this-worldly orientation, his younger contemporary makes one of the principal subjects of her work.

Byer (1944–) is the author of five award-winning book-length collections of poems and several chapbooks. Although raised on a farm in southwest Georgia, just four miles from another farm owned by her grandfather, Byer has made the mountains of western North Carolina her home since 1968, the year she completed her M.F.A. degree at the University of North Carolina at Greensboro. There Fred Chappell, whom she later succeeded as poet laureate of her adopted state, was among her teachers, as were Allen Tate and Robert Watson. Byer had read Tate and John Crowe Ransom, along with other Fugitives and Agrarians, while still an undergraduate at Wesleyan College in Macon, Georgia (L. Smith 305). But perhaps her most important early influence was James Dickey, whose work she also read at Wesleyan: "I recall sitting on the floor of the nearly deserted library on Friday night reading 'Cherry Log Road,' 'The Heaven of Animals,' 'In the Treehouse at Night.' Here was a poetry that pulsed with place, with a homeland so intense that I recognized it as my own. If Dickey could write about junkyards and fencewire, . . . I could begin to look closely at my own magical places, my grandparents' farm, the corn-fields I loved . . ." (Kennedy 9). Asked what she considers her most valu-able heirloom, Byer once responded, "a sense of belonging in a particular place at a particular time, a sense of connectedness. I can think of no more precious inheritance for a writer" (Johnson and Walden 30).

In moving to the mountains Byer remained deeply embedded in this sense of place, for she was pursuing her paternal grandmother's unful-filled desire to return to the landscape of her birth in Dahlonega, Georgia. As the poet comments in an interview with Lee Smith, "I knew that I wanted to live in the mountains after I got my education. I wanted to live where my grandmother had wanted to live" (301). In that same interview, Byer remarks that she found in the mountains a rural way of life that had largely disappeared from southwest Georgia by the time she left for col-lege (299, 306). Thus while Byer is a writer who considers at least two places "home"—the farm of her childhood and the mountains in which she has spent most of her adulthood—what links these two places is their close contact with the natural world, for which Byer expresses profound affection. About the landscape of her childhood she states in an early in-terview, "The land, nature, the fields and trees around me, were always like a haven, the 'hiding places of power,' as Wordsworth says. . . . The land helps us remember, keeps us rooted to what matters, and rises up in us as praise, pure celebration" (Johnson and Walden 30).

It is obviously that spirit of celebration that suffuses the opening po-ems in *The Girl in the Midst of the Harvest* (1986), Byer's first full-length collection. Divided into three titled sections ("The Girl in the Midst of the Harvest," "Search Party," and "Homecoming"), the book broadly traces Byer's movement from southwest Georgia to the mountains. The epigraph to part 1, taken from Rilke's *Stundenbuch*, includes the lines, "Who is not rich, with summer nearly done, / will never find a self that is his own" (1). The poet has decisively achieved such selfhood in poems like "Wide Open, These Gates," "Cornwalking," and "Daughter." In the first two she depicts herself as both walker and singer, whose song blends, significantly, with the songs she attributes to nature's creatures. "The gnats sing, and I'm going / to sing," she proclaims in "Wide Open" (3), while "Cornwalking" concludes with the poet's song joining that of "the gathering wind in the corn itself / singing, 'We are growing everywhere. / What is the world but our song?'" (5). This identification of self with nature is affirmed in "Daughter," which ends, "I am the girl in the midst of the harvest. // I am the harvest" (7). Byer's use of single-sentence lines here induces the reader's assent, especially when she places the concluding line in a separate stanza. The motif of singing, a conventional metaphor for poetry itself, is one Byer uses extensively in later books as well.

Part 1 of *Girl* also contains several poems about the poet's great-grandmother and grandparents, establishing a network of family relationships that tie the poet to both southwest Georgia and the mountain South. That section concludes, however, with "Drought," a poem that describes Byer's revisiting the farm of her birth after she has begun residing in the mountains. On this occasion the poet is eager to leave this setting where "Nothing has changed," where "water is / only illusion, an old trick / light plays on the highway that runs north . . ." (23). The poet has already followed that highway north to the mountains, north to the lineage of her paternal grandmother, as parts 2 and 3 reveal. The ambivalence evident in "Drought" also reflects what Byer acknowledges in her essay "A Thing Called Home": that not all southern writers want to go home, that the idea of home includes contradictions and dangers. Yet in that essay Byer also refers to home as "the bedrock, the Mother of all obsessions" (8) and argues that "Southern writers go searching unashamedly for those spirits of place" (10).

Part 2, "Search Party," records just such a quest. Winner of the 1978 Anne Sexton Prize and published as a chapbook in 1979, "Search Party" consists of eight poems in which Byer imagines the life of her great-grandmother as both that woman's daughter (Byer's paternal grandmother) and her great-granddaughter (Byer herself) attempt to reconstruct it. According to family legend, this great-grandmother was the first white child brought to the Black Hills, where "the sun blinds" (28), where "the wind sings of nothing // but rocks crumbling, / roots letting go" (29). The harshness of this landscape, together with Byer's depiction, in "Drought" and other poems, of the difficulties of agrarian living, attests to the poet's refusal to idealize nature. Yet for Byer the earth remains, quite literally, the ground of human being, as the epigraph to part 3, "Homecoming," implies. That epigraph, taken from Marie Luise Kaschnitz's "Dear Sun," speaks of "the undiminished / Daily witness" to "Dear sun / Good earth"—despite the temptation to despair, to "stop loving anyone / And give up our planet" (37).

Much of the critical commentary on Byer's work has understandably focused on her detailed examination of female identity and relationships among women. But from the beginning of her career Byer has also been committed to critiquing the philosophical dualism that sets body and mind, nature and spirit, earth and heaven in opposition to one another. Like feminist theologian Rosemary Radford Ruether, Byer has recognized the connection between a soul-body dualism that denigrates the body and the male-female dualism in both Classical and Christian thought that denigrates women. For Ruether, "the equation of woman with the body also made her peculiarly the symbol of sin," both as Eve yielding to temptation and as the personification of physical passion (*Liberation* 100). According to Ruether, one of the consequences of this subordination of women, as with any oppressed group, is that they "live in a culture of silence, as objects, never as subjects of the relationship" (102). One of Byer's principal aims as a writer has been to give voice to these long-silent women, like her great-grandmother and like Alma of *Wildwood Flower*. At the same time Byer has sought to subvert the otherworldly theology that Ruether rejects in urging the recovery of "a full-bodied sense of creation and incarnation" and of selfhood achieved "not merely against the body, but in and through the body" (113). As Ruether argues in *Sexism and God-Talk*, feminist theology must reject "the concept of spirit and transcendence as rootless, antimaterial, originating in an 'other world' beyond the cosmos, ever repudiating and fleeing from nature, body, and the visible world" (70).

While I don't mean to suggest that Byer is consciously adopting Ruether's ideas, her poems do evince a similar desire to affirm the body and the natural world. The "homecoming" to which she invites the reader in part 3 of *Girl* is multifaceted; it is not only a literal homecoming to her grandmother's beloved mountains but also a figurative turning to the "good earth" of the epigraph from Kaschnitz. Far more than Jim Wayne Miller and Jeff Daniel Marion, Byer foregrounds matters of religious belief and incorporates allusions to the Bible. In part 1, for example, in the "Elegy" for her grandfather, she recalls the night of his death and "the bare feet on which he set forth / as if told he must take up his mattress / and walk away, praising each step of the journey" (14; Matthew 9:6; Mark 2:11). The following poem, "Old Orchard Road Again," likewise portrays the poet's grandfather, concluding with her memories of "his sentence prayers muttered at morning devotion," prayers that include "*Thank you for green grass. / Thank you for clear water*" (16). The this-worldly orientation of these prayers is also evident in part 3's "Heaven," which begins with the poet comparing an oak tree "transfigured / by sun" to "Ghiberti's bronze doors into Paradise" in Florence (50). This poem also alludes to the Annunciation ("Mary's face turned away from the angel") and to Christ's raising of Lazarus (50). But such miracles as the Virgin birth and resurrection from the dead give way, in the poem's final line, to "a heaven of Tuscan leaves" outside the room where mother and daughter sit as autumn moves toward winter. "Heaven" is followed by "Solstice," set in winter, a poem in which Byer presents a telephone conversation between someone identified only as PCP, to whom "Solstice" is dedicated, and the poet herself, a more skeptical figure. Whereas PCP finds the Virgin Mary "easy to pray to" because "she is so human" (52), the poet is silent, noncommittal. But Byer gives the last word to PCP, who remarks, "Perhaps there is such a thing as grace, / the smallest twig kindling, / the empty hearth filling with light" (53).

This image of light, commonly linked to intellectual and spiritual illumination, recurs at various points throughout part 3, most notably in "Wings" and in the concluding sequence of eight poems entitled "I Inherit the Light of My Grandmother's House." In the former Byer refers to "turning toward light and what light / always promises: wings and more wings" (46). But if such wings are instruments of soaring, of transcendence, Byer brings the reader back to earth in the final sequence, which contains several biblical allusions. Here the grandmother's house has burned down after being struck by lightning, though the grandmother had abandoned it following her husband's death. Long vacant, it had been broken into by thieves, an allusion—in the sequence's larger context—to

Matthew 6:19. In the third poem, "Glory," Byer describes her grandmother's hair, echoing St. Paul's term for a woman's hair in I Corinthians 11:15 (King James Version) and thus calling attention to the irony of his injunction in the same chapter that women should keep their heads covered in church. This chapter also includes St. Paul's deplorable claims about the subordination of women to men: "The head of a woman is her husband. . . . [H]e is the image and glory of God; but woman is the glory of man. . . . Neither was man created for woman, but woman for man." Yet Byer presents her grandmother as a figure of self-sufficiency, whose house was a nurturing place, "the sun filling / it up like a milkbucket" (68), its windows seeing "clear to Kingdom Come" (71).

The sequence's (and thus the book's) penultimate poem is entitled "Prayer." In this poem Byer envisions her grandmother awakening on a Saturday morning in late June when "The house needs no cleaning," when "The cornfields are rustling / like water" (72). "May she live in that homeplace forever," the poem concludes, although the sequence in its entirety leaves little doubt that the actual house has been reduced to ashes. The poet's imagination, however, restores the house to wholeness—and does so not only by insisting on the granddaughter's right of inheritance but also by affirming the grandmother's own contentment with the life she had lived. "*Today she would change nothing,*" the final poem, "Kitchen Sink," begins (73). That poem's pivotal line, the eleventh of twenty-one, reads, "*The reward of a long life is faith.*" But in one of her characteristically apt uses of enjambment, Byer immediately adds, after a stanza break for heightened emphasis, "*in what's left*" (73). Rather than offer an endorsement of traditional religious belief, Byer subverts it, writing of her grandmother, "*She has been able // to lay up her treasures on earth, / as if heaven were here, worth believing*" (73). In these lines Byer highlights the immanent, not the transcendent. It is on the earth, in the temporal world, that she feels at home. That Byer herself has inherited this light, this truth, from her imaginative reconstruction of her grandmother's life is apparent from the emphasis she gives this poem by placing it at the end of her first book. Moreover, "Kitchen Sink" is also the final poem in Byer's 1983 chapbook *Alma*, which first introduced the persona of her second full-length collection, *Wildwood Flower* (1992). Thus Byer gives special prominence to this poem in two separate contexts and echoes its insistence on the here and now in two other poems in part 3 of *Girl*, "Potatoes" and

"Peaches," both poems of nature's plenitude that appear on facing pages immediately prior to "I Inherit the Light of My Grandmother's House." The former, in fact, uses the phrase "good earth," echoing the epigraph from Kaschnitz, and it closes with the lines: "Today, I keep saying. Today / and today. We live here / by this patch of plowed earth / and we'll eat potatoes all winter" (60).

The bountiful agrarian vision of these lines is not, however, the daily experience of Alma in *Wildwood Flower*, which won the Lamont Poetry Prize. In the essay "Deep Water" Byer comments on the genesis of this persona, "this solitary voice I could not get out of my head":

> When her first poems began to speak to me, I had no idea who was saying them, only that they had somehow originated on a hike up the Kanati Fork trail in the Great Smoky Mountains. Halfway up the trail, I happened upon a deserted homesite hidden away in the darkness of vines and brush. What sort of woman could live up here, I wondered. How could she stand it? Something of her persona followed me the rest of the hike, and by the time I had come back down the mountain, "Wildwood Flower" had written itself out in my head. Whoever this voice was, I knew she had been waiting a long time to speak. (68)

Alma emerges, then, out of the silence that has long afflicted women, as feminist thinkers, including Ruether, have emphasized.

In the book's prefatory poem, which Byer italicizes to set it apart from those in Alma's voice, Byer retells the story of Alma's initial appearance:

> *At Kanati Fork*
> *she was a face fading back into hemlock.*
> *I heard her long skirt rustle,*
> *knowing it sumac and witch-hobble.*
> *She was the wind in my ears,*
> *singing "Sail away, ladies,"*
> *and setting the maple leaves spinning.*

The texturing of sound effects in this opening stanza is typical of Byer's poetic craft. The alliteration of the *f* sound in "*Fork*," "*face*," and "*fading*" is heightened by the assonance of the long *a* sound in the last two of those words, and that long *a* reappears near the end of the stanza in "*sail*" and the first syllable of "*ladies*" and "*maple*." The hardships of Alma's life are anticipated by the harsh *k* sound of *"Kanati," "Fork," "back," "hemlock,"* *"skirt"* and the hard *c* of *"sumac"*—and also by the negative connotations of words like *"hemlock"* and *"sumac"* (both can prove poisonous) and of a term like *"witch-hobble."* Yet the alliteration of the sibilant *s* sound, especially in *"singing," "Sail," "setting,"* and *"spinning"* in the stanza's last two lines, instills a gentler tone, one consistent with Alma's identity as ballad singer. As wind, Alma provides poetic inspiration, and her capacity for endurance is hinted at in the ongoing action of Byer's present participles: *"singing," "setting," "spinning."* Almost as noteworthy in these lines is Byer's succinct evocation of place, not only through her use of Kanati Fork but also through such a distinctive term as *"witch-hobble,"* a species of viburnum (also known as hobble-bush and wayfaring tree) with long branches that root at their tips, thus hobbling passersby.

Alma is a mountain woman of the late nineteenth or early twentieth century, of Byer's grandmother's or great-grandmother's generation, not a contemporary figure. The Latin origin of her name is rich with significance, for *alma*, the feminine form of *almo*, means nourishing, kind, cherishing. When applied to a wet nurse, the term suggests the breast and thus implies uniquely female nurturing. As a poetic epithet, the term was often applied to goddesses such as Ceres, Venus, "and other patron deities of the earth, of light, day . . ." (Lewis and Short). Alma's name thus connotes traditional female roles in providing nurture, but it also reflects Byer's commitment to the natural world and to the body.

One of the ironies of *Wildwood Flower*, however, is that Alma, called by name only once in the entire collection, must often contend with an unaccommodating physical environment that severely limits her capacity to nurture. The volume's title poem, the first spoken by Alma, begins, "I hoe thawed ground / with a vengeance. Winter has left / my house empty . . ." (3). Springtime means work; it offers Alma an opportunity to combat hunger, but winter itself has been a season of bitter deprivation, as Byer also indicates by choosing as an epigraph to the first of the book's two parts God's question to Job: "Have you entered the storehouses of the snow?" (Job 38:22). Alma might well be inclined to answer yes, given all that she has endured. One of the functions of this epigraph is to link Alma with the suffering of Job. But Job at least had his so-called comforters, while Alma frequently experiences a horrible isolation. The epigraph to the book as a whole comes from Emma Bell Miles's *Spirit of the Mountains*

(1905) and aptly reads, "Solitude is deep water . . .," like the water into which Alma seems to vanish in the collection's final poem, "River Bed."

Byer has acknowledged the major influence on *Wildwood Flower* and *Black Shawl* (1998) of both Miles's book and Lee Smith's portrait of Granny Younger in the novel *Oral History* (1984): "I knew that . . . when Alma turned contrary and taciturn, I had those old prophetesses that Miles celebrates in 'Grandmothers and Sons' and Smith's irrepressible Granny Younger to help me out" ("Deep Water" 69). The term "prophetess" comes from Miles, and in the chapter to which Byer refers, Miles speaks of these women as "repositories of tribal lore—tradition and song, medical and religious learning. They are the nurses, the teachers of practical arts, the priestesses" (37), women to whom respect is paid because of their "superior holiness," Miles adds (38). Miles also remarks that for the mountain woman, whose "strength and endurance are beyond imagination to women of the sheltered life" (54), "nothing is trivial, all things being great with a meaning of divine purpose" (66). Such a passage is striking because while Byer clearly appropriates the strength and endurance Miles describes, Byer presents Alma's religious views in quite dissimilar terms. In fact, Byer endows Alma with a distinctively modern skepticism that sets Alma apart from Miles's archetypal mountaineer. In this connection the epigraph from Job is again pertinent, for Job is, among other things, someone who challenges both God and the religious orthodoxy of his era.

Byer underscores Alma's religious concerns by raising them in the very first poem that Alma speaks. "Wildwood Flower" includes the question, "Is there no place to hide / from His [God's] silence?" (3), a question she seeks to evade by immersing herself in grinding labor. Finding rebellion fruitless, at poem's end she concedes, "I will learn / to be grateful for whatever comes to me" (3). Little comes, however, as the title of the next poem, "Empty Glass," indicates, with its "black empty sky" (4). Similarly, in "Extremity" Alma declares, "I have no blessings to count" (14).

Most of the poems in part 1 are set in late fall or winter, so Alma has anything but an idyllic encounter with nature. Nevertheless, in "All Hallow's Eve," Alma grounds the spiritual, as Byer herself does, in the world of the senses, rejecting the traditional dualism that privileges spirit over body. In that poem's final stanza Alma envisions the ghosts of the dead departing in disgust:

> . . . complaining how little the living
> have learned, on our knees
> every night asking God for a clean heart,
> a pure spirit. Spirit? They kick
> up the leaves round the silent house.
> What good is spirit without hands for walnut
> to stain, without ears for the river
> to fill up with promises? What good,
> they whisper, returning to nothing, what good
> without tongue to cry out to the moon,
> "Thou hast ravished my heart, O my sister!" (8)

Byer's repetition of the phrase "what good" makes this passage all the more insistent. That Alma's husband shares the outlook of these dead, drawn back to the land they cultivated, becomes apparent when Alma recalls, in the very next poem, his reference to "this valley / you said was our Heaven" (9).

In the last two poems of part 1, Alma is depicted both as the "Lost Soul" of Byer's villanelle of that title, paralyzed at her kitchen sink (in contrast to the grandmother in the final poem of *Girl*) and as the keeper of a lonely vigil in "Quilt." "What else can I call it / but *Waiting for Spring*?" she inquires: "That old patchwork. The dead / sleep beneath it forever" (17). Although Alma perseveres, she is scarcely optimistic, let alone joyful.

Part 2 of *Wildwood Flower* fills twice as many pages as part 1 and bears a far more positive epigraph: "I went down . . . to look at the blossoms of the valley" (19). This epigraph comes from Song of Solomon 6:11, the Old Testament book noted primarily for its celebration not of divine but of human love, the latter portrayed in overtly carnal terms, although many biblical commentators have transformed this text into an allegorical or mystical vision of God's love for humanity or Christ's love for the church. The adverb "down" in this epigraph reflects Byer's emphasis on the immanent rather than the transcendent, and the first poem of part 2, "April," likewise begins with the injunction "Come down": "Come down / to bloodroot that blooms / for a day only" (21). The evanescence of this flower generates a sense of urgency, not of uneasiness, an urgency captured in Byer's effective use of enjambment as she describes the lively dance of Alma's quilts on this spring day. Though Alma turns to self-mockery when she looks at her unkempt reflection in a basin of rainwater, she is obviously reinvigorated by the arrival of spring and the hope of rebirth it offers.

Many of the poems of part 2 are set at a period in Alma's life earlier than that of the poems of part 1. Having established the difficulties of Alma's adulthood in the first third of the book, Byer turns to Alma's courtship and her married years prior to her husband's abandonment of her. Several of the poems focus on a time when Alma was still living at home with an older sister who eventually ran off to marry. Although "April" is followed by two other poems set in spring, both of them poems of sexual passion, those poems also foreshadow the disappointments and frustrations that await Alma. In "Ivory Combs," for example, she recalls her husband's professed yearning to travel and the way he walked toward her across the grass, "crushing the wildflowers under his feet" (23), an unconscious act of destruction repeated by male figures in other Byer poems as a sign of their alienation from nature and their disregard of anything beyond the moment's passion. Alma, in contrast, is attentive to spring's profusion of blossoms:

> How the ridges were rife with this word's [April's] blooming
> multitudes, sprung out of nothing
> and overnight, as if the souls of all creatures
>
> with wings buried under the leaf mold had risen
> and, but for our presence, might take to the sky
> singing praise! (22)

Like the God of Genesis, nature in this passage creates *ex nihilo,* and it also practices a type of resurrection. Alma's impulse, like that she ascribes to the flowers themselves, is to sing praise in the presence of April's wonders, an impulse to praise that is equally prominent, as we have seen, in the poetry of Chappell, Morgan, and Marion.

Succeeding these three poems of springtime is a sequence of four poems with the general title "Christmas," poems that continue to exhibit Alma's religious sensibility. In them a pregnant Alma finds herself identifying with the earthly Mary, not with the spiritualized Holy Virgin. The third poem in the sequence, "Whippoorwills," recounts Alma's observance of the mountaineers' "Old Christmas" (Epiphany), when the animals in barns are said to kneel in homage to the Christ child. But instead of indicating whether Alma experiences such a miraculous vision, Byer concludes the poem by having Alma consider her grandmother's words:

"She promised me / wonders if I'd but believe them" (26). The poem leaves that "if" unresolved, though obviously Alma has opened herself to such spiritual possibilities by being present in the barn. The question of belief is central to the final poem in the sequence, too, a poem whose title, "Snow," recalls both the wintry landscapes of part 1 and its epigraph from Job. Contemplating Christ's birth, Alma asks herself, "Can I believe in it?"—a question that goes unanswered, although in the poem's final stanza Alma longs to "conjure under a rising moon snow / like the light in the darkness the preacher says / faith is" (27). Critic Julie Kate Howard finds in Alma—and in Delphia of *Black Shawl*—a clear-cut embrace of what Howard terms "the Christian mythos," which Howard contends is "an integral part of Byer's canon" (24). But the unresolved questions about belief in the last two poems of "Christmas" argue against such a view.

Yet however skeptical Alma may be about conventional religious belief, Byer repeatedly underscores the varied ways in which Alma maintains an ongoing dialogue about—if not exactly with—God even amid His silence and her doubts. In four successive poems near the end of the book—"Cobwebs," "Easter," "Amazing Grace," and "Afterwards, Far from the Church—these facets of Alma's personality are reemphasized. In the first, "Cobwebs," Alma is sitting dressed for Easter services when suddenly a ray of sunlight makes the cobwebs on her porch rail shimmer and glisten. "Signs! God's signs / hide everywhere like / hooks," she exclaims (43). In this poem she admits that it is *her* eyes that are often "squinted," that there may be some "bright pattern" that she fails to detect "for looking out the wrong / way or not looking" (43).

But the following poem, "Easter," reiterates her distrust of a religion that deprecates both the world of the senses and women themselves:

> Where my father's house stood
> at the edge of the cove is a brown church
> the faithful call Bosom of God.
> I have come back to sit at the window
> where I can see apple trees bud
> while the preacher shouts death has no victory.
>
> Everywhere dogwoods are blooming
> like white flesh this man claims
> is devil's work: woman who tasted

the apple and disobeyed God. But for Christ
we are doomed to the worms waking under
these hills I would rather be climbing

again with my father's goats bleating
so loud I can't hear this man say
I must ask the Lord pardon for what
I've come back to remember—the sun
on my neck as I shook loose my braids
and bent over the washpot. My bare feet

were frisky. If wind made the overalls
dance on the clothesline, then why
shouldn't I? Who's to tell
me I should not have shouted for joy
on this hill? It's the wind I praise God for
today, how it lifted my hair like a veil. (44)

The reference to dancing in this poem may remind many readers of Appalachian literature of Gertie Nevels and her daughter Clytie in Harriette Arnow's *The Dollmaker* and of the fierce denunciation of both women by Gertie's fundamentalist mother. Alma's impulse, like Gertie's, is to praise God for the things of this world, not the next, and she is willing to be among the goats rather than the righteous sheep to preserve her allegiance to nature's beauty and vitality.

In the next poem of these four, "Amazing Grace," the congregation has been dismissed for a post-worship picnic, but Alma continues to meditate on the prophets' declaration that God speaks to human beings in thunder —that is, in condemnation and in the hellfire-and-damnation preaching of much mountain religion. "But why," Alma asks, "should He speak to us only in anger?" Like the Robert Morgan who emphasizes the necessity for coming out from under Calvinism, Alma envisions a different kind of divine presence:

That playing of wind
in the witch-hobble could be His drawing
nigh. Could be He's singing

like bees on the applecake,
soothing the children to sleep. (45)

Byer ends this poem with the image of fathers waking their children, calling each by name, and of children arising to see "everywhere / dogwood white flame" (46), a vision of resurrection that invokes God as loving parent, not thundering judge, and that substitutes for hellfire the dogwood's shining blossoms.

When Alma feels forced to choose between earth and heaven, she follows Emily Dickinson in embracing this world, which Dickinson calls "a magic prison" that engenders a "Happiness / That too competes with Heaven" (304). In "Afterwards, Far from the Church," the poem that succeeds "Amazing Grace," the reader once again finds Alma removed both spatially and emotionally from the community's religious views. Alma's "Promised Land" is not the one yearned for by those in the church pews but is rather "an earthly creek, late-blooming columbine, / bed of wet maple leaves we made / beyond any singing but that of the ravens" (47). Alma prefers the world of "meadow-sweet" (23) to what Wallace Stevens in "A High-Toned Old Christian Woman" calls "haunted heaven" (59), and like the Stevens of "Sunday Morning," who assures the woman to whom he speaks that no conception of the afterlife "has endured / As April's green endures" (68), so Alma in "Trillium" had earlier praised the creative power of the word "April."

While it is inaccurate to speak, as Howard does, of "Alma's Christianity"—even though Howard also recognizes Alma's rejection of "certain patriarchal tenets of Christianity" (27)—Byer's portrait of Alma highlights Alma's profound wrestling with her religious heritage. As noted earlier, such skepticism is not characteristic of the women whom Miles describes in *The Spirit of the Mountains*, one of Byer's principal sources of inspiration for Alma. Thus readers might justifiably conclude that these issues are as crucial to Alma's creator as to Alma herself, and Byer's subsequent books bear out such an assessment.

Like *Wildwood Flower*, *Black Shawl* is filled with the voices of mountain women of an earlier generation. In fact, the first of the book's three sections is titled "Voices," while the third, "Delphia," introduces another major persona in Byer's work, in this case one based on an actual person, Delphia Potts, whose daughters befriended the poet following Byer's move to western North Carolina. In her interview with Lee Smith, Byer indicates that many of the poems in *Black Shawl* are "spill-over" poems written during the composition of *Wildwood Flower:* "poems that went into *Black Shawl* rather than *Wildwood Flower* because the voice didn't seem quite like Alma's" (310). In "Deep Water" Byer says of this third book that it is comprised of "poems that kept coming after its [*Wildwood Flower's*] completion" (68). Both books illustrate what Sarah Kennedy has labeled Byer's "incremental monologues"; "her work builds," says Kennedy, "through the accretion of similar voices in poem after poem" (10). These voices powerfully articulate female experience of household labor, child-rearing, marital relationships, and such activities as quilting, cooking, and ballad singing.

In *Black Shawl* Byer particularly emphasizes quilting and ballad singing as expressions of female creativity as well as means of crafting identity and establishing continuity between past and present. The book's title and the epigraph to part 1 both come from Byer's poem of the same title in *Wildwood Flower*. There the black shawl is primarily a negative image linked to "rag / taggle gypsies," "stealing / away to their dirty / work" (41). In "Deep Water," however, Byer writes of the black shawl as an emblem of female community or solidarity; it represents "a larger web of voices, voices that I have come to see as connective tissue stretching across these hills" (63). Ballad singing is another manifestation of that connective tissue. Byer begins and ends *Black Shawl* with italicized poems about this activity, "The Ballad Singers" and "Síle," the latter dedicated to Sheila Kay Adams, a seventh-generation ballad singer from North Carolina's Madison County, *Síle* being the Gaelic for "Sheila" (52). But preceding "The Ballad Singers," which opens part 1, Byer places a prefatory poem, "Mountain Time," which introduces the quilter and reading teacher Delphia, whose name links her to the ancient Greek oracle at Delphi as well as to those "prophetesses" of Emma Bell Miles. According to Byer, Delphia serves as a model for poets: "This labor to make our words matter / is what any good quilter teaches. / A stitch in time, let's say" (x). As Robert West has pointed out, in the last of these three lines Byer puns on the prosodic term "stich," meaning a line of verse (21). In an essay entitled "Stitching the Past Together," Byer credits Willa Mae Pressley, one of Delphia Potts's daughters, with teaching her the "lexicon" of quilting (11), and she claims for quilting a restorative power to which her poetry likewise aspires: "Making the world whole again, perhaps that is really what quilting is all about" (13). Byer concludes this essay by listing such evocative quilt patterns as Heart's Seal, Winding Way, Rose of Sharon, and World Without

End (13). The last of these would allow for ongoing stitches in time, just as in "Mountain Time" Byer contrasts "prophets [who] discourse about endings" with Delphia, who is said to remind us that "the world as we know it / keeps calling us back to beginnings" (x), beginnings that attune readers to the temporal world.

Although *Black Shawl* contains fewer poems than *Wildwood Flower* that deal with explicitly religious subject matter, Byer reemphasizes this dimension of her work by placing "Circuit Rider" among the earliest poems in part 1. Significantly, the poem's speaker is not the itinerant preacher of the title but rather a woman he has encountered on his circuit. While the poem remains a monologue, the speaker both communicates with the preacher and ascribes various ideas to him. By excluding the preacher's voice, Byer imbues the speaker with greater authority, and that speaker, both rebellious and flirtatious, well versed in the Bible, is more than a match for the circuit rider. Stanza 1 reads:

> Handsome man, come with your black book to judge
> me, I'll not ask you down for so much as a sip
> from my bucketful. Stay in your saddle
> and preach God's arrival. I'll listen. (7)

This speaker sees the preacher—and presumably the God he represents—as primarily condemnatory. Yet she agrees to listen because any voice is preferable to the solitude of her daily round. Responding to an implied comment from the preacher and alluding to Proverbs 31:10 (King James Version), she says, "Yes, / I know my price. Beyond rubies and diamonds."

In the third and fourth stanzas Byer has the speaker compare soul and body—to the soul's disadvantage:

> Soul? Oh, that flimsy of silk hand-me-down,
> it does not want to snuggle in Abraham's
> bosom! It wants a strong wind. Let it fly
> with the smallest of God's many sparrows.
>
> This body you say will decay desires nothing
> but sally grass, sycamore shade. Where my grave
> waits is nobody's business. (7)

By poem's end, the speaker has evidently aggravated the preacher with her self-sufficiency and her resistance to his entreaties. "Don't shout!" she tells him at the end of the final stanza's initial line, and she goes on to both taunt and entice: "I believe every hair on my head has been numbered. / Lean closer. I'll untie my kerchief / and you can let God help you count them" (7). The stance of this speaker resembles that adopted by Alma in poems like "Easter" and "Amazing Grace," which reject the excessively judgmental, flesh-denouncing God of much of Western Christianity, as Chappell does through the figure of Uncle Body in *Midquest* and through the harsh portrait of the preacher Canary in *I Am One of You Forever*.

"Circuit Rider" is followed by "The Devil's Dream," a phrase that refers (as in Lee Smith's novel of the same title) to fiddle music, to secular rather than sacred song. The speaker is a woman, now abandoned by a former lover or husband, who addresses her words to that absent figure as she anticipates her death. Like the speaker of "Circuit Rider," she aligns herself with the physical world when she states, "What's the Devil's own / dream but to be / snagged forever on / April, like me among / blackberry briars" (8). Her lover, in contrast, is associated with the sacrament of baptism as a salvific act intended to distance the baptized person from the world of the senses:

> . . . . I know
> what you want. To wade into
> deep water with me,
> your hand on my head
> meant to save me from
> hearing again how
> the hatchling frogs down
> by the river sing
> some other god's resurrection. (8–9)

The frogs' song celebrates the natural world as a site of divine energy, though not one acknowledged as such by a Christian theology that considers nature a temptation or views nature as a manifestation of the profane rather than the sacred.

Byer opens and closes the first section of *Black Shawl* with poems about the moon, a conventional emblem of female identity but also a multivalent symbol of change, of flux, of madness, and of the natural and temporal in contrast to the sun as an image of the divine. In "She," the first of those poems, the moon is linked to passion, to the transgressing of restraints, to wolfish menace. The only place name in this poem is Hell's Thicket (5), a name in keeping with the speaker's impulse to prowl and howl. In "Full Moon," however, the speaker is the moon itself, which addresses "all you women who wait" (20), offering them benison, a baptism of light. Byer's imagery assumes a sacramental quality when the moon says, "give me / your empty glass, pour / all you want, drink," and states, "let light / pour like water upon your heads" (20). At poem's end the moon invites its auditors to "smile back at me / and so quietly nobody can hear you / but you, whisper, 'Here am I'" (20). "Here am I." These are the words young Samuel uses to respond to God's call in I Samuel 3 (King James Version). But Byer's women are invited to be nature's acolytes, nature's disciples, to find spiritual fulfillment within the bounds (and bonds) of the physical world.

When Byer turns her attention to Delphia in part 3, this persona has been engaged in spinning, an activity that joins her to the Moirai of classical mythology, though her work has produced "*length / upon length of the sweetest / black thread*" (33). In this section's title poem Byer immediately assigns Delphia the trait of truth telling and describes her crafting a quilt that will prove "Cullowhee Valley's most bountiful rose garden" (34). Whereas in Chappell's poetry such references to rose gardens generally invoke Dante's vision of Paradise, Byer seems content to limn nature as an end in itself. Delphia, in any case, eschews metaphysical speculation:

> Don't ask me the big questions
> none but a fool tries to answer
> straight. All I can tell you of why
> you were born is to take your own time
> once the needle's been threaded. (34)

"To take your own time" is, among other things, to seize the day, to live fully in the here and now. Delphia counsels patience and offers reassurance when she remarks, "Just remember the light will come back / for another day's labor" (34). One of the subtle narrative strategies Byer uses in this poem is to begin in the third person and then shift to first person by means of intervening imperatives, thus giving readers a compelling sense of the influence exerted by Delphia as this persona assumes control of the poem.

So strong an impact does Delphia make on others that the speaker of the subsequent poem, "The Morning of the First Day," credits her with having awakened the speaker, as the title implies, to new life: "Through her window / I saw, for the first time / to know it, the world outside / me" (36). For the speaker, that world is defined by its "refus[ing] to hold still," its fluidity, its subjection to change (36). That fluidity is made concrete in the lineation of the following poem, "Timberline," in which the lines begin at varying degrees of indentation across the page. Yet because those lines are divided equally among four nine-line stanzas, the poem's formal structure also suggests art's capacity to impose some measure of order upon the flux of experience. "Timberline" is one of the most accomplished poems in *Black Shawl,* and like "Easter" it uses dancing as a metaphor for vibrant life. Comparing the trees to women and noting "how the wind through their branches / keeps trying to make them sway," Delphia wonders, "What does wind whisper / up there of death? Or is dancing / the gist of it?" (37). In contemplating death, Delphia speaks of "my need to bear witness / to all I cannot keep from dying." Because such bearing witness is one of the traditional functions of poetry and storytelling more than of quilting, readers tend to hear Delphia as a spokesperson for Byer herself, a tendency supported by the book's opening poem, "Mountain Time." "Timberline" ends with Delphia identifying herself with the trees, seeing herself as an extension of the natural world rather than in opposition to it, and hence joining her "sisters up there on the ridge, / still in line for the next dancing lesson" (37). Insofar as the wind in this poem assumes any of its conventional associations with divine or poetic inspiration, Delphia is responsive to its influx but sees it as an invitation to relish the temporal world, where death is ultimately inevitable and resurrection unanticipated. Such an outlook places Byer in sharp contrast both to Chappell and Morgan, with their repeated emphasis on rebirth and resurrection, and to Wright, whose anguish in the face of death's apparent finality is almost palpable.

Perhaps the poem with the most explicitly religious content in part 3 is "Sea Change," a response to a ninth-century Irish poem in which Líadan renounces Cuirithir "for fear of the King of heaven" (Calder 64). The speaker of this poem, apparently Delphia herself, thinks of Líadan as either crazy or cursed when she first hears this tale as a child. God, says Delphia, "to me always meant so much Preacher / Talk: *Here on the al-*

tar of time will the Lord / thy God sacrifice all things most precious / to thee (39). Self-denial, renunciation—these are the traits Delphia associates with God. Yet this poem also recounts Delphia's own experience of such a paradoxical defiance of love in the name of love, although in her case the act is prompted by human prudence, not divine imperatives. The sea change to which this poem's title refers may thus be read as the shift from sacred to secular rationales for human action, as well as the shift in modern thought, including contemporary eco-theology, from heaven to earth as the locus of human allegiance.

That increasingly earthly religious orientation is evident in part through Byer's greater use of Cherokee mythology in *Black Shawl*. Whereas in *Wildwood Flower* the Native American influence on contemporary Appalachia was reduced to little more than the place names Kanati Fork and Cherokee Gap, in part 3 of *Black Shawl* Byer includes two poems that draw on Cherokee lore: "Wa'ya" (meaning *wolf*) and "Kanátï." Wa'ya was the watchdog of Kanátï the huntsman, who was married to Selu, goddess of maize. What Byer calls "the homefire / of words" (38) burns not only in Latin and Greek but in the many place names and other terms that European Americans, "searching for home in these mountains" (45), as Byer writes, borrowed from Native Americans. But Byer also builds on the religious sensibility of Native American thought, with its reverence for nature and its equanimity in the face of death. Part 4 of "Kanátï" opens with the lines, "Like cairns marking some ancient God's / visitation, these mountains in early spring / promise a way home" (46). That way home inexorably involves an encounter with death, and Delphia closes the poem with the comment: "I hear blood in my ears // drum the oldest / of riddles. The one unto / death demands I // be the answer" (47). The subsequent poem, "Backwater," which Byer calls in her notes to *Black Shawl* "an Appalachian version of the ninth-century Irish poem . . . 'The Hag of Beare'" (53), presents Delphia in old age. Unlike its Irish antecedent (Calder 62–64), Byer's poem omits any direct reference to God and the Son of God, focusing instead on Delphia's consciousness of imminent death, a death imaged in terms of "deep water" carrying her out to sea (49). But Delphia calmly accepts the prospect of death without holding out any apparent hope of resurrection. Gazing toward "that yonder / sea," she concludes the poem with the lines, "Blue nothing / I call it. Calling me" (49).

While *Black Shawl* ends, as noted earlier, with "Síle," returning readers
to the ballad tradition with which the book began and to the community
of female ballad singers across the centuries, the last poem in Delphia's
voice is "Tuckasegee," the only poem transplanted to *Black Shawl* from
the chapbook *Alma*. That poem takes its title from the Tuckasegee River
in western North Carolina, and this text thus extends the water imagery
of "Backwater" and so many of the poems in *Wildwood Flower,* including
that volume's closing poem, "River Bed." In the opening stanza of "Tuckasegee" Byer draws on the conventional association of water with time:
"Wherever I walk in this house / I hear water. Or time. / Which is water
. . ." (50). The fluidity of water and time leads Delphia not only to
thoughts of decay but also to reflections about the interminable cycles
of doing and undoing (or redoing) that constitute women's work: prepar-
ing daily meals and cleaning up afterward, washing clothes that will soon
need washing again, planting and harvesting and replanting, braiding and
unbraiding hair, giving birth and laying out the bodies of the dead. "It
has always been / done, this undoing / ongoing," Delphia observes. Yet
rather than plunging her into despair, this cyclical pattern fails to daunt
Delphia. "Our time is the music / the water makes," she declares, a music
that fills both the mountaineers' traditional ballads and Byer's own poems, the music of mortality.

That music achieves its diapason in Byer's fourth book, *Catching Light*
(2002). Here Byer deals with the experiences of an aging woman whom
she calls both Evelyn and Eve, thus evoking the archetypal mother in
Genesis. The book's three numbered parts are of unequal length, part 1
consisting of the ten-poem sequence "In the Photograph Gallery." Some
of the poems in this sequence and elsewhere in *Catching Light* originally
appeared in Byer's chapbook *Eve* (1998), accompanied by the photographs
of Louanne Watley, whose exhibition entitled "Evelyn" inspired these poems. Watley's photographs were of Betty Bell, a Chapel Hill resident with
a reputation for being rather eccentric. The only photograph by Watley in
Catching Light appears on the book's cover, which depicts Evelyn standing
at a light-filled doorway with her back to the viewer/reader. So intense is
the light that her right hand is raised, apparently to shade her eyes. "In
the Photograph Gallery" traces the approach of Evelyn's death and ends
with her asking, "how does my face look / confronting the light?" (12), a
seemingly unanswerable question that nevertheless invites speculation.

On one level, then, the book's title refers to photography's use of light, but it also suggests the quest for truth, for illumination, especially in terms of the human confrontation with old age and death.

Part 2 extends Byer's treatment of this issue by taking its epigraph from Strauss's opera *Der Rosenkavalier*, lines in which the Marshallin notes the abrupt transition from youth to old age. The speaker in the first poem in this section, "Old," thinks of herself as "Old as creation" (15), a phrase appropriate to the biblical Eve as well, while later poems in part 2 such as "Vanity" and "Eve" allude to that figure directly. But several of the poems rely not on Watley's photographs but on Byer's memories of her grandmother, as she mentions in an interview with Gary Cardin (22). "Her Porch," for example, situates the grandmother in that location, where she would sit on Sundays "rocking the sermon away," distancing herself from the preacher's words, having first "pour[ed] out her hair / from her Sunday hat," a gesture affirming her female identity (23). In "Open Casket" Byer raises the questions provoked for her by her grandmother's death:

> The cotton-
> stuffed silence of death,
> did it last, or would angels begin
>
> to trill louder than katydids,
> the sinking sun burning a hole in the sky
> through which I'd be borne heavenward? (28)

Because Christianity affords consolation in the face of death through its promise of resurrection, mortality is a key issue for Byer, as it was for Stevens in "Sunday Morning," as she seeks a more earth-oriented religious vision than the otherworldly perspective that Christianity has historically represented.

Several poems in part 2, most notably "Music Lessons" and "Aria," juxtapose such this-worldly and otherworldly outlooks. In the former grandchildren gather around the grandmother and sing *The Last Rose of Summer*, with its "faraway garden," meanwhile ignoring the grandmother's "own garden rife with petunias / and blossoming okra plants" in which "honeybees reveled / . . . all afternoon" (22). Busy "rehearsing the old endings" (22), including, by implication, the traditional Christian view of heaven as final destination, the grandchildren overlook the paradisal garden that surrounds them.

Similarly, in "Aria" Byer alludes to Puccini's opera *Tosca*, especially the protagonist's sense of betrayal as death approaches. The poem's epigraph, taken from the opera, reads, "I lived for art, I lived for love. . . . / Why, O Lord, why / Dost thou repay me thus?" (29). The poem's occasion is the poet's listening to Marie Callas sing Tosca's part on an old recording and hearing "time scratching counterpoint / into the art of her voice." The flawed vinyl denotes human limitation, though Byer comments ironically, "*La Divina*, the liner notes call her [Callas], / as if she were deathless" (29). This Italian epithet leads the poet, in the second stanza, to reflect on what she calls "The Goddess herself" who "crooned to us mortals" in creating nature. The poem's last two stanzas indicate that this Goddess's creative work persists:

> Come evening, I'll hear
> her chorus of frogs in the low
> pasture, long after Tosca
> has leapt to her death,
> singing not for the glory of art
> but for earthly awakenings
>
> into another spring.
> Thus does she sometimes repay
> us, her stubborn joy rising
> again out of thawed ground
> like the breath from a diva's
> throat spiraling into bel canto. (29)

The frogs in this passage recall those in "The Devil's Dream" in *Black Shawl* that "sing / some other god's resurrection" (9), though here that god has assumed distinctly female form. As these stanzas demonstrate, it is resurrection in nature, not in an afterlife, that Byer embraces, her musical imagery making such a prospect all the more attractive.

Part 3 of *Catching Light* returns to Evelyn as its dominant voice, although at times her voice all but merges with Byer's own. This final section opens with an epigraph from Louise Bogan's poem "Night." Thus, even though all three parts of this book are untitled, the epigraphs move from "days" and "light" in part 1 through the sudden awareness of old age in part 2 to the "narrowing dark hours" of the lines quoted from "Night" (33). In fact, the first poem in part 3 is entitled "Dark Hour," a title meant, perhaps, to remind readers of the dark night of the soul in St. John of the Cross. If so, Byer's speaker is not about to be intimidated by the encroaching darkness as Night "interrogates" her (35); she refuses to "be bullied, // or spooked, by Night's blank windows" (36). This personified Night, symbolic of death itself, does not induce the speaker to cease her epicurean pursuits. Instead she takes the initiative in confronting those blank windows "shining my ghost faces back at me // when I look straight through / myself into darkness / before I extinguish the lights" (36). The fearlessness of this glance ("straight through / myself into darkness") is characteristic of Byer's female personae.

The following poem, "Wedding," seems to present a different persona, a self-described "old maid" who is eager to escape the church in which this marriage ceremony occurs, an impulse to escape the confines of church also evident in several of Morgan's poems. As the service proceeds, Byer's speaker comments on "the blooming / world's psalmody" (37) outside the church, where "the new leaves / can't stop surging / over the graveyard" (38). She also thinks of God as "grown / hard of hearing," speaks of Judgment Day as "the big send-off," and irreverently imagines God with "his mouth full / of false teeth / and snuff, / his idle hands age-speckled," sitting alone and remote in the heavens (37, 38). While Byer clearly distances herself from this speaker, the God this poem depicts differs sharply from the actively nurturing Goddess of "Aria."

As in "Wedding," images of nature's vitality recur throughout part 3, which at key points invokes the archetypal Garden of Eden in Genesis. In "Wisteria," for instance, the speaker is intoxicated by the fragrance of these flowering vines and refers to "The secret of everything opening / over and over again / every April" (41), a pattern of repetition far more positive than that in "Tuckasegee" in *Black Shawl*. The speaker of "Wisteria" actually uses the image of a black shawl, seeing it as a garment she would slowly unwind and discard to "get on with the real work of dancing / this song to its end," a dance to which "Timberline" invites Delphia in that earlier volume.

The poem's immediately following "Wisteria" capture Evelyn's increasing consciousness of death. "El Día de los Muertos," set on November 2, the Mexican day of the dead, begins with the line, "In Frida's house, it was every day" (42). The death-haunted painter Frida Kahlo, the reader is told, "doted on skeletons." While Byer and her personae are scarcely enamored of death, mortality remains the great challenge to the kind of nature-based religious outlook that Byer espouses. At poem's end the living are left "begging the darkness / that takes us, *Adonde? Adonde?*" (43). Whither? Through Byer's repetition of *Adonde,* the question reverberates; yet it remains unanswered, as do those in the poem titled "Unanswerable" (46).

Catching Light concludes, however, with a half-dozen poems that lighten the book's tone considerably without denying the finality of death. The first of these, "Listen," directs the reader's attention to "This old hymn / of April again" (51). The term "hymn" links April to worship, to sacred rituals, and the light of this day's dawn instills a sense of rebirth, "rousing the birds / to a reveille" that the speaker imagines herself conducting, "wanting words to this music," she says,

> I know have been waiting
> for me all my life
> as if Jesus himself
> might spit onto his fingers
> and, touching my tongue,
> whisper
> *Ephphatha,*
> *Ephphatha!* (51–52)

Byer's note to this poem explains that the closing lines mean "Open, open!" and allude to Jesus's miraculous healing in Mark 7:34 of a man mute from birth (52). But the "as if" Byer employs in this passage makes it clear that nature, not the divine, prompts the speaker's outpouring of speech. This poem is clearly an important one for Byer because she presents a revision of it entitled "I Listen" in her most recent collection, *Coming to Rest* (2006).

The beautifully crafted sestina "Sleepless" further expands the paean to nature in "Listen" by invoking both Evelyn's garden and the Garden of Eden. Byer's careful choice of this poetic form's six repeated terms highlights the positive ("garden," "breath," "light," "wings") while also underscoring the hardships and contradictions that accompany human life ("sweat," "freeze"). "Sweat" is a particularly apt term because it recalls God's declaring to the fallen Adam, "In the sweat of thy face shalt thou eat bread" (Genesis 3:19; King James Version). "Sleepless" allows Byer to contrast Evelyn's sensibility with some of the negative features of the biblical creation story. Whereas for Evelyn "each next breath's a mystery," indeed a blessing, for Eve and her partner in sin consciousness of the act of breathing implicates them in human finitude: "first thing that out of the garden / gate Adam and Eve saw, the cold light // of their own mortality dawning" (57). For this pair, Byer writes, "God's light / seemed thrilling at first" (57)—until it served to expose their disobedience and led to the "hard freeze" of their expulsion from the garden. Although Evelyn herself remembers how her father "could freeze / me with one look, God turning me out of the garden," she is more inclined to be "amazed by the simplest things—light, / for example, or air, the way it's made for wings" (58). Yet she feels the weight of the creation story's tale of exile and its disenchantment of the temporal world, now conjoined with death, in favor of a transcendent, eternal realm. Thus in the sestina's closing tercet Byer writes, "That garden has always been breathing its myth / down my throat, its freezing light making my palms / sweat, my arms heavy with wanting to be wings" (58). In the context of traditional Christian theology, with its pervasive residue of Neoplatonic and Gnostic otherworldliness, Byer considers such a desire for wings misguided.

The following poem, the humorously titled "Eve Sings to the Okra," reflects Byer's vision of life's evanescence, with Eve/Evelyn seeming to taunt the okra blossom for its folly in continuing to bloom. Set in early autumn, this poem compares Evelyn's situation to that of this late-blooming plant. Eve's words to the okra ("nobody promised you September / lasted forever," "Let the wind take you") offer advice that Evelyn herself must heed (59). Byer's closing poem, too, emphasizes departure, and its title, "Open," both echoes Jesus's *Ephphatha* in "Listen" and suggests Evelyn's ultimate embrace of—not just resignation toward—the fact of death. The image of the open door first appears in the book's cover photo and then in the final poem of "In the Photograph Gallery" before reappearing in this book's concluding poem. Rebuking herself for looking back, for pausing at that door, Evelyn strides confidently through it. "*Lightly, / lightly,* I sing to myself," she remarks, the repeated *lightly,* as Byer's notes to *Catching Light* state, quoted from Randall Jarrell's "An English Garden in Austria." Evelyn also speaks of "shutting the door / ever after behind me," lines that can be read as an affirmation of death's finality. Yet the third of this poem's four stanzas appears to leave things more open-ended:

> The door on the other side's open,
> the day blazing through
> and beyond it another way
> into which I might keep going
> or disappear. (61)

The uncertainty that Evelyn expresses here is consistent with the "agnosticism" that Ruether recommends about what she calls "the 'immortal' dimension of our lives" in her chapter on "Eschatology and Feminism" in *Sexism and God-Talk* (258). For women, Ruether argues, the question of personal immortality, survival of the individuated ego, does not have the same urgency as it does for men. Ruether also critiques traditional Christian views of immortality and eschatology by citing Vine Deloria's *God Is Red*, with its Native American perspective on the unity of humanity and nature and its assumption that, in Ruether's words, "God/ess is the great Spirit that animates all things" (250). According to Deloria, the resulting sense of the integrity of the temporal world, of its fundamental interdependence rather than of human separation from nature, produces in Indian tribal religions "people unafraid of death" (180). For Deloria, "American Indian tribal religions certainly appear to be more at home in the . . . world than Christian ideas and Western man's traditional religious concepts" (109), and Byer herself, as we will see, draws heavily on Native American thought in her latest book, *Coming to Rest*.

Unlike Byer's preceding books, *Catching Light* rarely focuses on distinctly Appalachian materials. Nor does it project a strong sense of place or evince much concern for the idea of home, though Evelyn, as noted, does have an intimate relationship with the natural world and feels affection for many of the physical features of her house and yard. But in *Coming to Rest* the term "home" appears in at least twenty of the book's thirty-six poems. What might account for this renewed attention to the idea of home?

Two of the most important factors in this resurgence, I would argue, were the events of September 11, 2001, and the departure for college of the poet's only child, her daughter Corinna, to whom Byer dedicates *Coming to Rest*. That September 11 had a powerful impact on Byer is evident in her chapbook *Wake* (2003), which contains a dozen unpaged poems, five of them responses to the tragic circumstances of that day. The chapbook's title suggests both ritual mourning, a vigil beside the dead, and the need for wakefulness. In its second poem, "Critique," the poet voices her objection to another writer's attempt to provide religious consolation amid the devastating attack on the World Trade Center. "Your image of angels attending the ruins / fails to move me," Byer begins, and in the second of the poem's five sections she asks the perennial question that intrudes after such tragedies: "Where / was He?" "Too busy pouring the wine // for a new round of martyrs? Inspecting the sheen / on his solid gold cobblestones?" she wonders ironically. Rejecting religious consolation, Byer states, "I ask of a poem only this: / Give me dust unto dust." *Wake* is a death-haunted collection. In fact, in "Day after Thanksgiving" she confesses, "*Timor Mortis* . . . / . . . assails me," echoing the refrain of William Dunbar's "Lament for the Makers." Presiding over this chapbook is the Anglo-Saxon figure of fatality Wyrd, who gives the final poem its title. Imaged as one of the classical Fates, "her rusty shears clacking," and as "an old woman . . . casting dice" at a crossroads, this figure pronounces the chapbook's closing words, posing the crucial question, "*Which way?*"

The poems of *Coming to Rest* indicate that Byer's response to that question, at least in part, was to embed herself more deeply in family relationships, in ties based on home and memory and a heightened attachment to nature. At the same time, however, this book shows Byer utilizing the journey motif to explore Native American creation myths and thus leaving home to return enriched by this alternative to the Judeo-Christian tradition. The title of part 1, "Again," announces the collection's emphasis on memory and on the motif of return, both literal and figurative. The epigraph to this section comes from Seamus Heaney's "The Birthplace," lines that give the book its title and that focus the reader's attention on places of origin. Byer's opening poem, "Coastal Plain," refers to "Home that calls // and calls / and calls" (4), and this poem's unusual formal structure—couplets of identical rhyme—mirrors, stanza by stanza, the movement of return. In several of these poems Byer's grandmother is again a prominent figure. In "Hallows" Byer writes, for instance, "When I hear Pavarotti / sing *Panis Angelicus*, I see her hands / deep in the dough bowl" (7). Yet this grandmother bakes earthy cornbread, not the bread of angels, and in the final section of "Hallows" Byer describes the dead, as she did in "All Hallows Eve" of *Wildwood Flower*, as gravitating toward the earth, "this granary," not toward a heavenly afterlife. Here again Byer approvingly uses the phrase "laying up treasures on earth" and says of the dead, "they have nothing / to say beyond what's meant / to lie on the earth and be claimed by it" (8).

The final six poems of part 1 all deal with experiences involving the poet's daughter, experiences that range from infancy to Corinna's twenty-first birthday. The last of these poems, "Chicago Bound," anticipates a reunion to celebrate that birthday. Aloft in a plane, high above the clouds, the poet finds "Nobody at home up here" (21), a pointed reference to God's absence from the heavens of traditional cosmology. More importantly, however, thinking of her daughter waiting below, Byer writes, "if it's down / there on earth where you are, / it's Sweet Home" (22). Even into so seemingly mundane a poem as this one about an airplane trip, Byer injects her recurring thematic preference for the earth, identifying home in this case not with a particular locale but with a network of human relationships.

Part 2 of *Coming to Rest,* "Singing to Salt Woman," recounts a different journey, one closer to the pilgrimage of traditional Christian iconography, although this journey is framed in terms of Native American myth and legend. This sequence of fourteen separately titled poems, along with an untitled envoi, revolves around two substances essential to all life, water and salt, the Cherokee words for which give the first and last of the fourteen poems their titles. In the Cherokee language the two words mirror one another—*A-ma'* (water) and *A'ma* (salt)—and Byer may be using this parallel to suggest the interconnection of all living things, including human beings and nature. As with her work as a whole, so in "Singing to Salt Woman" Byer distances herself from the God of her Presbyterian upbringing, whom she describes as "distant, judgmental, cold" (letter to the author). In "Dreaming through Tennessee," for instance, she observes in the countryside "the same makeshift signs // that I've seen all my life / threaten God's coming back" (27), and in "Dead End in Pueblo, Colorado" the poet asks a deceased friend, "Tell me the truth, if you wanted // to howl with the ghost of some / long-extinct wolf, would He let you?" (31). The God envisioned in such passages is clearly Alma's God of wrath and of prohibitions. Of that deity the poet says, "I'm dreaming God's gone // for good to inhabit / the desert like wind / or like silence at noonday" (27). Perhaps the dead end of the latter poem cited above is the otherworldly theology that Byer repeatedly rejects in favor of what the poem "Black Road" terms "the sermon / of here and now" (29).

Like Deloria, Byer critiques both the exclusivity of Christianity's claims and the chasm it establishes between human beings and the rest of nature. The poet addresses the latter tendency in "Contemplation" when she writes of "the Christian re-vision of this land" which assumes that nature's creatures exist apart from God's plan of salvation because "they have no immortal souls" (32). In "Edge of Plains" she likewise objects to Christian exclusiveness when she refers ironically to "the only true God," in whose honor the Mormons christened the mesa now known as Zion (35). This poem contrasts the Mormons' quest for a "heavenly paradise" with the Anasazi Indians' vision of "earthly / repose" (35).

While Byer's physical journey in this sequence involves departing from and returning home, she also inquires, "what's native now?" (28), a question to which she responds in "Zuni," the central poem in part 2:

> Maybe *native* means nothing
> if not our own way of recovering,
>
> back to the first wind
> that quickened it, what we call
> home. . . . (33)

The legend of Salt Woman mentioned in "Zuni" directs readers to what the poem's closing lines call "a creation story / whose ripples keep spreading / beyond comprehension" (33). Over against the creation story in Genesis, with its account of human dominion over nature and estrangement from God, Byer sets "the earth herself / chanting her way back through time / to the dawn of the first morning" (35). Just as the trajectory of the airplane in "Chicago Bound" is earthward, so the trajectory of Byer's mythopoeic vision in part 2 comes to rest on the images of a linen tablecloth settling over a table and of Alice Mathews (Byer's former colleague at Western Carolina University to whose memory "Singing to Salt Woman" is dedicated) delighting in the sight and smell and taste of raspberries, relishing nature's goodness and the pleasures of the senses.

The title of part 3, "Closer," encourages readers to ask, "Closer to what?" Among many possible answers, two seem especially compelling: closer to death, the ultimate "rest," and closer to home, whether home denotes a particular place or the recovery of one's past or final union with the life force manifest on "the dawn of the first morning." Only two of the poems in part 3 deal overtly with religious concerns, but those poems are given prominence by their placement at the very end of the book. In "Halloween Again" Byer returns to one of her favorite times of the year:

> . . . All Hallows Eve
> when the veil
> between seen
> and unseen trembles
> sheer as silk
> through which
> we might, if
> we come close
> enough, see
> the other side
> waiting for us
> as a mirror waits
> to be filled
> with the bright
> face of forever. (60–61)

These lines move beyond Byer's usual emphasis on this world by positing an "other side" that generally remains unnoticed. According to Byer, the idea that autumn is a time when the boundary between the visible and invisible grows transparent occurs in Celtic mythology, and Byer refers to this season as "the visionary time, the poet's time, the seer's time" (Woloch 61).

The phrase "if / we come close / enough" in "Halloween Again" resonates in the title of the book's final poem, "Closer," the shortest poem in part 3. Here Byer underscores the motif of return by reprising the couplets (though in this case unrhymed) that she used in the book's initial poem, "Coastal Plain"; by repeating that poem's title phrase; and by again including images of travel and homecoming. "Closer" is among this volume's loveliest poems in terms of its tightly woven sound effects and its vivid images in such lines as *"old road dreaming me back home"* and *"maybe souls do flow into and out of the world— / that crow over corn stubble, scythe of light // off the truck's chrome"* (62). The statement *"maybe souls do flow into and out of the world"* is striking, however, given Byer's customary rejection of the dualism of body and soul that characterizes much of Western philosophy and religion. Visitations by the dead, of course, are an important feature of Byer's poetry over the course of her career, from "Ghost Story" in *Girl* and "All Hallows Eve" in *Wildwood Flower* to such poems as "Hallows" and "Los Muertos" in *Coming to Rest*, so Byer may be speaking primarily of memory's capacity to raise the dead. The epigraph to part 3 includes the phrase "the call / and response of memory" (41), and one of the poems in part 3 commends the power of "language [to] raise the world up / from the grave of our common amnesia" (56).

But whatever Byer may intend by her use of the term "souls" in "Closer," the majority of her poems testify to the wonders of this world, especially nature, the body, and human love. In her interview with Cecilia Woloch, the poet states, "We dare to whine about our human state and long for a heavenly home. Well, our home, paradise, is right here, and that is the value above all others that I would wish to base my life and my community upon" (61). Though she is cognizant both of political injustice and the hardships that nature can impose, Byer is ultimately a celebratory poet who realizes, as she comments to Woloch, "how blessed we are to live on this earth" (61). For Byer that blessing is bestowed by the earth itself and by the creative Goddess of "Aria" in *Catching Light*, who sings the way home to "earthly awakenings" (29).

6

CHARLES WRIGHT

"The Energy of Absence"

CHARLES WRIGHT (1935–) IS UNDOUBTEDLY the most widely known poet discussed in this book. *Country Music* (1982), his selected early poems, won the National Book Award, while *Black Zodiac* received both the Pulitzer Prize and the National Book Critics Circle Award for Poetry. Wright has also received the Ruth Lilly Poetry Prize and the Lenore Marshall Poetry Prize, among many other awards. Since 1995 two superb collections of essays and reviews on his poetry have appeared, and in 2008 Robert Denham published an invaluable companion to Wright's later poems (1988–2007). As many of these essays and reviews make clear, Wright's ties to the Appalachian region—and even to the wider South—have often been overlooked or minimized, in part perhaps because Wright lived outside the South from 1957, the year he completed his undergraduate degree at Davidson College, until 1983, when he began teaching at the University of Virginia in Charlottesville. His name did not appear in *The History of Southern Literature* (1985), for example, nor was his work included in the 1998 edition of the Norton anthology *The Literature of the American South*. Moreover, unlike the other poets discussed here, Wright did not tend, early in his career, to identify himself explicitly with Appalachia, as all the other poets examined in this study had done. Yet several of the poems in his second collection, *Hard Freight* (1973), are set in east Tennessee (where he was born and raised) and western North Carolina, including "Dog Creek Mainline," which Wright has described as the pivotal poem in his career (Suarez 45). Subsequent collections return regularly to the landscapes of his childhood, including the Holston River, one of the principal place names in Jeff Daniel Marion's poetry as well. But it was not until the 1998 publication of *Appalachia* that Wright underscored his continuing sense of identification with and indebtedness to the region of his childhood, a regional background that has dramatically shaped at least two of what he labels his three major themes: language, landscape, and the idea of God (*Quarter Notes* 122). To that triad readers should add mortality, for death is certainly among his most prominent subjects.

Wright's interest in landscape is not limited to Appalachian settings, of course, but ranges widely to include, among other places, Italy, where Wright was stationed in Verona from 1959–61 while serving in the U.S. Army Intelligence Corps; California, where he taught from 1966 to 1983; Montana, where his wife's family has land and a cabin; and his backyard in Charlottesville. What helps to connect many of Wright's beloved landscapes is the presence of mountains. In Charlottesville, for instance, the Blue Ridge Mountains are never far from view, and thus Wright's twenty-five-year residence there has strengthened, it seems, his childhood attachment to Appalachia. As for his fondness for the landscapes of Italy, the place where his vocation as a poet began, Wright says, "There was, and is, some strange balance for me between Italy, and Venice especially, and the wilderness of east Tennessee and western North Carolina" (*Half-life* 62). At the same time, as the title of one of the poems in *Appalachia* announces, Wright assumes that "All Landscape Is Abstract and Tends to Repeat Itself," an assumption, as Robert M. West notes, that has tended to diminish, for many readers, Wright's claim to be a distinctively Southern —let alone Appalachian—poet (97–98). For Wright, as the postscript to *Country Music* implies, landscape provides emotional and spiritual satisfactions which are otherwise absent. In that postscript (which also serves as the epigraph to *China Trace* [1977]), Wright quotes T'u Lung as saying, "And so, being unable to find peace within myself, I made use of the external surroundings to calm my spirit, and being unable to find delight within my heart, I borrowed a landscape to please it" (*Country Music* 157). Unlike T'u Lung, however, Wright speaks not of "borrowing" but of "inventing": "My landscapes have always been imaginary, invented and reconstructed" (*Halflife* 181). Those landscapes enable Wright to move from the visible to metaphysical and theological speculation about the "invisible"; yet they clearly reflect the poet's attachment to the physical world, what Wright refers to in one interview as his profound attraction to "the given world out there" (Gardner 99).

Only rarely does Wright focus on an agrarian landscape, however, for unlike the other poets examined in this book, Wright did not grow up on a farm or feel a strong connection to agrarian life. In fact, the words "farm" and "farmhouse" appear in Wright's seventeen full-length collections fewer than ten times, most recently in the opening poem of *Littlefoot* (2007), in which "the farm" is described as "far away," temporally as well as spatially (3). Yet like these other poets, Wright is drawn to the natural world. "Indenture yourself to the land," he advises his son Luke in "Firstborn"; "Surrender yourself, and be glad" (*Country Music* 26). The poet embraces nature both for its physical beauty and for its seeming testimony to spiritual presence, although what he discovers is often only nature's indifference—not evidence of the infinite but sure knowledge of human finitude. Wright's work stands in sharp contrast to Jim Wayne Miller's claim that Appalachian literature is "decidedly worldly, secular, and profane in outlook," for his poetry articulates an intense yearning for spiritual revelation and transcendent meaning, a yearning that typically goes unfulfilled. Asked what he hoped to accomplish with his poetry, Wright responded, "To be saved, but it won't happen" (Mayer 8). To another interviewer he remarked, "All my poems seem to be about the impossibility of salvation" (Clark and McFee 10). Despite so gloomy a prognosis regarding his spiritual dis-ease, Wright has continued to portray himself, throughout his forty-year career, as a religious "pilgrim," yet one impelled more by what he calls "the energy of absence" than by any conviction of God's presence (*Quarter Notes* 173). While he longs for an eternal home on "the other side of the river"—whether the River Jordan or the river of time—his thwarted spiritual quest has instead often led to his immersion in the physical world, what Buddhism calls "the world of the ten thousand things," the title Wright gave to his second trilogy of poems. Yet Wright's luminous imagery and figurative language, along with his frequent personification of nature, repeatedly transfigure the immanent, infusing it with an aura (if not the presence) of the divine in an age of what he calls "postbelief" (*Short History* 35).

Although the oldest (by one year) of the authors treated in this book, Wright has the most postmodern sensibility, especially in his skepticism about religious belief and about the inability of language to adequately reflect what lies outside words. Wright is also, paradoxically, the author among these six writers whose work most clearly bears the impress of the traditional dualism of Western philosophical thought, at least in his diction. Only Chappell, with his references to both "flesh tree" and "tree of spirit," so explicitly embraces the kind of dualistic vision that pervades Wright's poetry, in which the term "soul" appears almost as regularly as "body" and in which "the other side" ("there" vs. "here," eternity vs. time, heaven vs. this world) is mentioned some thirty times (Denham 220). Wright's profound doubts about God's existence notwithstanding, his poems frequently invoke God through prayers and petitions, as Chappell does too, though much less often, and Wright also regularly invokes the Virgin Mary and assorted saints, some of them fictive. Rilke-like, he refers casually to angels, thus naturalizing such spiritual beings, who appear much less often (in some cases, never) in the work of the other poets analyzed here. As Michael McFee was among the first to observe (94–95), Wright is likewise painfully conscious of sin and guilt and the need for redemption, much more so than any of the other poets in this study, as a title like "Peccatology" attests (*Negative Blue* 40). In *Scar Tissue*, for instance, he speaks of "our just meat being ash" (60), and in both *A Short History of the Shadow* and *Littlefoot* he employs Hawthorne's symbolic birthmark to characterize humanity's susceptibility to guilt, loss, and death (*Short History* 18; *Littlefoot* 22, 41).

Wright thus engages in an ongoing dialectic on the idea of God and expresses conflicting spiritual impulses shaped by his formative years in Appalachia, especially his high school years at private schools in western North Carolina. He spent his sophomore year at Sky Valley School, which was situated on two thousand acres of woodland near Hendersonville, not far from Robert Morgan's home. That year the school had an enrollment of just eight pupils "under the evangelical thumb," as Wright has said, "of the daughter of the Episcopal Bishop of South Carolina" (*Quarter Notes* 5). He spent his junior and senior years in Arden at Christ School, another Episcopal institution. Although Wright's religious outlook had already been instilled by his mother before these high school years, it would be hard to overestimate the influential role of the poet's experiences at these schools, especially in reinforcing his love of landscape and what he has called his "negative spirituality" (Gardner 96). As he once stated, "What Mrs. Perry [the director of Sky Valley] inserted into us is that there *is* a possibility of salvation, and I'm still arguing with her" (Clark and McFee 10).

Critics have characterized Wright's resulting theological perspective in varied, often conflicting ways. Henry Hart, for example, refers to Wright's *via mystica,* emphasizing Wright's reading in both Chinese poets of the T'ang Dynasty and Christian mysticism. Denham's *Companion* also cites those influences on Wright, arguing that in Wright's poems the terms "nothing" and "emptiness" are frequently linked to Buddhist thought, to the "*deus absconditus* of *The Cloud of Unknowing,* the abyss of Boehme's *Urgrund,* [and] the spirit of darkness in St. John of the Cross," among other sources (237). Denham sums up Wright's outlook in the phrase "Wright's unsystematic theology of immanence" (230). Peter Stitt, in contrast, writes of the poet's "naturalistic humanism" which "locat[es] the divine principle within nature rather than above it" (236). Floyd Collins similarly finds a "secular mysticism" in Wright's work that depicts "finite yet hauntingly numinous moments" (467). Yet for Bonnie Costello in her essay on Wright's *via negativa,* although "Wright has created a mysticism for the modern mind" (325), his poetry "is not theological or even confidently transcendental," culminating instead in what Costello calls "an eschatological naturalism" (328, 329). According to Costello, "the absolute" to which Wright attests "consumes and absorbs rather than radiates; its agent is death" (329). The title of Lee Upton's essay, "The Doubting Penitent: Charles Wright's Epiphanies of Abandonment," seems best to capture Wright's emotional entanglement in traditional religious belief while also highlighting both the poet's deep-seated skepticism and the visionary dimension of his work.

As previously mentioned, Wright decided to become a poet while serving in the U.S. Army in Italy. There, on the advice of a friend, he took his copy of Ezra Pound's *Selected Poems* to Sirmione on Lake Garda and read Pound's "Blandula, Tenulla, Vagula," which describes this Italian landscape. Pound's title echoes the opening line of Emperor Hadrian's poem addressed to his dying soul, "Animula vagula, blandula" (to which Chappell likewise alludes, as we've seen, at the end of *Spring Garden),* and Pound's poem begins with the line, "What hast thou, O my soul, with paradise?" (13). Pound's speaker chooses an earthly paradise of "terrene delight" over an otherworldly one, thus anticipating the apparent resolution of Wright's own spiritual quest. From Pound, Wright learned to write a highly condensed poetry that is structured associatively, through patterns of imagery and the emotions they invoke, rather than narratively. As with Robert Morgan, it was Pound's *Cathay* that first introduced Wright to Chinese poetry, and Wright shares with fellow east Tennessean Jeff Daniel Marion an affinity for that poetic tradition, which Wright praises as "a poetry of seeing" whose "spiritual strength is in that seeing and in the things of this world they [Chinese poets] look at" (*Quarter Notes* 41)—the "terrine delight," in short, that Pound commends.

As important as Pound's early influence was for Wright, Wright's spiritual pilgrimage and the content of his work are best illuminated by examining his poetry in relationship to such influences as Dante, Emily Dickinson, Wallace Stevens, and T. S. Eliot, along with Chinese poetry and Wright's extensive reading in Christian mysticism and the myriad texts that constitute the Nag Hammadi Library, the last an increasingly prominent source of allusions in Wright's poems. Of the author of *The Waste Land* and *Four Quartets*, for instance, Wright has said, "Eliot has much more to *say* to me than Pound" (Gardner 105). Like Chappell in *Midquest*, Wright is drawn to Eliot's image of "the still, small point of the turning world" (177), what Wright calls in *Buffalo Yoga* (2004) the "essential stillness at the center of things" (59). To reach that point is one major aim of Wright's spiritual journey, for that still point is an image of fulfillment toward which he yearns, though without attaining it. Dante is an even more important influence on Wright, as pervasive throughout Wright's poetry as in Chappell's. While Wright distances himself more from Dante's religious beliefs than Chappell does, Wright affirms a Dantean view of the function of poetry: "The true purpose and result of poetry," he has written, "is a contemplation of the divine and its attendant mysteries" (*Halflife* 5). In shaping his separately published collections into the "trilogies" *Country Music, The World of the Ten Thousand Things* (1990), and *Negative Blue* (2000), Wright drew ("loosely," he concedes) on the structure of Dante's *Commedia* (Di Salvo 42). "His [Dante's] poetry is relevant to me," he has said, "as I would hope to aspire to the condition his poetry lays down for us: spiritual quest and aspiration and attainment" (*Halflife* 124). As Wright told interviewer Morgan Schuldt, poetry "is a matter of 'soul-making,' as John Keats said. . . . It's either Atonement or At Onement, but it is one of them" (77).

Equally crucial in understanding Wright's themes are the examples of Dickinson and Stevens. Of the former Wright has said, "Emily Dickinson is the only writer I've ever read . . . whose work has influenced me at my heart's core" (*Halflife* 54), and he refers to her poem "There's a certain Slant of light" as perhaps "the ur-poem in my unconsciousness" (Gardner 97). For Dickinson that wintry slant of light brings "heavenly hurt" and creates "internal difference, / Where the Meanings are"; it is associated with both despair and death-in-life (36–37). What particularly appeals to Wright in Dickinson's poetry is her wrestling with issues of faith and doubt, "a kind of negative spirituality I have and that I find she had long before me" (Gardner 96). As Dickinson herself writes, "Narcotics cannot still the Tooth / That nibbles at the soul" (124), a statement that epitomizes the burden of Wright's entire oeuvre. Like Dickinson's, Wright's poems record conflicting moments of sensation, observation, and reflection, as one insight gives way to opposing points of view. Those readers impatient with Wright's repeated worrying of the same issues, his refusal to resolve the questions he raises, would do well to recall Dickinson's work and to consider her lifelong exploration of such subjects as the character and existence of God and humanity's relationship to nature. According to Wright, "[Dickinson] believed in the idea of God much more than I do" (Gardner 101); yet both poets seek to reassemble what Wright calls, in commenting on Dickinson's poetry, "the broken ladder to Paradise" (*Quarter Notes* 40).

The example of Stevens, in turn, reinforces that of Pound's "Blandula" by helping to orient Wright's vision of Paradise toward the physical world, an earthly paradise rather than an otherworldly one (the direction in which, as the preceding chapter noted, Byer's poetry also moves). Here Wright's probable ur-text is Stevens's "Sunday Morning," whose speaker insists "There is not any haunt of prophecy, / Nor any old chimera of the grave, / . . . that has endured / As April's green endures" (68). Stevens celebrates and accepts human mortality, naming death "the mother of beauty," and he sees human existence as an "island solitude, unsponsored, free" (70). Wright comes to view himself (and all human beings) as similarly unsponsored in a poem entitled "After Reading T'ao Ch'ing, I Wander Untethered through the Short Grass" (*Negative Blue* 183), a poem that originally appeared in *Appalachia*, a book that aims to reconcile both poet and reader to human finitude. The short grass of the title seems intended to allude to Isaiah's declaration that "All flesh is grass," with the shortness of this grass meant to underscore human transience. "I stand inside the word *here*," the poet announces, the *there* seemingly beyond him as he confronts the knowledge that "When it ends, it ends. What else?" Yet unlike Stevens, who seems comfortable in an exclusively secular world, Wright typically continues to yearn for a vision of the transcendent, the absence of which lends to much of his poetry its characteristic melancholy and elegiac tone. His metaphysical longing is frequently counterbalanced, however, by his recognition that, as Stevens put it, "the greatest poverty is not to live / In a physical world" (325). Yet at the same time, in the dialectical movement that defines his poetry, Wright suffers the distress occasioned by Stevens's insight into the ultimate origin of poetry: "From this the poem springs: that we live in a place / That is not our own, and much more, not ourselves" (383). Wright's sense of exile, of homelessness, is far more intense than Stevens's and prompts the journey, the pilgrimage, that his poetry depicts.

The contours of that pilgrimage have remained quite consistent over the course of Wright's career, as his three trilogies and the four subsequent individual volumes of poems through *Littlefoot* demonstrate. Wright's decision to title the first of those trilogies *Country Music* evinces not only the commitment he feels to rural landscapes and the natural world but also the influence of country music, including Gospel music, on his sense of his quest. In his first collection of essays, *Halflife*, Wright mentions songs such as Merle Travis's "I Am a Pilgrim" and A. P. Carter's "Higher Ground" and "Going Home," with their "God-haunted, salvation-minded" lyrics whose message was "change your life or heaven won't be your home" (53–54). The continuing influence of that musical tradition is particularly evident in *Littlefoot*, as Denham has shown (237), which alludes to or incorporates lyrics from at least nine different ballads, gospel songs, hymns, and other country music tunes. The book concludes, in fact, with a poem in which Wright simply quotes Carter's "Will You Miss Me When I'm Gone." As some of these song titles indicate, Wright's conception of home has always been tinged with a more otherworldly aura than that of Byer or Morgan, Marion or Miller, or even Chappell. Wright has come much more reluctantly, it would seem, to embrace the physical world because he is much less confident than Morgan or Marion or Chappell that nature reveals a divine presence.

Yet like Morgan, for instance, and Emerson before him, Wright has often depicted nature as embodying a language, though he is just as likely to underscore nature's silence, its failure to communicate or the indecipherability of its script. On the one hand, then, he writes of "the page that heaven and earth make," of "the silvery alphabet of the sea," and of "the labials of the sunlight"—images that seem to promise communication, revelation, as does his frequent personification of nature (*World* 27, 80, 84). On the other hand, the poet finds himself confronting "unbroken codes on the sun's wire" and proclaims that "nature, by nature, has no answers, landscape the same" (*World* 195, 208). Such images of nature as language and of the poet's inability to read nature's text recur in brilliant profusion throughout Wright's career, as the following passage from *Littlefoot* helps to illustrate:

> First character of the celestial alphabet, the full moon,
> Is a period, and that is that.
> No language above to aid us,
>   no word to the wise. (12)

Despite such difficulties in interpreting nature, Wright persists in keeping "one eye cocked toward heaven" (*Negative Blue* 147), an orientation evident in the titles of such collections as *The Southern Cross, Black Zodiac,* and *North American Bear,* the last of which became the concluding section of *Negative Blue.* In Wright's poetry skyscapes are one species of landscape, yet at the same time they enable the poet to reflect on the seeming emptiness of heaven and to read in the vastness of space the insignificance of human beings.

By analyzing the overarching structure of Wright's three trilogies, readers can detect both their double movement of ascent and descent and the poet's intention of reconciling himself and others to the apparent finality of death. The first trilogy, *Country Music,* is the one least resigned to human finitude. That volume reprints only five prose poems from Wright's first book, *The Grave of the Right Hand* (1970) but includes almost all the poems from *Hard Freight, Bloodlines* (1975), and *China Trace* (1977). The first of those reprinted prose poems, "Aubade," invokes "Saint Spiridion of Holy Memory," the patron saint of the island of Corfu, who is asked to exit his casket and emerge "from his grove of miracles" (*Country Music* 3).* Memory is a key concept in Wright's work as the poet explores the varied resources of the past, both personal and cultural. Here, at the very beginning of *Country Music,* the poet calls upon a figure from the Western

---

*In the following discussions of the poems within the various titles that compose Wright's three trilogies, *Country Music, The World of the Ten Thousand Things,* and *Negative Blue,* the page numbers are those of the trilogies, not of the individual titles that form them.

religious tradition, thus indicating the spiritual dimension of his quest. Yet the failure of that tradition to offer persuasive consolation is evident in such images and figurative language from *Hard Freight* as that of the clouds as "great piles of oblivion" that "darken whomever they please" (21), of "the stone / That no one will roll away" (20), and of the sky itself as "old empty valise" (36). The poem "Northanger Ridge," set at a Bible camp, is satirical in tone, with the words "nothingness" and "nothing" featured prominently as the poem opens and closes. "The children talk to the nothingness, / Crossrack and wound," the poet declares, while "Salvation again declines, / And sleeps like a skull in the hard ground" (43). The poet's skepticism about salvation is reinforced by the imagery of closed doors in a poem like "Primogeniture" (44). Nevertheless, Wright continues to seek "those few felicitous vowels / Which expiate everything . . ." (25; Wright's ellipsis), and he concludes *Hard Freight* with "Clinchfield Station," a poem of journeying that refers to Dante and that includes the prayer, "Father advise us, sift our sins" (48). Images of descent predominate in this poem, with the poet asserting in its final stanza, "The way back is always into the earth" (48), a statement that might be read as a commitment to the physical world, to the immanent, but that also might be seen as an image of death—though perhaps of death as preliminary to resurrection.

"Easter, 1974," the second poem in *Bloodlines*, offers little hope, however, of such rebirth. "What opens will close, what hungers is what goes half-full," the poet proclaims in the closing line of this brief lyric (*Country Music* 53). In *Bloodlines* Wright does indeed excavate the personal past, delineating some of its bleakest recesses in two complementary twenty-poem sequences, "Tattoos" and "Skins," both accompanied in *Country Music* by notes specifying the situation or incident that occasioned a particular poem. Several of the poems in "Tattoos" deal with religious experiences, including a snake-handling worship service, while nearly half the poems in "Skins," like Chappell's *Midquest*, are organized around images of earth, air, fire, and water. In "Tattoos" each free-verse poem consists of fifteen lines divided into three five-line stanzas (with the exception of the fourteenth poem, in which the middle stanza has just four lines). In "Skins" each poem has fourteen free-verse lines run together in a single stanza. Disjunctive, highly compressed, sometimes outright hermetic, the poems in these sequences are among the most obscure in *Country Music*—and would be even more challenging without Wright's notes.

Neither sequence, however, provides much hope of religious faith. Although the poet speaks of words as "Back stairsteps to God" in the twelfth poem in "Tattoos," that same poem concludes with a reference to "The news that arrives from nowhere: / Angel, omega, silence, silence . . ." (67; Wright's ellipsis), the last two words here indicative, it seems, less of the ineffable than of death's finality. The seventeenth poem in this sequence recounts a recurrent dream in which the poet encounters a figure referred to as "Faceless" (capital *F*), with the poem's speaker pleading, in the final line, "Faceless come back O come back," the urgency of this appeal conveyed by the poet's omission of punctuation (72). That faceless God becomes, in the fourth poem of "Skins," a figure depicted as "Original Dread" who presides over a universe moving toward entropy: "stars drifting into the cold," "washing into oblivion" amid "the indifferent blue" (85). The poet's quest continues nonetheless, as when he inquires, "Where is that grain of sand that Blake saw?"—a grain of sand in which the British visionary glimpsed eternity (88). Hoping to find "the thread that will lead [him] home" in the tenth poem of this sequence (91), the poet concedes in the following poem that the homecoming he envisions is "unworkable," that he must prepare "for the tilt and the blind slide" into nothingness (92). In fact, the fourteenth poem in "Skins" presents traditional religious visions of the afterlife as "alchemy," the phrase Wright assigns to this poem in his notes (102), and the seventeenth poem confirms death's apparent finality by referring to "That milky message of breath on cold mornings," the lesson of human transience, of inevitable disappearance (98).

Whereas the poet had imagined himself climbing, he comes to recognize that his path has been a descent (100), however intense his longing for a place "Where all is a true turning [whether conversion or some other type of transformation], and all is growth" (100). Thus Wright concludes "Skins" with the following passage:

> And what does it come to, Pilgrim,
> This walking to and fro on the earth, knowing
> That nothing changes, or everything;
> And only, to tell it, these sad marks,
> Phrases half-parsed, ellipses and scratches across the dirt?
> It comes to a point. It comes and it goes. (101)

These lines, which echo Job 1:7 in the phrase "walking to and fro on the earth," inaugurate Wright's career-long identification of himself as a pilgrim, with all the religious overtones that term implies. His concern with language and its limitations is also evident here, as is his recurring motif of appearance and disappearance, change and decay. The "point" at which this pilgrimage arrives may prove nothing more than the period that death stamps on each individual life amid the endless cycles of nature's seasonal alterations, seasonal cycles that become one of the major organizational principles in Wright's later books.

China Trace, the concluding volume in *Country Music,* expresses a powerful longing for salvation, yet charts the same attitude toward its unlikelihood that this chapter has already adumbrated. Wright's ambivalence is apparent in the two projected titles for this book that he considered and then rejected: "The Book of Yearning" and "Quotidiana" (*Halflife* 77–78), the former indicative of what Wright calls the collection's "full attempt at transcendence (and failure thereof)" (*Halflife* 29), the latter indicative of Wright's embracing of the physical world and its inexorable extinction of the personal self. Wright considers *China Trace* a single long poem composed of fifty parts, the second word of the title suggesting a path or road so that the book reconfirms his use of the motif of pilgrimage. In fact, of an earlier draft of the book Wright has said that he used the term "pilgrim" in almost every instance where the published version uses "you" (*Halflife* 84). This pilgrimage is not an April journey, however, like that of Chaucer's characters, and it concludes not in spring, the conventional season of rebirth, but in late autumn, the season most appropriate to "things in a fall in a world of fall," as the second poem in *China Trace* puts it (*Country Music* 112). (This postlapsarian outlook is implicit throughout Wright's work: the dust jacket of *Negative Blue,* for instance, presents Giovanni di Paolo's painting titled *The Creation and the Expulsion of Adam and Eve from Paradise.*) According to Wright, his pilgrim undertakes "an attempted ascension" but "ends up stuck in . . . a man-made heaven" because "he only believes what he can see" (*Halflife* 30).

The failures of this pilgrim make irony a major component of *China Trace* and thus of the closing portion of *Country Music.* In "Born Again," for instance, set on a Sunday evening, no spiritual rebirth occurs; instead, the poet directs his remarks to "Nothingness," who is told, "I am the wafer just placed on your tongue, / The transubstantiation of bone and regret" (*Country Music* 136). In "Captain Dog," similarly, Wright presents his pilgrim as "staked / In the shadow of Nothing's hand" (137), while "Stone Canyon Nocturne" opens by positing disbelief, not belief, as the norm: "Ancient of Days, old friend, no one believes you'll come back" (139). This categorical claim seems to implicate the poet as well, who concludes the poem by stating, "Like a bead of clear oil the Healer revolves through the night wind, / Part eye, part tear, unwilling to recognize us" (139).

Despite such assertions, *China Trace* exhibits Wright's characteristic wavering between faith and doubt, between earth and heaven, between what he calls in "Bays Mountain Covenant" "the sky my eye sees and the one that it cannot find" (106). Thus in "Going Home" Wright's pilgrim gives voice to the following prayer: "I ask for a second breath, / Great Wind, where everything's necessary / And everything rises, unburdened and borne away" (146). Oppressed by the radical contingency of human existence, with its downward thrust, the poet envisions a world of permanence and ascent. But unlike the grandmother in Chappell's "Second Wind," Wright's pilgrim achieves little sense of the presence or weight of grace and at best only manages to stand, as in the poem that follows "Going Home," on the verge of revelation, "Waiting for something immense and unspeakable to uncover its face" (147). Rather than reaching—or even successfully imagining—an eternal, celestial home, the pilgrim-poet of *China Trace* conceives of human beings as "slow orphans under the cruel sleep of heaven" (148) and declares, "I live in the one world, the moth and rust in my arms" (142), the final phrase in this quotation echoing Matthew 6:19–20. For Byer, as we've seen, laying up treasures on earth is an act of self-assertion, of freely chosen rebellion against the otherworldliness of the Christian tradition. For Wright, in contrast, such a gesture often seems made by default, the absence of the otherworldly compelling his decision. In fact, so desperate is his pilgrim for an incontrovertible sign of God's presence that in "Clear Night" he cries out, "I want to be bruised by God. / I want to be strung up in a strong light and singled out. / . . . / I want to be entered and picked clean" (152). But this longing goes unfulfilled in the poem's final stanza, which begins with the uncomprehending wind saying "what?" and ends with images of mechanistic cosmic forces like those Dickinson invokes in the closing lines of "Safe in their alabaster chambers" (26; second version). Ironically, then, this clear night—like the traditional dark night of the soul—eventuates in

doubt rather than belief. Although the final poem in *China Trace,* "Him,"
affords a modicum of hope in its own closing line, which speaks of release, lights, and being "lifted and laid clear" (156), the salvific vision it
hymns is undercut by the book as a whole, as Wright has acknowledged.
After the publication of *China Trace* and its incorporation in *Country
Music,* Wright sensed that he had reached a turning point in his poetry.
China Trace, he told an interviewer, "was such a dead-serious book. It's
still one of my two favorite books, . . . but I felt I had to lighten up. That's
when I started doing a longer line" (*Quarter Notes* 158). Whereas most of
the poems collected in *Country Music* are quite short, very few running
longer than two pages and the majority just a single page, the opening
poem in his next book, *The Southern Cross* (1981), ran to eight pages, with
the title poem nearly twice that length. While many of the others were
only a page long, they began to make greater use of what Wright has variously called the "dropped line" or "low rider," a type of lineation that occasionally occurs in his very first book, *The Grave of the Right Hand,* and in
China Trace but that Wright has gradually come to use so extensively that
it has become his trademark—a device that often disguises the uniformity
of his stanzaic patterns in the later books. Of the "low rider" Wright says,
"It is always one line, not two" (*Quarter Notes* 79). Yet as the following example shows, the low rider provides Wright with extraordinary opportunities for irony as well as elaboration, for the unexpected, for incremental
observation:

> I step through the alphabet
> The tree limbs shadow across the grass,
>
> > a dark language
> Of strokes and ideograms
> That spells out a different story than we are used to
> . . . .
> I think it's a happy story,
>
> > and not about us. (*World* 219)

Wright's desire to create a more "conversational line that is imagisti-
cally packed" (*Halflife* 164) eventuated in the poems collected in *Zone
Journals* (1988) and *Xionia* (1990), which he combined with *The Southern
Cross* and *The Other Side of the River* (1984) to form *The World of the Ten
Thousand Things,* a title that conveys Wright's increasing preoccupation

with the things of this world even as he remains tormented by his desire for the transcendent. The Eastern, indeed Buddhist, perspective reflected in Wright's title for this second trilogy should remind readers of his long-standing interest in Chinese poetry of the T'ang Dynasty, about which he has written: "Where our Western movement . . . tends to be upward, the Chinese aim deliberately downward, at the earth, at the landscape and the tactile world and their tenuous place within it. . . . Their sense of the permanence of the world is as strong as our sense of its transience" (*Quarter Notes* 41). Wright's second trilogy tries to come to happier terms with the transience of the self and the absence of God. In "Holy Thursday," for instance, the poet focuses not on the religious significance of that day but on the fact that the sun "doesn't believe in God / And still is absolved" (14). In another poem, Wright comments, "I want to complete my flesh and sit in a quiet corner / Untied from God" (22). Here the word "untied" echoes the poet's confession in "Reunion," "I write poems to un-tie myself, to do penance and disappear / Through the upper right-hand corner of things, to say grace" (*Country Music* 141), images that also reappear at later points in Wright's poetry. Yet the poet remains haunted by seemingly unfulfillable spiritual longing, a longing implicit in the poet's awareness that *untied* is an anagram for *united:*

> There is no sickness of spirit like homesickness
> When what you are sick for
> > has never been seen or heard
> In this world, or even remembered
> > except as a smear of bleached light. (131)

For Wright, unlike Marion and Byer, for instance, the term "home" does not primarily evoke memories of native ground, whether the region of his birth or, as in Byer's case, an adopted landscape. In *China Trace* the poem entitled "Going Home," while it may begin with a vision of physical landscape, of "dirt roads and small towns," concludes with a prayer addressed to the "Great Wind" for a transfigured world (146). The movement of ascent here reflects the poet's longing for a spiritual home of the sort that gospel music envisions. As Wright remarks in *Halflife,* "All the great poets of light . . . can be said to be 'going back.' All of them have the small, indestructible diamond of Neo-Platonism under their skins, . . . the ticket home" (31). In the opening poem of *Black Zodiac,* Wright again offers a petition for assistance in reaching his pilgrimage's goal: "St. John of the Cross, Julian of Norwich, lead me home" (*Negative Blue* 81). Yet elsewhere the poet recognizes that, given the absence of God, this longing for a home beyond the physical world is, in fact, a death wish: "the soul that desires to return *home*, desires its own destruction" (*Negative Blue* 162). Insofar as a temporal home supplants Wright's longed-for eternity, the poet finds himself consigned to oblivion: "One morning I'll leave home and never find my way back" (*Negative Blue* 183). Thus, while the overall thrust of Wright's work, like that of his beloved T'ang poets, is earthward, Wright retains a deep-seated ambivalence about humanity's relationship to the earth that finds him writing as late as *Littlefoot*, "My home isn't here, but I doubt that it's there either" (34). Although that doubt may counteract his earlier spiritual impulse toward the transcendent, his dis-ease remains, an Augustinian restlessness that the poet perceives as cureless because, as Hawthorne said of Melville, he can neither believe nor be comfortable with his disbelief.

In the journal poems reprinted in *World*, which include the forty-one-page "Journal of the Year of the Ox" (at almost the exact center of which Dante appears to the poet), Wright moves more explicitly toward affirmation of the natural world to the exclusion of the supernatural. The broken ladder to Paradise ceases to need repair because the pilgrim's movement is horizontal rather than vertical, although Wright continues to use traditional dualistic terminology as when he writes in "December Journal":

> What is important devolves
>   from the immanence of infinitude
> In whatever our hands touch—
> The other world is here, just under our fingertips. (211)

Or, as he puts it in "May Journal," "Paradise is what we live in / And not a goal to yearn for" (221–22). In the same poem, in striking contrast to the Marion of *Lost & Found*, Wright remarks, "That which was lost has not been found" (222), even though, like Marion, Wright draws on the example of St. Francis in addressing "Sister water, brother fire," whom he petitions to "gentle my way / Across" in *The Other Side of the River* (*World* 89). Yet the very poem in which the poet makes that request concludes with the line, "What gifts there are are all here, in this world" (93), a line made triply emphatic because it stands as a separate stanza, because it consists entirely of monosyllables, and because its ten-syllable length and five stressed syllables recall the iambic pentameter base of so much poetry in English. In a line like this one Wright again reiterates the outlook of the Stevens of "Sunday Morning," as he does near the close of *World* by professing his "Love for the physical world, *a liquid glory,* / Instead of a struck eternity / Painted and paralyzed" (224), a passage in which the italicized phrase is taken from Pound's "Blandula," with its celebration of "terrene delight."

Despite such expressions of allegiance to the natural world, Wright's characteristic uneasiness persists. He continues to waver between commitment to this world and an improbable next. In "A Journal of Southern Rivers," the same poem in which the preceding passage occurs, the poet writes, "We walk with one foot in each world, the isness of everything / Like a rock in each shoe" (224). Like the woman whom Stevens addresses in "Sunday Morning," Wright cannot quite convince himself that an earthly paradise adequately compensates for the utter dissolution that death brings. "This earth is a plenitude," he admits, "but it all twists into the dark, / The not no image can cut / Or color replenish" (158). At those times when Wright seems most strongly influenced by Buddhist thought, that not, that nothingness, becomes "The single spirit that lies at the root of all things," and he infuses his portraits of that negation with religious imagery: "How soon we become the acolytes / Of nothing and nothing's altar redeems us and makes us whole" (225, 226). More often for Wright, however, nothing simply annihilates rather than redeems, making all living things one in their subjection to death, in their mutual evanishment. Moreover, the final poem in *World,* "Last Journal," voices Wright's lingering fear of punishment for choosing this world over the next, a choice Dickinson likewise makes, with comparable anxiety, in a poem such as "Of God we ask one favor." In Wright's words as "Last Journal" opens, "Out of our own mouths we are sentenced, we who put our trust in visible things" (230). "Out of our own mouths we are sentenced," he repeats, in the closing statement of that poem and of the entire second trilogy.

Wright's third trilogy, *Negative Blue,* as its title suggests, once more inclines to skepticism about religious faith. Denham suggests that the title is reminiscent of Stevens's description of the sky in "Sunday Morning" as "this dividing and indifferent blue," the sky from which no voice is heard no matter how exquisite the celestial alphabet (23). *Negative Blue* collects the poems from *Chickamauga* (1995), *Black Zodiac* (1997), and *Appalachia* (1998), along with the chapbook *North American Bear* (1999). The "loosely" Dantean structure of the trilogies means that *Appalachia* is Wright's *Paradiso*, an intention he has acknowledged in interviews. To Martin Caseley, for example, the poet said, "I felt I should write a kind of Paradiso, or half-way house at least. The trouble was that everything the trilogies talked about refuted the idea, much less the actuality of a Paradiso. Besides, I wasn't really capable. So I hit upon the idea, at least to my mind the good idea of an ersatz Book of the Dead" (23). To another interviewer Wright explained, "Appalachia [the region] is the exact opposite of what one might think of as a paradisal place, but growing up in it, I loved it. I tend to think of western North Carolina, eastern Tennessee, southwestern Virginia, that part of Appalachia, as containing heavenly aspects" (Turner). Like *China Trace*, then, *Appalachia* limns the arc of spiritual yearning for ascent, though unlike the former, *Appalachia* does not conclude the trilogy to which it belongs.

Before examining this book in detail, it may be useful to consider briefly the two collections that precede it in *Negative Blue*, for if *Appalachia* is this trilogy's Paradiso, then *Chickamauga* and *Black Zodiac* might be seen as its Inferno and Purgatorio. Paradigmatic of the former—and of Wright's typical stance, I would argue, throughout his work—is the poem entitled "East of the Blue Ridge, Our Tombs Are in the Dove's Throat," a title that situates the poet outside the "paradise" of his native Appalachia and that raises the specter of death in a strikingly surrealistic image. While some readers might link the bird of this title to the dove of the Holy Spirit, thus lending the poem a salvific dimension, the reference to Lorca in the opening lines suggests that Wright associates the dove's throat primarily with the sound of mourning or lament. In the statement by Lorca to which Wright alludes, the Spanish poet says, "Our people cross their arms in prayer, look at the stars, and wait in vain for a sign of salvation" (qtd. in Denham 153). Later in the poem Wright states, "We'd like to disappear into a windfall of light. // But the numbers don't add up." Instead, in the poem's final line, "the earthly splendor roots our names to the ground" (43). Like Chappell, Wright repeatedly draws on the four elements to portray that earthly splendor, as when he itemizes "the colors of paradise, / Dirt-colored water-colored match-flame-and-wind-colored" (*Negative Blue* 6) in contrast to "the indeterminate colors of the divine"

(64). But that earthly paradise is located in the dominion of death, and the only resurrection the poet envisions in "Easter 1989" is seasonal recurrence in nature, not personal immortality. "Belief is a paltry thing and will betray us," contends the poet in this poem (8), or as the title of another poem in *Chickamauga* declares, "There Is No Shelter" (52).

In *Black Zodiac* Wright immediately highlights the religious dimension of his work by titling the book's lengthy opening poem "Apologia Pro Vita Sua," echoing the title of Cardinal Newman's famous autobiography. The poet speaks of being defined by Sundays, the day of the week on which he was born, but also of being dismantled by Sundays (*Negative Blue* 82), perhaps because the Christian Sabbath intensifies his awareness of his loss of God, his knowledge that the song he sings is what he terms "Exile's anthem" (74). Denham notes that as many of Wright's poems are set on Sunday as on the other six days of the week combined (215). In "Apologia" Wright again alludes to Eliot's "still point" (73), but he also emphasizes humanity's "Separation from what heals us" (74) and in the "Envoi" to the poem identifies the word of God as one of the things that "breaks down beneath its own sad weight" (87). That envoi finds Wright concluding, "I'll take as icon and testament / The daytime metaphysics of the natural world" (87), as he turns once more to the visible world while continuing to probe for its ultimate realities, which he later refers to, at least in part, as "the metaquotidian landscape of soft edge and abyss" (140).

That phrase appears in "Disjecta Membra," the closing poem of *Black Zodiac*, which like "Apologia" is composed of three numbered parts. Such symmetry of form is characteristic of Wright, for the poet must impose on the soft edges of the experienced world meaningful shapes. In this volume that impulse is apparent in such paired poems as "Lives of the Saints" and "Lives of the Artists," each of them consisting of five numbered sections, but it is also evident in the three poems that begin with the words "Meditation on" followed by two linked nouns (as in "Meditation on Summer and Shapelessness"). The poet longs to discover that "Deep Measure" (the title of another poem in *Black Zodiac*) "that runnels beneath the bone / . . . and sets our lives to music" (115), a harmony that Chappell and Morgan associate with the Pythagorean concept of the music of the spheres. For Wright, however, as for Stevens, in the absence of the divine that music becomes a product of the human imagination, not a feature of the external world. As the title "Disjecta Membra" [scattered parts] suggests, discord and fragmentation, not harmony and wholeness, typify the world Wright encounters.

Yet Wright never ceases to speak of God, for even when he views God as among the scattered parts, "syllable after syllable, his name asunder" (135), he also senses "God's blue breath" on his skin (134), and he ends both the first and second sections of the poem with prayers addressed to the "Lord." The divine being he envisions, however, does not seem to be the personal God of the Judeo-Christian tradition but rather an impassive Eastern deity who is "not concerned for anything, and has no desire" (135), a deity whom, in the following passage with its intentionally ambiguous phrasing, he yokes to the nothingness from which everything arises and to which it returns:

> Nothing regenerates us, or shapes us again from the dust.
> Nothing whispers our name in the night.
> Still must we praise you, nothing,
>   still must we call to you. (133)

Here God does seem to be linked to the concept of nonbeing as it appears not only in Buddhist thought but also in the negative theology of some Christian mystics, for whom God can be defined only by what God is not. But Wright's subsequent reference to "The cold, coercive touch of nothing" (135), while it personifies this abstraction, also indicates that this nothing may prove little more than a euphemism for death itself. At the end of "Disjecta Membra" the poet embraces, though somewhat tentatively, existence in the natural world (140), and instead of praying, as he has done at the close of the poem's first two sections, he takes his father-in-law's advice to relax, to "do what the clouds do," in the poem's closing words (141). This gnomic imperative is open to multiple interpretations, of course, but certainly among its meanings are the ideas of drifting along as the wind directs, of changing shape, and of dissipating. Dissolving into nothing is the measure of human movement in nature's processes.

To reconcile himself and others to that motion is one of the major functions of *Appalachia* and particularly of those poems that constitute or refer to what Wright calls "The Appalachian Book of the Dead." As a separately published book *Appalachia* was divided into three numbered sections of fifteen poems each, a structure reinforced by Wright's concluding each section with a poem entitled "Opus Posthumous," as if to underscore the collection's concern with mortality and the possibility of life after death. Wright's first poem titled "The Appalachian Book of the Dead" appeared in *Black Zodiac*, where its autumn landscape represents impending departure "Under the endlessness of heaven." "Such skeletal altars, such vacant sanctuary," the poet adds, although he also compares the stillness of the season to that of "the passageways of Paradise" (99). In creating his third trilogy, Wright placed this initial entry from the Appalachian Book of the Dead at the virtual center of *Negative Blue*. Unlike its predecessors, the Egyptian Book of the Dead and the Tibetan Book of the Dead, Wright's fictive volume serves less as a guide to the afterlife than as a consolatory text meant, "in part, to ease an exit" (186). *Appalachia* included five additional poems titled "The Appalachian Book of the Dead" and cited that title in four other poems offering comments on that imaginary book's purpose.

Despite the title *Appalachia*, readers expecting detailed descriptions of distinctively Appalachian settings are likely to be disappointed. Wright's landscapes omit the log cabins and hollers, the laurel slicks and mountain balds of regional stereotypes. His eyes turn instead toward more generic features of the natural world—clouds, rivers, trees, assorted birds and animals, the cycle of the seasons. Some of the poems are set in Italy, some in Montana, and some in the poet's backyard in Charlottesville, near the "dwarf orchard" that has become a major fixture of his poems since 1983, for that orchard is "God's crucible" (*Negative Blue* 149). As its name indicates, it may also be seen as Wright's modest relic of Eden, a version of Robert Frost's "diminished thing" in "The Oven Bird." Wright's backyard is the symbolic and thematic equivalent of Chappell's garden in *Spring Garden*, a crucial site of the poets' engagement with both nature and the divine.

Wright's interest in landscape and his ambivalence about it are emphasized in this volume's very first poem. "A love of landscape's a true affection for regret, I've found," the poet writes, "Forever joined, forever apart, outside us yet ourselves" (145). Enamored of the beauty of landscape, the poet nevertheless recognizes his estrangement from the natural world. In addition, as we have seen, it is often the *meta*physical landscape that engages Wright: "the secret landscape behind the landscape we look at here," a realm in which, he says, "We haven't a clue as to what counts" (150). That cluelessness leads Wright to question the revelatory power of nature, a power that is axiomatic for Emerson and many other Romantic poets. And it is not only the temporal landscape that eludes articulation; the same holds true of the secret landscape, "eternal and divine" (163), that presumably underlies the temporal world, as Wright confronts the "Indifferent silence of heaven, / Indifferent silence of the world" (162), with "God wandering aimlessly elsewhere" (165). Yet the poet's response to that silence is not to fall silent himself. Rather, in the first of the Appalachian Book of the Dead poems included in *Appalachia*, he voices one of the most intense spiritual longings of the Judeo-Christian tradition—a yearning, Wright's imagery implies, endorsed by nature itself: "Jerusalem, I say quietly, Jerusalem, / The altar of evening starting to spread its black cloth / In the eastern apse of things" (162). Such terms as "altar" and "apse," applied to elements of the landscape, enable Wright to suffuse nature with a religious dimension even amid his insistence that "everything works to our disregard" (153). That verbal strategy is utilized repeatedly in Wright's poems.

While the word "God" appears more often in *Appalachia* than in either of the preceding volumes incorporated in *Negative Blue*, God's presence is not a given, as the phrase "God wandering aimlessly elsewhere" indicates. In fact, in *Appalachia*'s opening poem, the poet assumes God's absence when he writes, "if God were still around, he'd swallow our sighs in his nothingness" (145). It is "the sure accumulation of all that's not revealed" (145) that troubles the poet in this poem even as he acknowledges that "God is the fire my feet are held to" (156), a striking single-stanza line whose power is reinforced by its use of iambic tetrameter with an initial trochaic foot. *Appalachia* begins in winter, in February, and its opening poems have a subdued tone appropriate to that season, an uncertainty of purpose or direction evident in their use of the phrase "Stray Paragraphs"—not lines or stanzas—in their titles. Yet the poet's stance, as so often in Wright's work, is one of expectancy, of hoped-for revelation, even as he concedes the unlikelihood of any epiphany. In "Star Turn," for instance, he echoes—and qualifies—Emerson's praise of the stars in the opening chapter of "Nature" by stating, "Nightly they give us their dumb show, nightly they flash us / Their message and melody," though that message and melody (portrayed, tellingly, as *dumb* show, hence mute) are also described as "frost-sealed" and thus scarcely comforting (148).

The poems that precede the first "Opus Posthumous" poem move from February to early September, and thus to the verge of fall, "set to set foot on the other side," Wright notes, in that initial "Opus Posthumous," which is also the first poem in *Appalachia* to use that place name (159). By the time readers reach this poem, Wright has heightened their awareness of both human finitude and humanity's ignorance of what lies beyond the grave. Given the fact of mortality, "what's the body to do, caught in its web of spidered flesh?" he asks in "Venetian Dog" (153), a poem that concludes with the image of St. Lawrence on a bed of burning coals lifting his arm in supplication to the heavens. Elsewhere in the opening third of *Appalachia* Wright raises another of the many questions that fill his poems, reinforcing their interrogatory nature: "who knows where the soul goes, / Up or down, after the light switch is turned off, who knows?" (158). Although the image of the light switch tends to subvert the gravity of the soul's plight, the cumulative effect of these early poems in *Appalachia* is to revitalize the basic philosophical and theological issues pervading Western thought.

Wright's skepticism about traditional religious belief precludes his offering any definitive answers to the questions he poses, but he persists in asking those questions and thereby reminds his readers of the possibility of belief. At times, he appears to go even further, as when he refers, in "The Writing Life," to "Restitution of the divine in a secular circumstance— / Page 10, The Appalachian Book of the Dead, the dog-eared one" (165). "The Writing Life" is set in December, the month of God's incarnation in Christian theology, but the winter landscape Wright describes does not lend itself to any epiphany: "Short days. Short days. Dark soon the light overtakes. Stump of a hand" (165). The inverted syntax of the one independent clause in this line makes that statement all the more prominent, while the terse fragments and the brutal closing image suggest broken (and broken off) lives. "Stump of a hand" also stands alone as a low rider in Wright's structuring of the poem, thus intensifying the impact of that image, which may mirror the poet's sense of his own diminished powers. But that final image is just as likely to derive from Wright's precursor Dickinson, who says in one of her poems:

> Those—dying then,
> Knew where they went—
> They went to God's Right Hand—
> That Hand is amputated now
> And God cannot be found— (298)

Restitution of the divine is clearly no easy matter in the world of either Dickinson or Wright, both of them poets of religious doubt who return again and again to what might be called the problematics of faith. Dickinson goes on, in the second stanza of her two-stanza poem, to lament the "abdication of Belief" and to state her preference for "an ignis fatuus" rather than "no illume at all." More often, though, like Wright, Dickinson elects to tell what she perceives to be the truth, however harsh, rather than offer an illusory consolation.

At the center of *Appalachia* Wright places "Giorgio Morandi and the Talking Eternity Blues," a title whose playfulness lightens the tone of this meditation, as Wright's titles of the 1990s and beyond, under the influence of Stevens, frequently do. This poem, according to its second line, is "The entry of Giorgio Morandi in The Appalachian Book of the Dead" (167), an entry that consists of a photograph of Morandi contemplating four objects, a photograph that has itself become an iconic object for Wright, referred to as "the ur-photograph" in the opening poem of *A Short History of the Shadow* (2002), the collection that followed *Negative Blue*. Morandi, along with Cézanne and Mondrian, is one of the visual artists whose work has become a touchstone for Wright, with one of Morandi's drawings appearing on the cover of *Country Music*. In "Talking Eternity Blues" Morandi embodies a Hardy-esque stoicism, a figure "oddly comforted by the lack of comforting": "Landscape subsumed, language subsumed, the shadow of God / Liquid and indistinguishable" (167). These closing lines reiterate Wright's major themes, just as his title foregrounds talk of eternity no matter how painful or disappointing (blues-inducing) such talk may prove. In this poem, in fact, "Eternity's comfortless, a rock and a hard ground," the poet proclaims (167). Yet in "The Appalachian Book of the Dead III," Wright glimpses, among the "Hieroglyphs on the lawn" and the "Egyptology in the wind," a light "mind-of-Godish" and states:

Surely some splendor's set to come forth,
Some last equation solved, declued and reclarified.
South wind and a long shine, a small-time paradiso . . . (173; Wright's ellipsis)

While the unusual adjective "mind-of-Godish" and the term "small-time" tend to diminish the potential impact of this imminent revelation, the radiance Wright anticipates here is linked, in "Ostinato and Drone," to "the bush on fire," both a particular quince bush and the burning bush from which God spoke to Moses (169). But that divine voice, which Wright hopes to find immanent in nature, is often either inaudible or untranslatable. And it is the difficulty, if not the impossibility, of progressing from this sensation of the sublime to an affirmation of the existence of the divine that leads the poet, in the following poem, to wonder, "What mask is the mask behind the mask / The language wears and the landscape wears" (170). The infinite regress that awaits all such queries is implicit not only in this poem's allusion to Borges but also in its very title: "It's Turtles All the Way Down."

Such doubts notwithstanding, "Opus Posthumous II" offers a visionary moment, for after asserting that "There is no acquittal, there is no body of light," "No pardon, no nourishment," this poem ends with a stanza that opens with the Latin phrase from Aquinas quoted twice in Pound's Canto 90—*Ubi amor, ibi oculus* (where there is love, there is vision). That stanza concludes with an ecstatic outburst: "the gates of the arborvitae / The gates of mercy look O look they feed from my mouth" (174). The absence of punctuation in this final line mirrors the poet's heightened emotion, as the physical (the arborvitae, whose name also recalls Eden's Tree of Life) and the spiritual (the gates of mercy, a phrase that recurs in Wright's subsequent books) are fused to the benefit of the "starvelings" first mentioned in line 8 of the poem. The final stanza thus transforms the poem's earlier denial of nourishment into an image of succor, a moment of grace.

The final third of *Appalachia* contains three additional poems titled "The Appalachian Book of the Dead" and two others that refer to that volume. Although this section of the book uses the word "God" less often, it does include several explicit references to Christianity, including such terms as "Eastertime," "Good Friday," and "The Holy Ghost," as well as an allusion to Jesus in "The Appalachian Book of the Dead IV" in the line "*there's a man there that's walking on the water*" (177). In that poem, set in April, the Chaucerian month of pilgrimages and the month in which Easter ordinarily falls, Wright presents a traditional Christian perspective on the transition to the afterlife—but largely to distance himself from such belief. Quoting lines from Mac Wiseman's gospel song "Let's All Go Down to the River," Wright responds to them by saying:

They'll have to sing louder than that.

They'll have to dig deeper into the earbone

> For this one to get across.
> They'll have to whisper a lot about the radiant body. (177)

That radiant body is the transfigured post-resurrection body, but the poet finds himself far from believing in "That dry-shod, over-the-water walk" through which such a body arises (177). Nevertheless, the "Rumor of luminous bodies" persists in a subsequent poem, one of the two that refer to the Appalachian Book of the Dead without using that book as their title. Calm and reassuring in tone, straightforward in its diction, that poem closes with an account of the children's game Red Rover, Red Rover, with its cry of release "let Billy come over" (179), a situation reminiscent of Eliot's scene of children at play in the final lines of "Burnt Norton" (Eliot 181).

"The Appalachian Book of the Dead V" likewise offers quiet assurance about the process of "crossing over," although the comfort it provides may be little more than the certainty of dissolution:

> When your answers have satisfied the forty-two gods,
> When your heart's in balance with the weight of a feather,
> When your soul is released like a sibyl from its cage,
> Like a wind you'll cross over,
>   not knowing how, not knowing where,
> Remembering nothing, unhappening, hand and foot. (181)

Wright's use of anaphora here suggests the orderly progress of the soul into the afterlife, however ignorant the soul remains of its ultimate fate. This poem's reference to the forty-two gods and the feather on the balance scales is Wright's most explicit allusion to the Egyptian Book of the Dead, which, like Christianity, anticipates a time of judgment. The potential threat of such judgment darkens the mood of the poem's closing line, in which the poet announces, "And here's the Overseer, blue, and O he is blue . . ." (181; Wright's ellipsis). No bland Emersonian Oversoul, this Overseer, as the epithet indicates, is as much taskmaster as loving deity, a divinity who perhaps overlooks (that is, ignores) humanity rather than oversees us, an interpretation consistent with the third trilogy's title, *Negative Blue*. In any case, this poem's final stanza reemphasizes mutability ("The landscape's a flash and fall") more than permanence.

The principal function, then, of the Appalachian Book of the Dead is not to give guidance about the afterlife but to prepare the reader for death itself, its inexorable arrival, its probable finality. Yet Wright also continues to seek light amid death's darkness, to keep his eyes "on the turning stars," those emblems of eternity for Dante and Chappell (184). It is toward those stars that Wright directs the reader's gaze in the seven poems that comprise *North American Bear*, which serves as a coda to *Appalachia* and the other two volumes preceding it in *Negative Blue*. As Robert West was the first to observe, the word "God" never appears in this section of the book, in sharp contrast to *Appalachia* and *Black Zodiac* (101), nor do readers find the poet praying or offering petitions to the divine. The physical and metaphysical orientation of these poems, however, is clearly heavenward, toward the "blurred star chart in the black light" as the poet notes in the evocatively titled "Step-Children of Paradise" (193). "We live our lives like stars, unconstellated stars" Wright declares in that poem, "ungathered, uncalled upon" (193), images that convey fragmentation, not wholeness, separation from the divine, not God's presence. In another of these poems Wright invokes Tu Fu's image of himself "Drifting, drifting, a single gull between sky and earth" (195), an image comparable to that of the clouds with which Wright concludes *Black Zodiac*. The title poem of this sequence opens with the words "Early November in the soul," thus paraphrasing Melville's Ishmael in the opening chapter of *Moby-Dick*. Just as Ishmael assumes that "Meditation and water are wedded forever," so Wright seems to assume that meditation and the stars are inextricably conjoined, for he speaks of "Heaven remaining my neighborhood" (198).

But it is in the final poem of *North American Bear*, a poem titled "Sky Diving," that Wright most explicitly addresses the spiritual aim of his quest:

I've talked about one thing for thirty [now forty] years,

and said it time and again,

. . . .

I mean the still, small point at the point where all things meet;
I mean the form that moves the sun and the other stars. (201)

The second of these lines again echoes Eliot, while the last line parallels the final line of Dante's *Commedia* (although Wright replaces Dante's term "love" with the word "form"). Chappell also incorporates Dante's line in the final poem of *Midquest*, a text in which spiritual desire achieves greater fulfillment than in Wright's work, for Wright's very next line adds self-deflatingly, "What a sidereal jones we have!" (201). The slang term in this passage undercuts the solemnity of the preceding statement of purpose, and yet Wright goes on to say, "Immensity fills us," one translation of Giuseppe Ungaretti's epigrammatic "Mattino" (*M'illumino / d'immenso*), a poem to which Wright also alludes in section 33 of *Littlefoot* and about which he has stated that it "says about all there is to say on the subject of epiphanic discovery" (*Quarter Notes* 33). That immensity continues to intrigue and perplex Wright, as the four collections that have followed *Negative Blue* amply illustrate.

While the scope of this study precludes detailed examination of those four books—*A Short History of the Shadow* (2002), *Buffalo Yoga* (2004), *Scar Tissue* (2006), and *Littlefoot* (2007)—they extend Wright's exploration of the polarities that have shaped his entire career, particularly those involving body and soul, immanence and transcendence, the visible and the invisible, the temporal and the eternal, presence and absence, belief and disbelief, life and death. Denham refers to these volumes collectively as Wright's "fourth trilogy and its coda" (134), but the poet has not yet combined these collections into a single volume as he did with his preceding books. Unlike *North American Bear*, these volumes again utilize prayer and petition to invoke the divine, though at times those prayers have attenuated to such an appeal as "O Something, be with me, time is short" (*Short History* 28). Here Something clearly seems preferable to Nothing, although when the same poem states that "something is calling us, something not unlike unbeing," the boundary between something and nothing blurs. The poet's anxiety about mortality is evident in the multifaceted symbol of the shadow, suggestive of time and death, of materiality, of the body itself ("the shadow of flesh," as one poem puts it), and of Platonic and Neoplatonic conceptions of this world as a mere shadow of the realm of Ideal Forms. Yet because possessing a shadow, seeing one's shadow, means that one is still alive, however tenuously, the image can have positive connotations, too. In *A Short History of the Shadow*, Wright acknowledges his "thirst for the divine" in a poem tellingly entitled "Lost Language," a thirst that remains largely unassuaged to judge by that title and such others as "On Heaven Considered as What Will Cover Us and Stony Comforter" (a title that echoes Stevens's "Of Heaven Considered as a Tomb") and "If This Is Where God's At, Why Is That Fish Dead?" Wright's skyward gaze is greeted by the "wordless, encrypted blue" (60), and his observation of the natural world leads him to label it "the underworld" in the book's title poem and elsewhere (38, 74), both because it is a realm of death and because it stands apart from "the things of the other side" for which he still longs despite "the daily paradise" he inhabits (40). Like Whitman before him, Wright often seems to contradict himself as he oscillates between the polarities that configure his poems. Thus, the physical world is both "the underworld" and "the daily paradise," and the claim that "The visible carries all the invisible on its back" (38) is later qualified, if not negated, by Wright's reference to "The thing invisible brought to naught" (43). In "Charlottesville Nocturne," however, Wright portrays himself as "Leaning against the invisible" (17), a phrase he uses twice and that itself derives from Dickinson's image of herself as "leaning against the sun." For Wright, paradoxically, in contrast to Dickinson, "Sunlight darkens the earth," for its rays cast shadows (17). Twice in this collection Wright again refers to the Gates of Mercy, in one instance simply to use that phrase in a sentence fragment as an example of "Words stuttered by hand" (19). In the other instance Wright addresses those Gates, pleading with them to "stop breaking down" (65) in a world where "everything nudges our lives toward the coming ash" (64). Wright's inability to affirm religious faith manifests itself again when he confesses, "It is a kind of believing without belief that we believe in" (50). All the same, the title of the fifth and final section of this book, "Body and Soul," returns readers to one of the fundamental dichotomies that has shaped religious thought, and in the first of the poems with that title Wright professes his continuing conviction that "language [can] lead us inexplicably to grace" (71).

That conviction is sharply qualified in Wright's next book, *Buffalo Yoga*, a title whose paired terms combine the physical and the spiritual as well as Western and Eastern experience. Wright links this book with *A Short History* when he asks in its title poem, "Who thought that words were salvation?"—a question clearly aimed at the poet himself and a question to which he responds decisively, if indirectly, in the low rider appended to it: "We drift like water" (15). This lengthy title poem, occasioned in part by the early death of Wright's former student and fellow poet Tom Andrews, is marked by Wright's pervasive consciousness of mortality. In its final section, however, Wright also speaks of what he calls "The formalist implications of the afterlife" that necessitate "a black voyage / To rediscover our names, / Our real names, imperishably inscribed in the registry of light" (22). The diction of this final section presents the physical world itself as a text far more accessible to interpretation or translation than Wright typically assumes. The "radiant lettering" of "afternoon's alphabet" (22) helps prepare the reader for Wright's embracing, in "Buffalo Yoga Codas," of that physical world, "the luminous, transubstantiated world, / That holds me like nothing in its look" (27). In a pattern of repetition highly unusual in Wright's work, the poet repeats the entire stanza in which these words appear at the end of both the first and the third of these three codas. The adjective "transubstantiated" clearly implies the presence of the divine within this world just as the word "luminous" indicates that here Wright experiences one of those epiphanic moments of "splendor" that he ardently seeks. But the ambiguous phrasing "That holds me *like nothing* in its look" adds an unsettling element, for if Wright means that he is literally held as strongly by the prospect of nothing as he is by the prospect of this luminous world, then he will remain haunted by human finitude and by absence, as he is when he depicts the soul itself as a divided entity: "The lonely half looks up at the sky, / The other stares at the dirt," a dirt symbolizing both the earth that sustains life and the grave that terminates it (18). As the poet succinctly notes in the final "proem" to *Buffalo Yoga*, "A minute of splendor is a minute of ash" (6).

Wright's ongoing argument with and about God—to whom he refers at least twice in this book as "the light that shines without shadow" (39)—reaches a climax in "Dio Ed Io," God and I. Set on a Sunday, appropriately, this poem opens with the line, "There is a heaviness between us" (50). "There is a disappearance between us as heavy as dirt," the poet adds in the second stanza, while the final stanza of eight begins: "Such heaviness. The world has come and lies between us. / . . . / Unbearable absence of being" (50, 51). Although the Italian *Io* is contained within the word *Dio*, Wright's poem emphasizes the separation between self and God, a gulf his pilgrimage, it would seem, cannot bridge. Yet Wright finds a remarkable array of images for this fugitive or often absent God. One of the pleasures of reading Wright's poetry arises from the vividness of his description and the sheer inventiveness and evocative power of his figurative language, as when he writes: "God's ghost taps once on the world's window, then taps again / And drags his chains through the evergreens" (9). Implicit in this image is both the death of God (now become a ghost) and the persistence of the idea of God, which survives that death but in a diminished state. Another such example occurs in "La Dolceamara [bittersweet] Vita," in which Wright hears "church chimes like empty villages, ruin-riddled, far away, / Where nobody goes" (67), an image of vacancy and absence that stands in striking contrast to the church bells in Chappell's *Midquest* with their repeated call *home home home home.*

When Wright thinks of home in *Buffalo Yoga*, he presents it both literally and figuratively; it is both his house on Locust Avenue in Charlottesville and the celestial home of gospel songs, country music, and hymnody, although that heavenly home is often displaced by thoughts of the utter oblivion that death brings. In the humorously titled "Charles Wright and the 940 Locust Avenue Heraclitean Rhythm Band," for instance, Wright quotes the line *"I'm on my way back home"* from Roy Acuff's "Streamlined Cannonball," but given the reference to Heraclitus in the title, it is temporality, not eternity, that preoccupies the poet here, an assumption seemingly confirmed by the fifth stanza's lines about the stars, a conventional image of eternity:

> The stars have opened their bottomless throats, and started their songs.
> They are not singing to us,
> It turns out, they are not singing their watery songs to us. (55)

The music of these spheres is what Stevens would call "inhuman." Wright's allusion to Prufrock's mermaids (Denham 178) should remind readers of another abortive journey ("Let us go then, you and I," says Prufrock, in Eliot's opening line) and another failed pilgrim.

That Wright hungers for much more than 940 Locust Avenue is evident in the title "Little Apokatastasis," one of the three poems that serve as "Postscripts" in the final section of *Buffalo Yoga*. The Greek theological term in this poem's title refers to the gathering together of all living creatures in an act of universal salvation, but it can also suggest restoration to one's original condition, a return or homecoming. The apokatastasis in Wright's poem is "little" both in the brevity of the poem (just four lines long) and in the nature of its homecoming (residents of Charlottesville returning from work). But the poem's final phrase, "everyone coming home," evokes this theological concept's inclusiveness and attests to Wright's deep-seated yearning for divine welcome, a welcome that his reference to "the lost highway" seems to preclude (73). Instead of such an image of arrival or restoration, which presumes a metaphysical desti-

nation and/or point of origin, Wright speaks in "Sinology" of "This float-
ing life, no anchor at either end" (70), an image similar to the notion
of being "untethered" that he advances in one of the Chinese-inspired
poems in *Negative Blue* (183). But that Chinese influence proves empow-
ering in the final poem of *Buffalo Yoga*, "In Praise of Han Shan," a poem
in which Wright celebrates the T'ang poet also known as Cold Mountain
because of his identification with the landscape he inhabited. After the
poet's death, his writing remained, his only immortality and "Nothing's
undoing" (76). Wright hopes for a comparable immortality and a comparable sense of oneness with the landscapes he so vividly depicts, but as his
trilogies and more recent books reveal, he also continues to long for the
consolations—mercy, forgiveness, eternal life—of the Judeo-Christian
tradition in which he was raised even as he labels himself, in his interview with Turner, "a God-fearing non-believer."

That longing is present again in *Scar Tissue*, with its three untitled
parts, the first and third each consisting of twenty shorter poems and the
middle section composed of two lengthier poems bearing the book's title.
In the first of those title poems Wright admits that "There is a desperation
for unknown things, a thirst / For endlessness that snakes through our
bones" (38), lines in which the noun "desperation" and the verb "snakes"
call into question the appropriateness of such yearnings. Yet Wright's desire to live wholly within the confines of the physical world founders, in
this book as elsewhere, upon his recognition of nature's indifference to
humanity. In "Inland Sea," for instance, with its wasteland imagery and
its evocation of Matthew Arnold's retreating "sea of faith" in "Dover
Beach," Wright states, "The constellations ignore our moans, / . . . / No
cries of holy, holy, holy" (5). "The world is a desolate garden," he writes
in another poem (14), an image that starkly contrasts with the lush gardens in Chappell's and Marion's poems. While at times, as in "High Country Canticle," Wright experiences ecstatic moments when "Everything's
benediction, bright wingrush of grace" (8), he generally concedes, as in
"Wrong Notes," that human beings err if they assume that nature's music
is playing their song (27–28). Although enlightenment is possible, suggests "Saturday Morning Satori," the insight attained may be grim. "We're
Nature's nobodies," not the Rapture's child, says the poet in "Matins,"
"children of the underlife," though only temporarily, he adds in "Vespers"
(56, 59). The latter poem opens by quoting the twelfth-century mystic

Hildegard of Bingen, whose words attest to the longing for "*the fiery life of divine substance.*" In this case the poet resists the impulse toward transcendence, instead noting that "The world in its rags and ghostly raiment calls to us" and at poem's end accepting the reduced circumstances that the temporal world, with its rags, represents.

Wright's alignment with this world rather than a hoped-for next is also highlighted in "A Short History of My Life," which centers upon the motif of birth and rebirth. Contrasting the birth of Lao-tzu, reputedly of divine origin, with his own "untouched by the heavens" (11), Wright speaks of two experiences of rebirth: the first into his poetic vocation in Italy in 1959, the second forty-five years later in a spring landscape, a secular conversion into the "Nowhere but here, my one and only, nowhere but here" (12). "The world in its dark grace," the poet concludes, "I have tried to record it" (12). In later poems in *Scar Tissue*, however, poems such as "The Narrow Road to the Distant City" and "Pilgrim's Progress," juxtaposed on facing pages, Wright returns to the motif of pilgrimage. The former addresses the Lord, to whom Wright had also "whisper[ed]" earlier in *Scar Tissue* despite "knowing he's not around"—a claim made more emphatic by its placement in a low rider following the poet's question, "Are you there, Lord?" (16). The latter poem testifies not to progress but to regress, to the poet's recognition that the distant city, Wright's version of Augustine's city of God, is unattainable. The poem's final stanza reads:

> In the end, of course, one's a small dog
> At night on the front porch,
> > barking into the darkness
> At what he can't see, but smells, somehow, and is suspicious of.
> Barking, poor thing, and barking,
> With no one at home to call him in,
> > with no one to turn the light on. (61)

For Wright, this heavenly home is unhaunted, however haunting, a site of darkness rather than light. Wright's use of final prepositions in these sentences is one of his characteristic devices to lend his poetry a conversational tone, a colloquialism that invites readers into the philosophical and theological speculation which the poems enact.

If what Wright calls in *Buffalo Yoga* "the radiant root of all things" is to be found (63), it will be amid what the title of the poem that follows

"Pilgrim's Progress" calls "Little Landscape," a title reminiscent of the earlier book's "Little Apocalypse" and "Little Apokatastasis." The revelation that this little landscape with its iconic heron brings "is just is, just is," the poem's final phrase, which points to the mystery and wonder of being itself (*Scar Tissue* 62). Earlier in this poem the poet inquires which way he should go, but the closing phrase focuses his attention on the here and now, not the remote celestial city. As Wright remarks in one of the interviews reprinted in *Quarter Notes:* "What we have, and all we will have, is here in the earthly paradise. How to wring music from it, how to squeeze the light out of it, is, as it has always been, the only true question" (120).

Yet once again, characteristically, the poet in *Scar Tissue* cannot rest with such insights, cannot overcome his sense of exile and the anxiety induced by his consciousness of mortality. His estrangement from nature is evident in the twice-repeated phrase "Strange flesh in a stranger land" in "Heraclitean Backwash" (53) and in the exclamation in the book's penultimate poem, "How quickly and finally the landscape subsumes us" (68), a poem that concludes with imagery of ravens, conventional emblems of death. "This is the executioner's hour," the final poem, "Singing Lesson," begins, and the lesson that "the Great Mouth with its two tongues of water and ash" seems to teach is acceptance of dissolution, embrace of death's darkness (69). Thus, the scar tissue of this book's title results from the wounds inflicted by this world as well as by the apparent absence of the otherworldly.

Wright's *Littlefoot* is unique among his published collections because it consists of thirty-five numbered but untitled poems. Of varying lengths, these poems generally function individually rather than as a sequence, although the first seven originally appeared under the title "Appalachian Autumn" in *The American Scholar* (2005). As the reader learns in the twenty-eighth poem, the book's title is the name of a horse, and the collection is thus named for a figure from the natural world, with which the poet finds himself at peace in this poem, "the evening's homily" summed up in the word "praise," which Wright repeats five times in as many lines, four times as the first word in a line (67). The emphasis that this anaphora provides encourages the reader to join the poet in celebrating the visible, the tangible, even as Wright continues to conceive of the landscape as "a windowpane / Into the anteroom of all things untouchable" (14). The Littlefoot of the book's title also seems to represent all finite creatures whom death awaits, especially in contrast to "Bigfoot, the north wind" (51), for in *A Short History of the Shadow* Wright says, "The song of the north wind fills our ears with no meaning" (24). The poet often, in fact, describes wind less as an emblem of spirit than as a resistless natural force. The contrast between the names Littlefoot and Bigfoot—and between the kinds of natural phenomena that each represents—suggests the fragility and brevity of human and animal life, of "those who walk slip stitch upon the earth and lose their footprints," as Wright puts it in *Scar Tissue* (42).

The opening lines of *Littlefoot* raise the issue of return, of what Wright also links elsewhere to the theological concept of apokatastasis. Those opening lines insist, however, that "You can't go back" (3), a position Wright later qualifies when he remarks, "Outside of the church, no salvation, / St. Cyprian says. / Outside of nature, no transformation, I say, no hope of return" (9). In the latter lines Wright once more looks for transformation not in spiritual rebirth but in nature's cyclical recurrence. Yet for human beings, as he recognizes, such seasonal cycles offer little consolation; they cannot satisfy the longing for eternity. "Like clouds, once gone in their long drift," he writes, "there's no coming back" (22). While the winds of North America usually drive those clouds from west to east, the dominant movement Wright depicts in *Littlefoot* is westward, and he draws on the conventional association of the west, the realm of the setting sun, with death. In this collection the Great Mouth of the final poem in *Scar Tissue* becomes "the great mouth of the west" that eventually devours all living creatures. In a metaphor that reveals the mechanistic quality of nature's processes, Wright portrays the constellation-filled night sky as a dark player piano and comments, "No stopping the music, east to west, no stopping it" (27). Rather than a resonant music of the spheres, Wright seems to hear a funeral march. While he also contemplates "Reunion in Heaven," the title of a gospel song by Lester Flatt and Earl Scruggs for which he recalls a fugitive, unrecorded verse (77), such religious consolation appears as improbable as survival amid nature's cyclical renewal. "Faith is a thing unfathomable," says the poet (19), and yet like the Stevens who wrote, "It can never be satisfied, the mind, never" (247), Wright confesses that "There is no end to longing," a longing that is intensely spiritual as well as intellectual.

Like Wright's other books, *Littlefoot* is filled with prayers and petitions of various kinds. Among the most striking in this book is his appeal to the "Master of words, Lord of signs" to "Step out of the Out" (37). Characteristically for Wright, that prayer goes unanswered; instead what is revealed is "The perpetual presence of absence" (51). In *Littlefoot* this enduring dilemma leads the poet to a keener acceptance of mortality than was evident in his earlier collections, an acceptance evident in a phrase such as "The salve of nothingness" and in his reference to "The emptiness of nonbeing" as "something to shoot for" (15, 82). The wind bears testimony to that void, for it is an "Unstoppable storyteller with nothing to say" (59). And yet the poet affirms the splendor and satisfactions of the physical world, however evanescent its beauty, however temporary human lives may be. "We are the generations of the soil," he writes; "it is our destination, our Compostela" (56), lines in which he both alludes to and subverts the biblical story of Adam's creation out of the dust of the earth and in which he puns on the place name Compostela, the goal of one famous medieval pilgrimage but here also the Whitmanian compost from which all life arises and to which it returns. Wright's pun makes death itself the endpoint of this pilgrimage.

Like Hamlet, however, Wright cannot evade discomfort at the prospect of somehow surviving death and chancing dread dreams. Longing for "a finitude to count on" (58), the poet is haunted by Franz Kafka's parable of the Hunter Gracchus, to whom Wright refers or alludes in all four of his collections published since *Negative Blue*. Kafka's tale is paradigmatic for Wright because the dead Gracchus's ship is condemned to endless wandering, unable to reach its port in the afterlife. Asked, then, if he has no part in the other world, Gracchus replies, "I am forever on the great stair that leads up to it" (Kafka 129). Whereas for Dante that stairway might well represent the ascending rounds of Purgatory, with heaven the soul's eventual, if deferred, destination, Kafka holds out no such hope for Gracchus, whose rudderless ship "is driven by the wind that blows in the undermost regions of death" (135). For Wright, too, the journey into death holds no assurance of either salvation or stasis. Although he expects death to be final, he remains uncertain whether he can effect a total disappearance. As he says in one of the sestets that he has published since *Littlefoot*, "The entrance to hell is just a tiny hole in the ground, / . . . soul-sized, horizon-sized. / Thousands go through it each day" ("Hasta" 107).

The preceding quotation helps to reveal that, among the six poets treated in this book, Wright is the one who seems to have the greatest difficulty "coming out from under Calvinism," in Robert Morgan's phrase.

Wright is more concerned about sin and guilt than the other five authors, and he is also the poet most tormented by the loss of transcendence, most fearful that in choosing the things of this world he has somehow betrayed God's will, which another recent sestet characterizes as "renounce this, / Renounce that" ("Gospel" 110). By identifying God with renunciation, Wright tends to align himself with the otherworldly impulse in Christian theology, but in those moments when he comes to doubt both God's existence and the possibility of an afterlife, he gravitates toward the physical world as an earthly paradise. Ordinarily, however, he finds himself unable to locate divine presence within or through nature, though he certainly strives to do so. If, as Wright has said, "The textures of the world *are* an outline of the infinite" (*Quarter Notes* 120), then what is ultimately infinite for Wright seems to be nonbeing itself, whether defined as death or nothingness, together with nature's cyclic processes.

In a revealing reformulation of his tripartite subject matter for a recent interviewer, Wright spoke of it as "the idea of God behind the language of the landscape" (Di Salvo 45). As should now be apparent, however, for Wright that landscape is often as mute as God, though certainly more easily imaged and loved. Yet Wright finds himself unable to celebrate unreservedly an earthly paradise; instead, his sense of exile, of homelessness, persists. To an interviewer who inquired about Wright's stance in relation to Gerard Manley Hopkins's poetry, Wright noted that while for Hopkins, as that poet wrote, "The world is charged with the grandeur of God," "I am charged by the *absence* of God" (Gardner 98). The energy of that absence—and the concomitant quest for divine presence—has driven Wright's poetry for over forty years, lending it much of its thematic significance and underscoring the poet's ongoing engagement with the religious sensibility so prominent in Appalachia, a region that has enriched the literary imaginations of all the writers discussed in this study.

Like the larger South, the mountain South remains a region of strong religious traditions, traditions that continue to influence, sometimes overtly, sometimes quite subtly, the literary texts produced by the region's writers. For most of the poets analyzed in this book, the pronounced otherworldliness and harsh judgmentalism of mountain religion have led them to a spirituality more attuned to creation and to an affirmation of nature and the temporal world as loci of divine presence. The poetry of all these writers, with the exception of Jim Wayne Miller's, regularly ad-

dresses religious concerns: whether it be the Dantean spiritual quests
envisioned by Chappell and Wright, quests with strikingly different out-
comes; or the rituals of rebirth to which Morgan attests; or Marion's vivid
detailing of the grace-full wonders that suffuse nature; or Byer's celebration of an immanent, not transcendent, creative power drawn from Native American spirituality.

What Byer calls "earthly awakenings" is a central theme for all these
poets, including Miller, as they seek to recover a sense of the beauty and
goodness of the physical world and a renewed recognition of humanity's
dependence on nature. Clearly, the resulting texts, far from being simply
"worldly, secular, and profane," as Miller had argued, are both worldly and
intensely religious, invoking the sacred amid the secular, interfusing the
natural and the supernatural—or seeking in vain to do so in Wright's case.
These poets thus participate in a long tradition of theological reflection
in American literature, a tradition that originates with the Puritans, was
sustained throughout the Romantic era, and extends over the twentieth
century and beyond. Although what Chappell variously calls the "tree of
spirit" and "the Mountains Outside Time" remains a part of the poetic vision of some of these authors, it is the recovery of creation that lies at the
heart of their spiritual quests as they map the route home to *this* world.

WORKS CITED

Andrews, Tom, ed. *The Point Where All Things Meet: Essays on Charles Wright.* Oberlin, OH: Oberlin College P, 1995.

Arnold, Edwin T. "An Interview with Jim Wayne Miller." *Appalachian Journal* 6 (1979): 207–25.

Arnow, Harriette. *The Dollmaker.* New York: Avon, 1972.

Bain, Robert, and Joseph M. Flora, eds. *Contemporary Poets, Dramatists, Essayists, and Novelists of the South: A Bio-Bibliographical Sourcebook.* Westport, CT: Greenwood, 1994.

Beattie, L. Elizabeth, ed. *Conversations with Kentucky Writers.* Lexington: UP of Kentucky, 1996. 240–61.

Berry, Wendell. "Christianity and the Survival of Creation." *Sex, Economy, Freedom & Community.* New York: Pantheon, 1993. 93–116.

Bizzaro, Patrick. "Introduction: Fred Chappell's Community of Readers." *Dream Garden: The Poetic Vision of Fred Chappell.* Ed. Patrick Bizzaro. Baton Rouge: Louisiana State UP, 1997. 1–5.

Bizzaro, Patrick, ed. *More Lights Than One: On the Fiction of Fred Chappell.* Baton Rouge: Louisiana State UP, 2004.

Bizzaro, Patrick, and Resa Crane Bizzaro. "'The Poetics of Work': An Interview with Robert Morgan." *North Carolina Literary Review* 10 (2001): 173–90.

Booker, Suzanne. "A Conversation with Robert Morgan." *Carolina Quarterly* 37.3 (1985): 13–22. Rpt. in Morgan, *Good Measure.* 131–43.

Bourne, Louis M. "On Metaphor and Its Use in the Poetry of Robert Morgan." *The Small Farm* 3 (1976): 63–79.

Broughton, Irv. "Fred Chappell." *The Writer's Mind: Interviews with American Authors.* Vol. 3. Fayetteville: U of Arkansas P, 1990. 91–122.

Brown, Fred, and Jeanne McDonald. "Fred Chappell." *Growing up Southern: How the South Shapes Its Writers.* Greenville, SC: Blue Ridge, 1997. 117–34.

Buell, Lawrence. *Writing for an Endangered World: Literature, Culture, and Environment in the U.S. and Beyond.* Cambridge: Harvard UP, 2001.

Byer, Kathryn Stripling. *Alma.* Cullowhee, NC: Phoenix, 1983.

———. *Black Shawl.* Baton Rouge: Louisiana State UP, 1998.

———. *Catching Light.* Baton Rouge: Louisiana State UP, 2002.

———. *Coming to Rest.* Baton Rouge: Louisiana State UP, 2006.

———. "Deep Water." *Bloodroot: Reflections on Place by Appalachian Women Writers.* Ed. Joyce Dyer. Lexington: UP of Kentucky, 1998. 61–70.

———. *The Girl in the Midst of the Harvest.* Lubbock: Texas Tech P, 1986.

———. Letter to the author. September 13, 1996.

———. "Stitching the Past Together: The Heritage of Western North Carolina Mountain Quilts." *Smoky Mountain Living* 2.1 (2002): 10–13.

———. "A Thing Called Home: Broodings on Southern Writing at the Turn of the Millennium." *Appalachian Life* 46 (August 2000): 8–10.

———. "Turning the Windlass at the Well: Fred Chappell's Early Poetry." *Dream Garden: The Poetic Vision of Fred Chappell.* Ed. Patrick Bizzaro. Baton Rouge: Louisiana State UP, 1997. 88–96.

———. *Wake.* Sylva, NC: Spring Street, 2003.

———. *Wildwood Flower.* Baton Rouge: Louisiana State UP, 1992.

Calder, Daniel G., et al. *Sources and Analogues of Old English Poetry II: The Major Germanic and Celtic Texts in Translation.* Cambridge: D. S. Brewer, 1983.

Cardin, Gary. "Shutting the Door Forever After." *Smoky Mountain News* 24–30 April 2002: 22.

Caseley, Martin. "Through Purgatory to Appalachia: An Interview with Charles Wright." *PN Review* 27.1 (2000): 22–25.

Chappell, Fred. *Backsass.* Baton Rouge: Louisiana State UP, 2004.

———. *C.* Baton Rouge: Louisiana State UP, 1993.

———. *Family Gathering.* Baton Rouge: Louisiana State UP, 2000.

———. *First and Last Words.* Baton Rouge: Louisiana State UP, 1989.

———. "The Function of the Poet." *Plow Naked: Selected Writings on Poetry.* Ann Arbor: U of Michigan P, 1993. 26–39.

———. *I Am One of You Forever.* Baton Rouge: Louisiana State UP, 1985.

———. "Jim Wayne Miller: The Gentle Partisan." *North Carolina Literary Review* 6 (1997): 7–13.

———. *Midquest.* Baton Rouge: Louisiana State UP, 1981.

———. *Moments of Light.* Los Angeles: New South, 1980.

———. *More Shapes Than One.* New York: St. Martin's, 1991.

———. "The Poet and the Plowman." *Plow Naked: Selected Writings on Poetry.* Ann Arbor: U of Michigan P, 1993. 73–79.

———. Review of *Lost & Found. Now & Then* 12 (Spring 1995): 34–35.

———. *Source.* Baton Rouge: Louisiana State UP, 1985.

———. *Spring Garden: New and Selected Poems.* Baton Rouge: Louisiana State UP, 1995.

———. "Too Many Freds." *More Lights Than One: On the Fiction of Fred Chappell.* Ed. Patrick Bizzaro. Baton Rouge: Louisiana State UP, 2004. 256–71.

———. "Towards a Beginning." *The Small Farm* 4 & 5 (1976/77): 93–99.

———. "The Two Ministries." Printed in Casey Howard Clabough's *Experimentation and Versatility: The Early Novels and Short Fiction of Fred Chappell*. Macon, GA: Mercer UP, 2005. 147–58.

———. "Wind-Voices: Kathryn Stripling Byer's Poetry." *Shenandoah* 55.1 (2005): 64–82.

———. *The World between the Eyes*. Baton Rouge: Louisiana State UP, 1971.

Christianson, Christine. Unpublished transcript of interview with Jeff Daniel Marion. April 4, 2003.

Clark, Jim. "'Unto all generations of the faithful heart': Donald Davidson, the Vanderbilt Agrarians, and Appalachian Poetry." *Mississippi Quarterly* 58.2 (2005): 299–13.

Clark, Miriam Marty, and Michael McFee. "The Impossibility of Salvation: A Conversation with Poet Charles Wright." *Arts Journal* February 1989: 10–13.

Collins, Floyd. "Metamorphosis within the Poetry of Charles Wright." *Gettysburg Review* 4 (1991): 464–79.

Cornett, Sheryl. "A Conversation with Robert Morgan." *Image* 43 (Fall 2004): 65–76.

Costello, Bonnie. "Charles Wright's *Via Negativa*: Language, Landscape, and the Idea of God." *Contemporary Literature* 42 (2001): 325–46.

Coward, John. "Jeff Daniel Marion and His Poetry: Mapping the Heart's Place." *Encyclopedia of East Tennessee*. Ed. Jim Stokely and Jeff D. Johnson. Oak Ridge, TN: Children's Museum of Oak Ridge, 1981. 312–13.

Deloria, Vine, Jr. *God Is Red*. New York: Dell, 1980.

Denham, Robert D. *Charles Wright: A Companion to the Late Poetry, 1988–2007*. Jefferson, NC: McFarland, 2008.

Dickinson, Emily. *Final Harvest: Emily Dickinson's Poems*. Ed. Thomas H. Johnson. Boston: Little, Brown, 1961.

Di Salvo, Thomas. "An Interview with Charles Wright." *Writer's Chronicle* 39.6 (2007): 40–45.

Easa, Leila. "A Conversation with Fred Chappell." *The Archive* 108 (Fall 1995): 49–60.

Einstein, Frank. "The Politics of Nostalgia: Uses of the Past in Recent Appalachian Poetry." *Appalachian Journal* 8 (1980): 32–40.

Eliot, T. S. *Collected Poems, 1909–1962*. New York: Harcourt, Brace & World, 1963.

Elliott, David L. "An Interview with Robert Morgan." *Chattahoochee Review* 13.2 (1993): 78–97.

Emerson, Ralph Waldo. "Nature" and "The Poet." *The Norton Anthology of American Literature*. Vol. B. Ed. Nina Baym et al. Sixth edition. New York: W. W. Norton, 2003.

Frost, Robert. *Complete Poems*. New York: Holt, Rinehart & Winston, 1964.

Gardner, Thomas. "Interview with Charles Wright." *A Door Ajar: Contemporary Writers and Emily Dickinson*. New York: Oxford UP, 2006. 95–108.

Giannelli, Adam, ed. *High Lonesome: On the Poetry of Charles Wright*. Oberlin, OH: Oberlin College P, 2006.

Hall, Wade. "Jim Wayne Miller's Brier Poems: The Appalachian in Exile." *Iron Mountain Review* 4.2 (1988): 29–33.

Harmon, William. "Imagination, Memory, and Region: A Conversation." *Iron Mountain Review* 6 (Spring 1990): 11–16. Rpt. in Morgan, *Good Measure*. 158–70.

———. "Robert Morgan's Pelagian Georgics: Twelve Essays." *Parnassus* 9 (Fall/ Winter 1981): 5–30.

Hart, Henry. "Charles Wright's *Via Mystica*." In Giannelli, *High Lonesome: On the Poetry of Charles Wright*. 325–44.

Hatch, James V. "Jeff D. Marion and Michael Weaver: Two Poets Down Home." *Artist and Influence* 10 (1991): 190–212.

Heyen, William, and Stanley Rubin. "'The Rush of Language': A Conversation with Robert Morgan." *The Post-Confessionals: Conversations with American Poets of the Eighties*. Ed. Earl G. Ingersoll et al. Rutherford, NJ: Fairleigh Dickinson UP, 1989. Rpt. in Morgan, *Good Measure*. 144–57.

Hinton, David. *Mountain Home: The Wilderness Poetry of Ancient China*. New York: Counterpoint, 2002.

Hovis, George. "An Interview with Fred Chappell." *Carolina Quarterly* 52.1 (1999): 67–79.

———. "'When You Got True Dirt You Got Everything You Need': Forging an Appalachian Arcadia in Fred Chappell's *Midquest*." *Mississippi Quarterly* 53.3 (2000): 389–414.

Howard, Julie Kate. "In Her Own Image: Characterizing Theology in Kathryn Stripling Byer's Poetry." *Iron Mountain Review* 18 (2002): 24–29.

Jackson, Richard. "On the Margins of Dreams." *Acts of Mind: Conversations with Contemporary Poets*. Tuscaloosa: U of Alabama P, 1983. 153–57.

Johnson, Don. "The Appalachian Homeplace as Oneiric House in Jim Wayne Miller's *The Mountains Have Come Closer*." *An American Vein: Critical Readings in Appalachian Literature*. Ed. Danny L. Miller, Sharon Hatfield, and Gurney Norman. Athens: Ohio UP, 2005. 125–33.

———. "Coming 'the Long Way Around': Marion's Chinese Poems." *Iron Mountain Review* 11 (1995): 17–22.

———. "The Cultivated Mind: The Georgic Center of Fred Chappell's Poetry." *Dream Garden: The Poetic Vision of Fred Chappell*. Ed. Patrick Bizzaro. Baton Rouge: Louisiana State UP, 1997. 170–79.

Johnson, Jennifer, and Karen Walden. "Interview with Kathryn Stripling Byer." *Mossy Creek Journal* 11 (1987): 28–31.

Jones, Loyal. "The Brightest and Best." *Appalachian Heritage* 25.4 (1997): 45–46.

———. *Faith and Meaning in the Southern Uplands*. Urbana: U of Illinois P, 1999.

———. "In Quest of the Brier." *Appalachia and Beyond: Conversations with Writers from the Mountain South.* Ed. John Lang. Knoxville: U of Tennessee P, 2006. 53–72.

Jones, Roger D. "Robert Morgan." *Dictionary of Literary Biography, Vol. 120: American Poets since World War II, Third Series.* Ed. R. S. Gwynn. Detroit: Gale, 1992. 213–19.

Kafka, Franz. *Parables and Paradoxes.* New York: Schocken, 1961.

Kennedy, Sarah. "'That Little Gal's Not Going Anywhere': Kathryn Stripling Byer's Incremental Monologues." *Iron Mountain Review* 18 (2002): 9–15.

King, Winston L. "Religion." *Encyclopedia of Religion.* Ed. Mircea Eliade. New York: MacMillan, 1987.

Lang, John. *Understanding Fred Chappell.* Columbia: U of South Carolina P, 2000.

Lee, Ernest. "The Journey a Poem Makes: Interviewing Jeff Daniel Marion." *Appalachian Journal* 31 (2004): 194–211.

Leidig, Dan. "On the Rim of Knowing: The Achievement of Jeff Daniel Marion." *Appalachian Journal* 10 (1983): 142–56.

———. "pro tempore." *Iron Mountain Review* 4.2 (1988): 2.

Lewis, Charlton T., and Charles Short. *A Latin Dictionary.* Oxford: Clarendon, 1962.

Lutwack, Leonard. *The Role of Place in Literature.* Syracuse: Syracuse UP, 1984.

Makuck, Peter. "Chappell's Continuities: *First and Last Words.*" *Dream Garden: The Poetic Vision of Fred Chappell.* Ed. Patrick Bizzaro. Baton Rouge: Louisiana State UP, 1997. 180–97.

Marion, Jeff Daniel. *Almanac.* Jefferson City, TN: Small Farm Press, 1976.

———. "Appalachia." *One Hundred Years of Appalachian Visions.* Ed. Bill Best. Berea, KY: Appalachian Imprints, 1997. 113–14.

———. "Biographical Note [and interview]." *The Small Farm* 3 (1976): 40–43. Rpt. in Morgan, *Good Measure.* 127–30.

———. *The Chinese Poet Awakens.* Lexington, KY: Wind, 1999.

———. *Ebbing & Flowing Springs: New and Selected Poems and Prose, 1976–2001.* Knoxville: Celtic Cat, 2002.

———. *Letters Home.* Abingdon, VA: Sow's Ear Press, 2001.

———. "Listening for the Hello of Home: A Conversation with Linda Parsons Marion." *Her Words: Diverse Voices in Contemporary Appalachian Women's Poetry.* Ed. Felicia Mitchell. Knoxville: U of Tennessee P, 2002. 180–90.

———. "The Long Way Around: Circling Back Home, A Metaphor for Writing." *Appalachian Journal* 31 (2004): 214–20.

———. *Lost & Found.* Abingdon, VA: Sow's Ear Press, 1994.

———. *Miracles of Air.* New Market, TN: Mill Springs Press, 1987.

———. "Our Daily Bread." *Iron Mountain Review* 11 (1995): 5–6.

———. *Out in the Country, Back Home.* Winston-Salem, NC: Jackpine Press, 1976.

———. "Poetry Magazines." *Encyclopedia of East Tennessee*. Ed. Jim Stokely and
    Jeff D. Johnson. Oak Ridge, TN: Children's Museum of Oak Ridge, 1981.
    383–85.

———. *Tight Lines*. Emory, VA: Iron Mountain Press, 1981.

———. "Try to Picture It: Poetry, Photography, and the Long View." *Now & Then*
    15.2 (1998): 21–24.

———. *Vigils: Selected Poems*. Boone, NC: Appalachian Consortium Press, 1990.

———. *Watering Places*. Knoxville: Puddingstone Press, 1976.

Marion, Stephen. "Fishing in the Language." *Appalachia and Beyond: Conversa-
    tions with Writers from the Mountain South*. Ed. John Lang. Knoxville: U of
    Tennessee P, 2006. 175–94.

Mayer, Barbara J. "Six Davidson Poets: The Consolation of Some Memorable
    Language." *Davidson Journal* 15 (Fall 1993): 7–13.

McCauley, Deborah Vansau. *Appalachian Mountain Religion: A History*. Urbana: U
    of Illinois P, 1995.

McFee, Michael. "Wright's Pilgrimage." *Seneca Review* 14.2 (1984): 85–97.

Middleton, David. "With Modesty and Measured Love." *Sewanee Review* 104.1
    (1996): x–xiii.

Miles, Emma Bell. *The Spirit of the Mountains*. 1905. Knoxville: U of Tennessee P,
    1975.

Miller, Jim Wayne. "Accepting Things Near." *Appalachian Heritage* 13.1–2 (1985):
    16–23.

———. "Anytime the Ground Is Uneven: The Outlook for Regional Studies and
    What to Look Out For." *Geography and Literature: A Meeting of the Disciplines*.
    Ed. William E. Mallory and Paul Simpson-Housley. Syracuse: Syracuse UP,
    1987. 1–20.

———. "Appalachian Education: A Critique and Suggestions for Reform." *Appala-
    chian Journal* 5 (1977): 13–22.

———. "Appalachian Literature at Home in This World." *An American Vein: Criti-
    cal Readings in Appalachian Literature*. Ed. Danny L. Miller, Sharon Hatfield,
    and Gurney Norman. Athens: Ohio UP, 2005. 13–24.

———. "Appalachian Studies Hard and Soft: The Action Folk and the Creative
    People." *Appalachian Journal* 9.2–3 (1982): 105–14.

———. "Appalachian Writing: A Region Awakening." *A Gathering at the Forks*. Ed.
    George Ella Lyon, Jim Wayne Miller, and Gurney Norman. Wise, VA: Vision
    Books, 1993. 416–21.

———. *Brier, His Book*. Frankfort, KY: Gnomon, 1988.

———. *The Brier Poems*. Frankfort, KY: Gnomon, 1997.

———. *Brier, Traveling*. Louisville: White Fields, 1993.

———. *Copperhead Cane*. Nashville: Robert Moore Allen, 1964.

———. *Dialogue with a Dead Man*. Athens: U of Georgia P, 1974.

————. *His First, Best Country.* Frankfort, KY: Gnomon, 1993.

————. *I Have a Place.* Pippa Passes, KY: Alice Lloyd College, 1981.

————. "I Have a Place." *Sense of Place in Appalachia.* Ed. S. Mont Whitson. Morehead, KY: Morehead State University, 1988. 81–99.

————. "Jim Wayne Miller." *Contemporary Authors Autobiography Series.* Vol. 15. Ed. Joyce Nakamura. Detroit: Gale, 1992. 273–93.

————. "A Letter on Poetry from Jim Wayne Miller." *Kentucky Poetry Review* 18–19 (1982–83): 54–61.

————. *The More Things Change the More They Stay the Same.* Frankfort, KY: Whippoorwill, 1971.

————. *The Mountains Have Come Closer.* Boone, NC: Appalachian Consortium Press, 1980.

————. *Nostalgia for 70.* Big Timber, MT: Seven Buffaloes, 1986.

————. "Nostalgia for the Future." *Kentucky Review* 8.2 (1998): 18–39.

————. "A People Waking Up: Appalachian Literature since 1960." *The Cratis Williams Symposium Proceedings.* Boone, NC: Appalachian Consortium Press, 1990. 47–76.

————. "A Post-Agrarian Regionalism for Appalachia." *Appalachian Heritage* 8.2 (1980): 58–71.

————. "Reading, Writing, Region: Notes from Southern Appalachia, an American Periphery." *Thinker Review* April 1992: 119–34.

————. "Regions, Folk Life, and Literary Criticism." *Appalachian Journal* 7 (1980): 180–87.

————. "Small Farms Disappearing in Tennessee." *Appalachian Journal* 2 (1974): 63–65.

————. "Unsalaried, He Deals in a Service." *Hemlocks and Balsams* 2 (1981): 5.

————. *Vein of Words.* Big Timber, MT: Seven Buffaloes, 1984.

Mooney, Stephen. "Tapping the Possibilities of the Appalachian Experience in the Contemporary Age: Jim Wayne Miller's 'Brier Sermon: You Must Be Born Again.'" *CrossRoads* 1.2 (Spring/Summer 1993): 63–68.

Morgan, Robert. *At the Edge of the Orchard Country.* Middletown, CT: Wesleyan UP, 1987.

————. "The Birth of Music from the Spirit of Comedy." *More Lights Than One: On the Fiction of Fred Chappell.* Ed. Patrick Bizzaro. Baton Rouge: Louisiana State UP, 2004. ix–xiv.

————. *Bronze Age.* Emory, VA: Iron Mountain Press, 1981.

————. *Good Measure: Essays, Interviews, and Notes on Poetry.* Baton Rouge: Louisiana State UP, 1993.

————. *Groundwork.* Frankfort, KY: Gnomon, 1979.

————. *Land Diving.* Baton Rouge: Louisiana State UP, 1976.

————. Letters to the author, February 10, 1991, and March 31, 1991.

———. "Nature Is a Stranger Yet." *The Jordan Lectures, 1998–99.* Roanoke, VA: Roanoke College, 1999. 27–42.

———. *Red Owl.* New York: W. W. Norton, 1972.

———. *Sigodlin.* Middletown, CT: Wesleyan UP, 1990.

———. *The Strange Attractor: New and Selected Poems.* Baton Rouge: Louisiana State UP, 2004.

———. *This Rock.* Chapel Hill: Algonquin, 2001.

———. *Topsoil Road.* Baton Rouge: Louisiana State UP, 2000.

———. *The Truest Pleasure.* Chapel Hill: Algonquin, 1995.

———. *Trunk & Thicket.* Fort Collins, CO: L'Epervier Press, 1978.

———. *The Voice in the Crosshairs.* Ithaca, NY: Angelfish Press, 1971.

———. *Zirconia Poems.* Northwood Narrows, NH: Lillabulero Press, 1969.

Palmer, Tersh. "Fred Chappell." *Appalachian Journal* 19.4 (1992): 402–10.

Patterson, Sarah, and Dan Lindsey. "Interview with Fred Chappell." *Davidson Miscellany* 19 (Spring 1984): 62–76.

Payne, Robert, ed. *The White Pony: An Anthology of Chinese Poetry.* New York: Mentor, 1947.

Pound, Ezra. *Selected Poems.* New York: New Directions, 1957.

Powell, Lynn. "'Climb the Mountain Daily and Remember': Lessons for Young Poets from the Poems of Jeff Daniel Marion." *Iron Mountain Review* 11 (1995): 11–16.

Quillen, Rita. *Looking for Native Ground: Contemporary Appalachian Poetry.* Boone, NC: Appalachian Consortium Press, 1989.

Rasmussen, Larry L. *Earth Community, Earth Ethics.* Geneva: World Council of Churches, 1996.

Richman, Larry. Interview/Review of *Vigils. Sow's Ear Poetry Review* 3.3 (1992): 12–15.

Ruether, Rosemary Radford. *Liberation Theology: Human Hope Confronts Christian History and American Power.* New York: Paulist Press, 1972.

———. *Sexism and God-Talk: Toward a Feminist Theology.* Boston: Beacon, 1983.

Schuldt, Morgan Lucas. "An Interview with Charles Wright." *Sonora Review* 43 (2002): 74–80.

Schurer, Norbert. "An Interview with Robert Morgan." *Pembroke Magazine* 36 (2004): 252–60.

Shackelford, Lynne P. "Jeff Daniel Marion." *Contemporary Poets, Dramatists, Essayists, and Novelists of the South: A Bio-Bibliographical Sourcebook.* Ed. Robert Bain and Joseph M. Flora. Westport, CT: Greenwood, 1994. 319–29.

Smith, Lee. "Singing the Mountains." *Appalachia and Beyond: Conversations with Writers from the Mountain South.* Ed. John Lang. Knoxville, U of Tennessee P, 2006. 293–311.

Smith, Newton. "Going back to the Mountains from *Topsoil Road*: A Retrospective Look at Robert Morgan's Poetry." *Pembroke Magazine* 35 (2003): 55–63.

Stevens, Wallace. *The Collected Poems*. New York: Knopf, 1954.

Stitt, Peter. "Resurrecting the Baroque." In Giannelli, *High Lonesome: On the Poetry of Charles Wright*. 230–54.

Stuart, Dabney. "Spiritual Matter in Fred Chappell's Poetry: A Prologue." *Dream Garden: The Poetic Vision of Fred Chappell*. Ed. Patrick Bizzaro. Baton Rouge: Louisiana State UP, 1997. 48–70.

Suarez, Ernest. *Southbound: Interviews with Southern Poets*. Columbia: U of Missouri P, 1999. 39–61.

Thoreau, Henry David. *Walden*. In *The Norton Anthology of American Literature*. Vol. B. Ed. Nina Baym et al. Sixth edition. New York: W. W. Norton, 2003.

Turner, Daniel Cross. "Oblivion's Glow: The (Post)Southern Side of Charles Wright, an Interview." *storySouth*, summer 2005. June 16, 2008. http://www.storysouth. com/summer2005/wright_interview.html.

Upton, Lee. "The Doubting Penitent: Charles Wright's Epiphanies of Abandonment." In Giannelli, *High Lonesome: On the Poetry of Charles Wright*. 255–84.

Waggoner, Hyatt H. *American Poets: From the Puritans to the Present*. New York: Dell, 1970.

Weaks-Baxter, Mary. *Reclaiming the American Farmer: The Reinvention of a Regional Mythology in Twentieth-Century Southern Writing*. Baton Rouge: Louisiana State UP, 2006.

West, Robert. "The Art of Far and Near: An Interview with Robert Morgan." *Carolina Quarterly* 49.3 (1997): 46–68.

———. "Everywhere but His Own Country: Three Essays on Charles Wright and the American South." *Asheville Poetry Review* 9.1 (2002): 93–103.

———. "'That Has a Ring to It': Song in the Poetry of Kathryn Stripling Byer." *Iron Mountain Review* 18 (2002): 16–23.

White, Lynn. "The Historical Roots of Our Ecologic Crisis." *Science* March 10, 1967: 1203–7.

Williams, Mary C. "Inside-Outside in Robert Morgan's Poetry." *The Poetics of Appalachian Space*. Ed. Parks Lanier, Jr. Knoxville: U of Tennessee P, 1991. 149–60.

Williamson, J. W. "Appalachian Poetry: The Politics of Coming Home." *Southern Exposure* 9.2 (1981): 69–74.

Wirzba, Norman. "Placing the Soul: An Agrarian Philosophical Principle." *The Essential Agrarian Reader: The Future of Culture, Community, and the Land*. Ed. Norman Wirzba. Lexington: UP of Kentucky, 2003. 80–97.

Woloch, Cecilia. "Interview." *New Southerner: An Anthology, 2005–06*. 58–61.

Wood, Gerald C. "The Poetry of Jeff Daniel Marion." *Appalachian Heritage* 13.1–2 (1985): 39–45.

Woodhull, Kenny. "Old Wine in New Bottles: An Interview with Jim Wayne Miller." *Mossy Creek Journal* 9 (1985): 13–19.

Worthington, Marianne. "Epistolary Exchanges: The Personal and Poetic Journey of Jeff Daniel Marion in *Letters Home.*" *Journal of Appalachian Studies* 9 (2003): 406–14.

———. "'Lost in the American Funhouse': Magical Realism and Transfiguration in Jim Wayne Miller's *The Mountains Have Come Closer.*" *Journal of Kentucky Studies* 22 (2005): 144–51.

Wright, Charles. *Appalachia.* New York: Farrar, Straus & Giroux. 1998.

———. *Black Zodiac.* New York: Farrar, Straus & Giroux, 1997.

———. *Bloodlines.* Middletown, CT: Wesleyan UP, 1975.

———. *Buffalo Yoga.* New York: Farrar, Straus & Giroux. 2004.

———. *Chickamauga.* New York: Farrar, Straus & Giroux, 1995.

———. *China Trace.* Middletown, CT: Wesleyan UP, 1977.

———. *Country Music: Selected Early Poems.* Middletown, CT: Wesleyan UP, 1982.

———. "The Gospel According to Yours Truly." *Virginia Quarterly Review* 83.3 (2007): 110.

———. *The Grave of the Right Hand.* Middletown, CT: Wesleyan UP, 1970.

———. *Halflife: Improvisations and Interviews, 1977–87.* Ann Arbor: U of Michigan P, 1988.

———. *Hard Freight.* Middletown, CT: Wesleyan UP, 1973.

———. "Hasta la Vista Buckaroo." *Virginia Quarterly Review* 83.3 (2007): 107.

———. *Littlefoot.* New York: Farrar, Straus & Giroux, 2007.

———. *Negative Blue: Selected Later Poems.* New York: Farrar, Straus & Giroux, 2000.

———. *The Other Side of the River.* New York: Random House, 1984.

———. *Quarter Notes: Improvisations and Interviews.* Ann Arbor: U of Michigan P, 1995.

———. *Scar Tissue.* New York: Farrar, Straus & Giroux, 2006.

———. *A Short History of the Shadow.* New York: Farrar, Straus & Giroux, 2002.

———. *The Southern Cross.* New York: Random House, 1981.

———. *The World of the Ten Thousand Things: Poems 1980–1990.* New York: Farrar, Straus & Giroux, 1990.

———. *Zone Journals.* New York: Farrar, Straus & Giroux, 1988.

INDEX

Agrarianism: influence on Byer, 125–126;
  influence on Chappell, 38–39, 52–53, 55–
  56, 60–61, 68; influence on Marion, 99–
  101, 104, 106; influence on Miller, 12–14,
  16–18, 22–23; influence on Morgan, 73;
  lack of influence on Wright, 158–59
Ammons, A. R., 112
Andrews, Tom, 185
"Animula vagula, blandula" (Hadrian), 69,
  161
Appalachian Literary Renaissance, 5, 8,
  25, 34
Appalachian out-migration, 14, 19–20, 113
Arnold, Matthew, 188
Arnow, Harriette, 1–2, 5, 10, 113, 137

Berry, Wendell, 3–4, 79, 99
Blake, William, 50–51, 72, 86, 95, 167
"Blandula, Tenulla, Vagula" (Pound),
  161–62, 173
Buddhism, 112, 119, 159, 161, 171, 173, 176
Byer, Kathryn Stripling: Alma as persona in
  Wildwood Flower, 130–38, 141, 153; April
  as emblem of rebirth in, 134–35, 138,
  141, 148–49; Delphia as persona in Black
  Shawl, 136, 138–40, 142–45, 148; Native
  American spirituality as influence in,
  125, 144, 151–54; quilting as motif in, 134,
  139–40, 142–43; singing as motif in, 127,
  131–32, 135, 139, 141, 145, 147
—works: "Afterwards, Far from the
  Church," 138; "All Hallow's Eve," 133–34,
  152; Alma, 130, 145; "Amazing Grace,"
  137–38, 141; "Aria," 147, 156; Black Shawl,
  133, 136, 138–45, 147, 148; "Black Shawl,"

139; Catching Light, 145–51, 156; "Chicago Bound," 153–54; "Circuit Rider,"
  140–41; "Cobwebs," 136; Coming to Rest,
  149, 151–56; "The Devil's Dream," 141,
  147; "Drought," 127–28; "Easter," 136–37,
  141, 143; Eve, 145; Evelyn/Eve as persona
  in Catching Light, 145–51; The Girl in the
  Midst of the Harvest, 126–30, 134, 156;
  "Halloween Again," 155; "Hallows," 152–
  53; "Heaven," 129; "I Inherit the Light
  of My Grandmother's House," 129–31;
  "In the Photograph Gallery," 145; "Listen," 149–50; "Music Lessons," 147; "Sea
  Change," 143–44; "Search Party," 127–28;
  "Singing to Salt Woman," 153–54; "Sleepless," 149–50; "Solstice," 129; "Timberline," 143, 148; Wake, 151–52; "Wedding,"
  148; "Wide Open, These Gates," 127;
  Wildwood Flower, 8, 128, 130–39, 144–45,
  152, 156; "Wildwood Flower," 131–33;
  "Wisteria," 148

Carter, A. P., 164
Cathay (Pound), 75, 161
Chappell, Fred: death as theme in, 42–43,
  45–47, 49–52, 57, 60, 66–69, 72; influence on Morgan and Byer, 74, 125–26;
  music as motif in, 46, 50, 55–57, 61; rebirth motif in, 43–47, 50, 53–54, 58–69;
  stars as major image in, 38, 41–42, 46,
  49, 63–64, 66, 70, 72; Uncle Body as
  character in, 4, 50–52, 61, 72, 141; use of
  four elements (earth, air, fire, and water)
  in, 43–47, 53, 61, 78; Virgil Campbell as
  character in, 44, 51, 53, 61, 69

Chappell, Fred (*continued*)
—works: "Agenda," 71–72; "An Old Mountain Woman Reading the Book of Job," 59,
64, 117; "The Autumn Bleat of the Weathervane Trombone," 47, 50–52; *Backsass*,
71–72; *Bloodfire*, 43, 46–47, 50; *C: Poems*,
65–67, 71; "Bringing in the Oaks," 71;
"Daisy," 65–66; *Earthsleep*, 43–44, 46, 51–
53, 66; "The Evening of the Second Day,"
56; *Family Gathering*, 69–71; "The Farm,"
41, 68; "Firewood," 47, 49–51, 53; *First
and Last Words*, 7, 59–65, 67; "Forever
Mountain," 58–59, 69; "The Garden,"
62–63; "The Gift to Be Simple," 60–61; *I
Am One of You Forever*, 39, 42, 54, 62, 140;
It Is Time, Lord, 41, 44; *Midquest*, 6–7,
39, 42, 43–55, 57–58, 60, 67, 69–70, 72,
117, 162, 166, 183, 187; *Moments of Light*,
57; "Morning Light," 65; "O Sacred Head
Now Wounded," 58, 117; "Patience," 60,
68; "The Peaceable Kingdom of Emerald
Windows," 47, 50–53; "The Poet and the
Plowman," 5, 38–39; "A Prayer for the
Mountains," 4, 55–56, 69; "Resolution
and Independence," 71; *River*, 43–44, 46–
47; "Scarecrow Colloquy," 60, 64–65, 117;
"Second Wind," 46, 169; *Source*, 55–59,
67; *Spring Garden: New and Selected Poems*, 41, 59, 62, 67–70, 72, 161, 177; "The
Strain of Mercy," 70; "Susan Bathing,"
47–49; "A Thanksgiving Invitation," 71;
"The Transformed Twilight," 57, 60; "The
Two Ministries," 39–40; *Wind Mountain*,
43, 47, 56; *The World Between the Eyes*,
40–43, 47, 57, 67–68
Chinese poetry as influence: on Marion,
107–13; on Morgan, 75; on Wright, 158,
161–62, 171, 188
Copland, Aaron, 60–61
creation, doctrine of, 3–4, 52, 86, 119, 128

Dante: as influence on Chappell, 6–7,
44–46, 53, 62, 68–70, 72; as influence on
Wright, 162, 166, 172, 174, 183, 192
Davidson, Donald, 5, 10–11

Dickey, James, 126
Dickinson, Emily, 8, 30, 75, 77–78, 85, 92,
138, 162–63, 169, 179–80, 185
Donne, John, 48, 54
dualism of body and soul, matter and spirit,
3–4, 6; as theme in Byer, 128, 133, 140,
155–56; as theme in Chappell, 39, 44, 48,
50–54, 72; as theme in Wright, 159–60,
172, 179, 184–85

earthly paradise as motif: in Byer, 154, 156;
in Chappell, 46, 53–54, 68; in Wright,
161–63, 172–74, 185, 190, 193
Eliot, T. S., 62, 64, 85, 162, 175, 182–83, 187
Emerson, Ralph Waldo, 4, 6, 11, 23–24, 27,
50–51, 75–76, 78, 80–83, 85–86, 95–97,
116, 123, 164, 177–78, 182

Faulkner, William, 8
Four Quartets (Eliot), 62, 162, 182–83
Frost, Robert, 26, 103, 177

Garden of Eden motif: in Byer, 148–50; in
Chappell, 86, 93, 96; in Marion, 122–23;
in Morgan, 46, 62, 68; in Wright, 177, 181
Georgics (Vergil), 5, 38–39, 52, 60, 68
Gnosticism, 39, 50, 77, 150

Hadrian, 69, 161
Hardy, Thomas, 57, 61, 65, 75, 180
Hawthorne, Nathaniel, 8, 46, 160, 172
Hell, 2, 33, 39, 66, 71, 83, 89, 137–38, 192
Heraclitus, 187, 190
Holston River, 105, 115, 157
Hopkins, Gerard Manley, 193
"The Hunter Gracchus" (Kafka), 192

Idealism (Platonic, Kantian, Emersonian),
4, 47, 50–51, 63, 75, 184
I'll Take My Stand, 11, 38
Incarnation, doctrine of, 3, 47, 58, 86, 119,
128

Job, allusions to, 59–60, 132–33, 136, 168
Johnson, Don, 23

Joyce, James, 71
judgmentalism in religion, 1, 29, 33, 42, 71,
    84–85, 87–88, 140–41, 153, 193

Kafka, Franz, 192

Lazarus, allusions to, 45, 92, 129
Lucretius, 43, 49–50, 52, 57–58, 61

Marion, Jeff Daniel: bird imagery in, 105–
    6, 112, 120–23; Chinese poet as persona
    in, 104, 107–13, 120; home as motif in,
    100–101, 104–6, 108–14, 122–24; influ-
    ences on, 103, 107–10, 112; sacramental
    vision of nature in, 113, 115–24; water
    imagery in, 102–3, 106–7, 109, 112, 116,
    118–20
—works: Almanac, 100, 108; "The Ar-
    bor," 123; "Aunt Clara's Credo," 122–23;
    "Boundaries," 103–4, 108; "Brakeshoe
    Spring," 102–3; The Chinese Poet Awakens,
    108, 112–13, 115, 120, 121; "Ebbing and
    Flowing Spring," 103; Ebbing & Flowing
    Springs: New and Selected Poems and Prose,
    1976–2001, 115–16, 119, 121–22; "The
    Farm Wife's Aubade," 119, 122; "Gifts,"
    120–21; "In a Southerly Direction," 100;
    "In Passing," 109; Letters Home, 113–15;
    Lost & Found, 107–12, 119–21, 124, 172;
    Miracles of Air, 105; "Nocturne: Rogers-
    ville, Tennessee, 1947," 106–7; "On the
    Banks of the Holston," 115–16; Out in the
    Country, Back Home, 100–105, 107, 120–
    21, 124; "Rambling Rose," 102; "Song for
    Gene," 101, 107; Tight Lines, 105–6, 107,
    111, 118, 122–23; "Tight Lines," 118; Vigils,
    105–8, 119–20; Watering Places, 100, 103,
    105, 109, 118–19, 121
Melville, Herman, 8, 43–44, 172, 183
Miles, Emma Bell, 132–33, 138–39
Miller, Jim Wayne: the Brier as persona in,
    14–15, 17, 20–26, 31–36, 108, 110, 112;
    conversion motif in, 16–17, 20–22, 32–
    34; "cosmopolitan regionalism" in, 11–12,
    21, 24–26, 104; influences on, 9–10, 11;

other religious elements in, 27–36
—works: "Bhagavad-Brier," 36; "Bird in the
    House," 17–18; "Brier Ambassador," 24;
    Brier, His Book, 15, 22–26, 35; "The Brier
    Moves to a New Place," 22, 35; The Brier
    Poems, 26, 35–36; "Brier Sermon," 19–21,
    24, 28, 31–34; Brier, Traveling, 36; Copper-
    head Cane, 12–13, 29–31; "The Country
    of Conscience," 24–26, 35; Dialogue with
    a Dead Man, 13–15, 21, 26, 29–31; "Down
    Home," 17–18; "Family Reunion," 14, 31;
    "Going South," 16; "Harvest," 19–20;
    "He Remembers His Mother," 32–33; His
    First, Best Country, 9, 22; "His Hands,"
    18, 27; "A House of Readers," 16–17; The
    More Things Change the More They Stay
    the Same, 12, 31; The Mountains Have
    Come Closer, 14–21, 24, 26–27, 31–34;
    "Names," 23; Nostalgia for 70, 26, 34; "On
    Native Ground," 31; "Original Red: A
    Short Story," 34–35; "Restoring an Old
    Farmhouse," 17–18; "The Reverend Mr.
    Thick," 28–30; "Shapes," 20, 32; "Trellis,"
    13; "Turn Your Radio On," 17; "A Turn-
    ing," 22; Vein of Words, 26, 34; "Written
    on the Land," 23
Morgan, Robert: influences on, 75–76, 82,
    87; interest in science, 74–75, 94–95, 97;
    music as motif in, 80; rebirth as motif in,
    81, 83–86, 89, 92, 97–98
—works: "After Church," 85, 117; At the
    Edge of the Orchard Country, 89, 92–95;
    "Besom," 77–78; "Blowing Rock," 78;
    Brave Enemies, 90; Bronze Age, 89;
    "Brownian Motion," 94–95; "Chicken
    Scratches," 77–78; "Church Pews," 84,
    88, 117; "Convection," 79; "Easter Algae,"
    85–86; "Face," 85, 117; "Fulgurite," 76,
    82; Gap Creek, 8; "The Gift of Tongues,"
    89–90, 117; Groundwork, 4, 86, 92;
    "Heaven," 90–92, 117; "Inertia," 96; Land Div-
    ing, 4, 74, 85–87; "Lightning Bug," 95–96;
    "Mockingbird," 87–89; "The Music of the
    Spheres," 80; Red Owl, 74, 83–85; Sigod-
    lin, 89, 96–98; "Sigodlin," 96; The Strange

Morgan, Robert *(continued)*
    Attractor, 97; "The Strange Attractor," 97;
    "Stretching," 96–97; *This Rock,* 76, 90;
    Topsoil Road, 4, 76–82; *The Truest Plea-*
    sure, 82, 90; *Trunk & Thicket,* 74–75, 87–
    89; *The Voice in the Cross Hairs,* 83–84;
    "Wind from a Waterfall," 78–79; *Zirconia*
    Poems, 74, 83–84
music of the spheres, 57, 80, 175, 187, 191

"Nature" (Emerson), 4, 6, 50–51, 76, 80,
    82, 116, 178
nature as a language, 4, 41, 62–63, 76–77,
    94, 122–23, 164–65, 170, 186
neo-Platonism, 51, 171, 184

otherworldliness in religion, 1–4, 6–8, 31,
    36, 39–40, 42, 50, 75, 82, 86, 93, 96, 99,
    119, 125, 128, 146, 150, 153, 164, 169, 193

Plato (Platonism), 3, 47, 50, 52, 184
Plotinus, 50
"Poet, The" (Emerson), 24, 80, 82
Pound, Ezra, 75, 161–62, 173, 181
Pythagoras, 43, 80, 175

Rash, Ron, 8, 23
Rilke, Rainer Maria, 58, 127, 160
Rimbaud, Arthur, 43, 49, 53
Ronsard, Pierre de, 67, 69
Ruether, Rosemary Radford, 128, 131, 151

St. Agnes, 70
St. Augustine, 88, 96, 172, 189
St. Francis, 112, 120, 172
St. John of the Cross, 161, 172
St. Paul, 39, 48–49, 130
Shakespeare, William, 48, 53, 70, 192
Small Farm, The, 8, 39, 97, 99–100
Smart, Christopher, 87
Smith, Lee, 133, 141
Stafford, William, 11, 99
Stevens, Wallace, 63, 138, 146, 162–64, 173,
    175, 180, 184, 187, 191
Still, James, 1, 5, 10

Stuart, Jesse, 5, 10
"Sunday Morning" (Stevens), 138, 146,
    163, 173

Tate, Allen, 39, 126
Thoreau, Henry David, 19, 22, 24, 44, 75,
    71, 83–84
Transcendentalism, 51, 116

Ungaretti, Giuseppe, 65, 184

Vanderbilt Agrarians, 5, 10, 39, 126
Vergil, 5, 38–39, 52, 60, 68
Virgin Mary, 48, 50, 129, 135, 160

Warren, Robert Penn, 34–35
Watauga Drawdown (Johnson), 23
Whitman, Walt, 8, 23, 75, 78, 83, 85, 106,
    108, 110, 112, 123, 185, 192
Wilbur, Richard, 119
Williams, William Carlos, 107
Wolfe, Thomas, 10, 75
Wordsworth, William, 71, 126
Wright, Charles: homelessness as motif
    in, 164, 167, 169, 172, 187–89, 193; in-
    fluences on, 160–64; landscape as sub-
    ject, 157–58, 165, 177–78, 188, 190, 193;
    mortality as theme in, 158, 163–64, 173,
    176–77, 182–83, 185–86, 190, 192; nature
    as subject, 159, 164–65, 178, 181, 190–91;
    pilgrimage motif in, 159, 164, 167–69,
    187, 189–90, 192; use of four elements
    (earth, air, fire, and water) in, 166, 174
    —works: "After Reading T'ao Ch'ing, I
    Wander Untethered through the Short
    Grass," 163; "Apologia Pro Vita Sua," 175;
    Appalachia, 157–58, 163, 174, 176–83;
    "The Appalachian Book of the Dead,"
    176–83; "Aubade," 165–66; *Black Zodiac,*
    8, 157, 171–72, 174–77, 183; *Bloodlines,*
    165–68; "Born Again," 168–69; *Buffalo*
    Yoga, 162, 185–89; *Chickamauga,* 174–75;
    China Trace, 158, 165, 168–70, 174; "Clear
    Night," 169–70; *Country Music,* 8, 157–59,
    162, 164–70; "December Journal," 172;

"Dio Ed Io," 186; "Disjecta Membra,"
175–76; "Dog Creek Mainline," 157; "East
of the Blue Ridge, Our Tombs Are in the
Dove's Throat," 174; "Giorgio Morandi
and the Talking Eternity Blues," 180;
"Going Home," 169, 171; *The Grave of the
Right Hand*, 165–66, 170; *Hard Freight*,
157, 165–66; "A Journal of Southern
Rivers," 173; "Last Journal," 173; "Little
Apokatastasis," 187–88; *Littlefoot*, 159,
160, 164–65, 172, 184, 190–92; "May
Journal," 172; *Negative Blue*, 160, 162,
172–84; *North American Bear*, 165, 174,
183–84; "Northanger Ridge," 166; "Opus

Posthumous," 176–79, 181; *The Other Side
of the River*, 170, 172–73; "Peccatology,"
160; "Pilgrim's Progress," 189; "Reunion,"
171; *Scar Tissue*, 160, 188–91; "A Short
History of My Life," 189; *A Short History
of the Shadow*, 159–60, 180, 184–85, 191;
"Singing Lesson," 190; "Skins," 166–68;
"Sky Diving," 183; *The Southern Cross*, 165,
170; "Step-Children of Paradise," 183;
"Stone Canyon Nocturne," 169; "Tattoos,"
166–67; "Venetian Dog," 179; *The World
of the Ten Thousand Things*, 162, 170–73;
"The Writing Life," 179; *Xionia*, 170; *Zone
Journals*, 170